FODENS

REPLACEMENT

ISBN 1 898432 14 7

In the same series or in preparation –

80 Years of Guy
Bedford Volume I 1923-1950
Bedford Volume II 1950-1995

Produced for the Publishers
Venture Publications, Glossop, Derbyshire,
by Mopok Graphics, Glossop SK13 8EH
using computerised origination

Foden
My Life with the Company

by

Harold Nancollis

Series Editor and Designer

Alan Townsin

Venture *publications*

CONTENTS

The annual London to Brighton run provides an opportunity for owners to show their treasured vehicles in a working environment and the type C steam lorry shown below is a prime example of the restorer's art. Built in 1922 as a box van it was in use until 1928 when it passed to a quarry company who left it to become derelict when they no longer required it. It was purchased for restoration in 1958 but such was the extent of work required that it remained derelict until it was purchased by Tate and Lyle in March 1968. They completely rebuilt it and it is seen here about to leave Battersea Park, London, in May 1971. It was later placed on display in the National Motor Museum at Bealieu.

CONTENTS

Another fine example of a restored vehicle is shown here. This model S4 was new in 1933 being supplied to Portsmouth and Brighton United Breweries Ltd. It gave good service with its original owner and after they sold it it had two more commercial users before spending twelve years in a derelict state. It was purchased by R. L. Scard of Ash Vale, Aldershot, who restored it and in so doing rebuilt the cab to its original specification. It is also seen in Battersea Park, London, this time at the start of the 1974 London to Brighton run. By 1988 ownership had changed to Mills of Mitcham.

INTRODUCTION

My time at Fodens spanned a total period of 45 years; from September 1937, when I joined the Company as a seventeen-year-old apprentice, through to July 1982 when I retired from the renamed, American-owned, 'Sandbach Engineering Company'. To me and to many others, it was still 'Fodens' and sometime later the Company was, in fact, more appropriately renamed 'Foden Trucks', the trading title currently in use. My time at Fodens covered a period of continual constructional and applicational development in the British commercial vehicle industry.

Design and legislative changes respectively improved performance, reduced unladen weight and increased payloads and earning capacity. Applicational design and development increased the range of home and overseas sales markets available to the company for both road haulage and contractors' plant vehicles.

Fodens' design team frequently pioneered these developments and thereby provided our sales force with unique opportunities to be first in the field.

To be part of this design team for 32 of my 45 years at Foden was a most satisfying and at times, exciting experience which I will always remember with some considerable pride, and if, as my story unfolds through the pages of this book, I can pass on to you, the reader, at least some of the sense of pride and achievement in this example of our commercial vehicle industry, then I will be pleased with a final job well done.

However, when I joined Fodens in 1937, the Company had already been in existence for over three quarters of a century and over the years, had established a fine reputation for quality engineering throughout the era of steam powered road haulage and into the early years of the internal combustion engine. My knowledge of this period in the Company's history must obviously be second hand, but at least I did have the opportunity, through conversations with my senior workmates over the years and through surviving copies of recorded events during this time, without which no version of the Foden Saga would be complete.

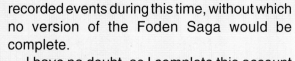

I have no doubt, as I complete this account of my working life at Fodens some few days prior to my 75th birthday, that I may have failed to recall all of the important events in the history of the company during this period of 45 years between 1937 and 1982, but at least I hope that this account of my own recollections will be of interest to the many former Foden customers, employees and historical commercial vehicle enthusiasts who still have a high regard for the old Company and the extensive range of quality vehicles produced over the years.

ACKNOWLEDGMENTS

When I retired from Sandbach Engineering Company, the American-owned successor to Fodens Ltd in 1982 after spending 45 years at Elworth Works, I had no intention of recording that specific period of my life in any way, shape or form.

I had retired, as planned, shortly after my 62nd birthday, which would have been my retirement date under the Foden regime, in order to spend more time with our growing family, which now included seven grandchildren. I also planned to pursue my various hobbies and see a little more of my favourite football and cricket teams. All perfectly normal, simple, possibly selfish ambitions which certainly did not include the long-term grinding chore of preparing and writing a book on Fodens.

However, some months after my retirement one of my former colleagues in the Technical Sales Department, Brian Lomas, asked if I could give a short slide presentation on the history of Fodens to a local group of Foden vehicle enthusiasts who had set up a museum of old vehicles and other Foden memorabilia in a section of the former Recreation Club in Elworth. I eventually collected sufficient slides to cover the period from the founding of the Company through to the termination of World War II and, some time later, completed the story with an additional presentation covering the period from 1945 through to 1982 when I retired. Each presentation included a full magazine of 80 slides and, with a normal commentary, covered a period of 60 to 90 minutes. The subsequent interest generated by these relatively limited versions of Fodens' engineering history clearly indicated that the preparation of a more comprehensive account would be a worthwhile project, particularly from a viewpoint within the Company.

This was my principal reason for taking on this project which has required a significant degree of external assistance to complete successfully. In this respect I am particularly grateful to my former chief, Jack Mills for confirmatory information and the loan of original vehicle specification data, also to David Foden for information relating to his record-breaking double Atlantic crossing; to John Sanderson for providing, from his comprehensive collection of Foden literature, the major proportion of the illustrations included in this publication, and finally, to my former secretary Janice Boulton for converting my original notes into a legible manuscript.

This former Warrington Corporation Foden PVD6 model, with bodywork built by Massey Bros of Wigan, has been fully restored and is now a regular attendee at rallies, giving an opportunity to see one of the few surviving examples of the marque. It was photographed during 1994 at the St Helens event, having for some time been kept in the Transprt Museum in that town. Another preserved Foden bus appears on the title page of this book, one of two supplied to Llandudno Urban District Council to operate its service around the Great Orme headland. Sprag gears were incorporated in the chassis specification to prevent any possibilty of a runaway on the steep gradients involved. The splendid eight-wheeler on the cover, another preserved example, was specially posed for photographer Peter Durham to whom we record our thanks.

1 THE STEAM AGE

Fodens' engineering history dates from the year 1856, when the fifteen-year-old Edwin Foden, son of a shoemaker and general dealer in the village of Smallwood near Sandbach, and with no apparent engineering heritage, finally persuaded his father to allow him to take up an apprenticeship with Plant and Hancock, who had a small engineering workshop and foundry at Elworth, another small village on the other side of Sandbach.

He had, in fact, left school at the age of thirteen and at his father's insistence, worked as the village post boy for two years, despite his often expressed ambition to take up an engineering career. His initial weekly wage at Plant and Hancock was four shillings, his weekly lodging cost six shillings and sixpence, the resultant deficit of two shillings and sixpence being made up by an allowance from his father. Any further cash requirements had to be earned by lodging at home and walking the three miles to and from work each day, or by working overtime.

Plant and Hancock, with a total workforce of around 30, manufactured and serviced a wide variety of equipment for the local farms and salt works, including a range of portable steam engines for driving threshing machines, water pumps and turnip and chaff cutters. When this type of work was scarce, they took on sub contract work for the thriving railway workshops at Crewe. Edwin Foden had been born in an era dominated by rail transport.

Passenger transport, previously handled by stage coaches at average speeds of 10 miles per hour with horses changed every hour, were now superseded by passenger trains, providing a more frequent and more comfortable service at average speeds of 20 miles per hour or more. The Manchester to Liverpool Railway, opened with much pomp and ceremony in 1830, was carrying over 1,000 passengers per day by 1831. Similarly, raw material and manufactured goods transport, formerly handled by the countrywide river and canal network, was also transferred to a large extent to the railways for similar reasons.

In 1844, a Government Select Committee summarised the changing situation as follows:–'From the immense superiority of the locomotive engine, railway companies may be taken, for all practical purposes, to possess a complete monopoly as regards the conveyance of passengers. As regards the conveyance of goods, this is not the case to the same extent, since railways are, in many cases, exposed to effective competition from canals and other waterways, and also since the saving of time does not give such a decided superiority over the old modes of conveyance'.

To all practical intents and purposes, it was, in fact, a complete rail transport monopoly. Steam powered road transport was never seriously considered as a viable third alternative at this time, despite the fact that both Telford and Macadam had already demonstrated that sound, high load bearing roads could be built and effectively maintained, and Goldsworthy-Gurney, Sir Charles Dance and

Edwin Foden.

Walter Hancock had designed and built steam powered road carriages capable of carrying twenty passengers at 20 miles per hour in the 1820s and 1830s.

Excessive road tolls and restrictive legislation had virtually eliminated steam powered road transport before Edwin Foden was born.

Walter Hancock, who had designed and built over a dozen steam driven road coaches at his London workshops, retired, no doubt with some considerable regret, in the mid 1840s and it was his son, George Hancock who came up to Cheshire to establish his own engineering workshop in Elworth around 1848 and eventually, in 1856, to inaugurate the Foden Saga by taking on the fifte-year-old Edwin.

The young apprentice developed his practical engineering and design skills remarkably quickly and at the early age of nineteen was made workshop foreman. He was now in a position to have some influence in the day-to-day operation of the company, but, unfortunately, after a disagreement with George Hancock over his right to engage and dismiss the men who worked under his

direction, he resigned, and quickly found alternative employment at the London and North Western Railway Company's much more comprehensively equipped workshops at Crewe, supervised at that time by a brilliant Chief Mechanical Engineer, John Ramsbottom. In addition to his principal achievement of designing and introducing a more standardised range of goods and passenger locomotives to the LNWR system, Ramsbottom invented the metallic split piston ring to replace the former hemp packing used on steam engines; the water scoop and trough pick up device to replenish locomotive water tanks at speed, and he also built the first U.K. Bessemer steel producing plant at Crewe.

There is no doubt that the young Edwin Foden gained a good deal of valuable steam engineering experience during his short period at Crewe and when George Hancock invited him to return to Elworth as a full partner in the company in 1862, he was better equipped to take on his wider responsibilities. At this time, the company was accordingly renamed 'Foden and Hancock' and the new partnership set about the task of consolidating its position in the agricultural and industrial steam engine business. An extract from a catalogue of the period sets out the company engineering

William Hancock's Automaton, built in 1836, successfully completed over 500 trips between Paddington and Moorgate.

policy as follows:- 'To obtain the highest amount of power with the smallest quantity of fuel is the most important point aimed at in the manufacture of our portable and fixed steam engines and it will be found in practice that the engines are both thoroughly efficient in working power and economical in the consumption of fuel'.

There was no practical incentive at this time to design and build a steam-powered road vehicle. The Locomotives Act of 1861 laid down the conditions that any mechanically driven road vehicle must not exceed speeds of 4mph on rural highways and 2mph in towns and at all times had to be preceded by a person carrying a red warning flag.

Further prohibitive measures in 1865 and 1867 underlined the Government's pro-railway transport policy and virtually precluded any viable form of mechanical road transport.

The partners, therefore, concentrated their attention on the agricultural and industrial application of their products and the company continued to prosper. One particular area of expansion was the design and manufacture of industrial steam engines for a wide variety of applications.

From the surviving drawing office records of the early 1870s, we note the following examples of customers and equipment supplied at that time:-

36in air compressing engines for the London and South Wales Coal Company.

16in hauling engine 36in stroke for the Cesna Sulphur Company.

12in pumping tackle for Messrs. Stubbs Bros. Winsford.

All drawings were made on cartridge paper, both sides of the paper were used and scales were ½in, 1in or 1½in to a foot. Draughtsmanship was of a very high standard and well detailed, and master drawings were colour tinted.

From the condition of surviving master drawings, it would appear that they never left the drawing office; in which case detail drawings would have to be prepared for the workshop to manufacture the individual components. The machine tools used in the manufacturing process were all 'home made' and steam powered, and undoubtedly crude by modern standards, but the components produced were 'hand finished' and selectively fitted to ensure that the company's high product standard was maintained.

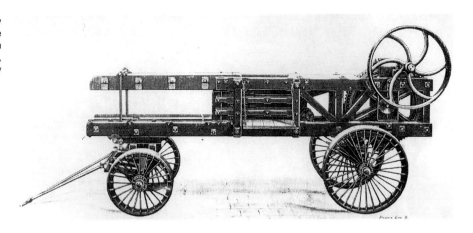

Foden's Improved Perpetual Straw or Hay Baling Press was an example of the Company's products at the time Edwin Foden took over sole charge of the company in 1876, although this illustration dates from shortly after the formation of Fodens Ltd in 1901.

In 1876 George Hancock decided to retire and the company was again renamed 'Edwin Foden and Son', the son being the eight-years-old William, destined, much later, to be Managing Director during my own time at Fodens.

Edwin Foden, now in sole charge of the company at 35, decided to extend the range of products from the Elworth factory to include a baling press for straw or hay and also a range of threshing machines, initially powered by horse drawn, portable steam engines and later, driven by a small integrally mounted steam engine.

The new Foden products were designed and built to meet the stated requirements of the young manager that 'Nothing but the best' was good enough for his customers. The expanding order book and the favourable reports of various comparison trials

carried out by the Royal Agricultural Society at that time, gave clear indication that his objectives were being achieved.

The products of Elworth Works at this time were not, of course, destined solely for agricultural use. Industrial steam engine orders were received on a regular basis and in 1877 two of the largest engines built at the factory were delivered to a tin plate rolling mill at Kidwelly in South Wales. With a 43in cylinder bore, 42in stroke and 25ft diameter flywheel weighing over 30 tons, the two engines continued to operate successfully, albeit intermittently, due to trading conditions, up to 1938, and are currently preserved as prime examples of 19th century engineering.

In 1878, after a considerable amount of organised pressure by farmers and landowners on the Tory government of the day, some

Foden's First Prize Thrashing Machine. High standards of design and manufacture were a feature of Foden products from the early days, as was care in the economical use of power. This was recognised by the award given after trials by the Royal Agricultural Society, underlining the Company's good reputation. Note that Foden used 'thrashing' rather than the spelling 'threshing' commonly used in this context.

One of the two steam engines built by Foden in 1877 for a rolling mill at Kidwelly. They ran until 1938 and are now preserved.

of the restrictive legislation relating to the operation of agricultural steam engines on the road, were repealed and it became obvious to Edwin Foden that there would now be an increasing demand for an efficient steam engine to haul and power the various items of farm machinery.

He was, at this time, developing a compound steam engine, using the exhaust steam from the high pressure cylinder to charge a larger diameter lower pressure cylinder and thereby utilising energy which was previously wasted, but, as the reliability of the new power unit was still in question, all of the original agricultural engines made in the early 1880s were powered by single cylinder engines.

One other feature of the early agricultural steam engines was the solidly mounted rear driving axle. On later models, designed more specifically as road locomotives, a 'Patent Spring Arrangement' was introduced, and the advantages of this feature are clearly defined in the illustrated description.

In 1884, a series of traction engine trials was arranged by the Northern Agricultural Societies at Stockport, and the Foden entry, powered by a 6hp two-cylinder engine, gave an outstanding

This single-cylinder agricultural engine introduced an early form of sprung mounting of the rear axle, shown in more detail on the opposite page. The company's name is quoted as 'E. Foden Sons & Co Ltd', the form adopted from 1887.

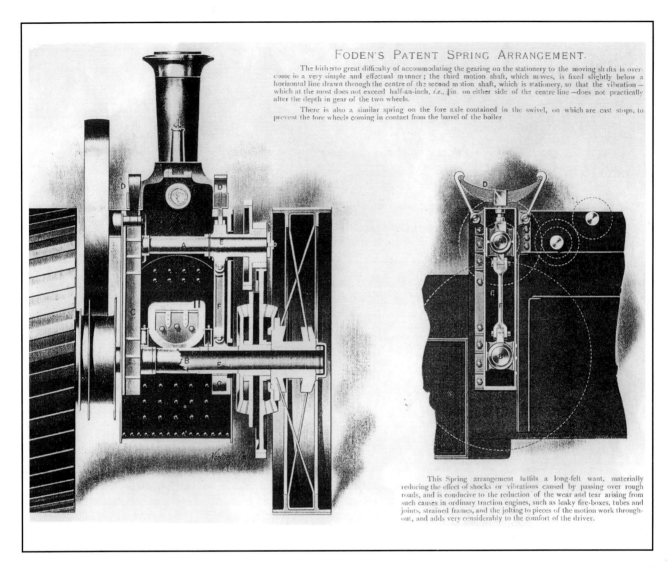

The layout of 'Foden's Patent Spring Arrangement' is shown in these views. The description indicates that the main motivation that lay behind the innovation was the protection of the structure of the engine from the effects of passing over rough roads, apt to cause "leaky fire-boxes, tubes and joints, strained frames, and the jolting to pieces of the motion work throughout", and "adds very considerably to the comfort of the driver." Even so, the description indicates that the total spring deflection did not exceed half an inch, so the absorption of road shock can only have been very limited. It is noteworthy that despite the general simplicity of design, the drive incorporated a differential mechanism to allow the driving wheels to rotate at slightly different rates when the engine was negotiating a turn.

performance, particularly in relation to fuel consumption. An account of the trials was reported in considerable detail by 'The Engineer' and orders for the Foden product immediately increased. Three years later in 1887, the Royal Agricultural Society arranged a similar series of engine trials at Newcastle on Tyne and on this occasion Edwin Foden entered a traction engine fitted with his twin cylinder compound engine. Operating at a working pressure of 250 psi, the Foden entry returned an overall fuel consumption of 1.86 lbs of coal per horse power hour, and this factor, plus the vehicle's overall performance throughout the trial, won a Society Gold Metal.

This successful trial marked a significant point in Foden's history and, as the orders poured into the factory, not only from the farming community, but also from a continually increasing demand for industrial steam engine applications, it was realised that additional capital would be required to re-equip the factory and increase production.

A new company was accordingly formed that same year, 1887,

with Thomas Cliffe, a local farmer, as Chairman, Robert, John, William, Reuben and James Stubbs from the local salt company as Directors, and Edwin Foden as Managing Director. Edwin Foden's two sons, William and Edwin were both now employed in the company, which was accordingly titled Edwin Foden Sons & Co Ltd.

During the early 1890s, the restructured company continued to expand the range of traction engines and road locomotives to meet the various requirements of their customers and the sales literature of the period indicates quite clearly that the Foden vehicles compared favourably with their competitors at that time, particularly in relation to fuel consumption, always a prime factor in any product designed by Edwin Foden.

Foden's main competitors in the traction engine market at that time were Charles Burrell of Thetford, John Fowler of Leeds, Ransomes of Ipswich and Aveling and Porter of Rochester.

Many had started in the same manner as Fodens, with the simple portable steam engines for driving farm machinery, but

The prototype two-cylinder compound engine was in the Foden tradition of seeking greater efficiency, much of the energy remaining in the steam exhausted from the high-pressure cylinder being recovered by allowing it to expand further in the larger low-pressure cylinder.

This page from a brochure spells out the virtues of the compound engine, in particular the better controllability when manoeuvring at slow speeds and the gain in economy. The note at the foot extolling the performance over 15 3/4 miles on 1394 lb (equivalent to nearly 140 gallons) of water and using 148½ lbs (1 1/3 cwt) of coal, although impressive by contemporary standards, underlines the quantities of water and coal needed on even a modest journey, admittedly with a load designed to keep the engine working quite hard.

GENERAL DESCRIPTION OF TRACTION ENGINES.

THE engravings herein illustrate the construction of our Patent Spring Traction Engines, which are of two classes, viz., Simple and Compound ; the former being made with single or double cylinders, the latter with cylinders side by side or tandem, and are designed to meet the requirements of the user, being narrow across the travelling wheels, short, and therefore capable of turning in a small space, compact, powerful, and easily handled. They are constructed of the best materials, by experienced workman, are equal in finish to the best Locomotive work, and stand unequalled for economy and durability.

ADVANTAGES OF THE DOUBLE AND TWIN COMPOUND CYLINDERS are—The strain on the gearing is reduced to a minimum, or less than half required to move the same load with a single engine.

The annoyance of reversing is done away with, which is evidently a great advantage in starting, and is thus more under the control of the driver.

The slow rate at which these Engines can be moved gives them an important advantage in hooking on, they are able gradually to start a heavy load, whereas with the single engine the load is started with a jerk which often breaks the drawbars and pulls the under-carriage-work and numerous other parts to pieces, besides endangering the life of the man hooking on.

The strain on the gearing, and therefore on the travelling wheels, being uniform throughout the stroke of the Engine, enables it to carry better over soft, greasy ground. The irregular snatching pressure of the single Engine is one of the prime causes of slipping.

Also—Priming is practically done away with, by drawing the steam off the water surface gradually instead of by snatches.

ECONOMY.—In this respect we claim to stand unequalled. We base our claim to this honour on the performances of our Engines at the two last great engine trials held in this country, viz. :—The Stockport Traction Engine Trials, a report of which will be found on page 12, taken from *The Engineer*, September 19th, 1884, and also at the Newcastle Engine Trials, held by the Royal Agricultural Society, 1887. The results were most satisfactory, our coal consumption being only 2¼lbs. per brake H.P. per hour in the single, and 1lb. 13½ozs. in the compound per brake H.P. per hour, showing an advantage in our Engines by compounding of 29.7 per cent.

It is well known that economy of fuel means a corresponding saving in wear and tear of firebox, tubes, stays, &c., a most important item in the maintenance of a Traction Engine, and well worthy of the careful consideration of intending purchasers.

At the above trials our Engine drove an 18 H.P. load, consuming only 1lb. 13½oz. of coals, and barely 18¼lbs. of water per brake H.P. per hour, which is equal to making a journey of 15¾ miles (fast speed) on 148½lbs. of coals and 1,394lb. of water, the Engine exerting 18 H.P. all the time. The tank capacity is 1,440lbs., and this journey could be performed without stopping to take up water. This is the highest point in economy yet obtained by any Traction Engine.

Telegraphic Address:
"Foden, Sandbach."
Telephone, No. 7, Sandbach.

FODENS LIMITED, ELWORTH WORKS, SANDBACH.

23

PRICE LIST DELIVERED F.O.B. AT ANY OF THE ENGLISH PORTS.

(SUBJECT TO ALTERATION WITHOUT NOTICE.)

AGRICULTURAL TRACTION ENGINES.

Nominal Horse Power.	Price with Single Cylinder, including Winding Drum, 50 yards Steel Wire Rope, Steam Water Lifter, Suction Hose, and Outfit. £	Extra for Double Crank Compound. £	Extra mounted on Foden's Patent Spring Arrangement, hind & foreaxle. £	Injector. £	Awning over Tender. £	Awning over Engine. £	Coal Rack. £	Front Tank. £	Brake acting on Rims of Hind Wheels. £	Cover for Flywheel and Motion. £	Water Heater. £	3rd Speed Road Gear. £	Copper Top on Chimney. £
6	460	60	50	8	10	20	5	18	15	5	10	25	3
7	485	70	50	10	11	20	5	18	15	5	10	25	3
8	520	80	50	10	12	25	5	25	15	5	10	25	3
10	595	100	50	12	15	25	5	25	15	5	10	25	3 10

SPECIAL ROAD LOCOMOTIVES.

Nominal Horse Power. £	Price with Single Cylinder. £	Extra for Double Crank Compound. £	Extra mounted on Foden's Patent Spring Arrangement, Hind and Foreaxle. £	Awning over Tender. £	Awning full length of Engine. £	3rd Speed Road Gear. £	Dynamo Fixing. £	Water Heater. £	Packing for Shipment. £
6	545	60	70	10	20	25	10	10	9
7	580	70	70	11	20	25	10	10	11
8	620	80	70	12	25	25	10	10	12
10	700	100	70	15	25	25	10	10	15

The above prices include Winding Drum, 75 yards Steel Wire Rope, Steam Water Lifter and Hose Pipe, Injector, Front Tank, Side Covers for Motion, Special Brake acting on both Driving Wheels, extra large Coal Bunker, Driver's Seat and Outfit.

PATENT EXHAUST & BLAST FINISHING THRASHING MACHINES.

Size of Drum.	Price.			Chaff Sifting and Backing Apparatus. £	Mounted on Springs. £	Improved Lubricators. £	Packing for Shipment. £
	Small Size. £	Large Size. £	Extra Large Size. £				
4 ft. 6 in.	145	155	175	5	15	5	10
5 0	155	165	185	5	15	5	12
5 6		175	195	5	15	5	14

TRACTION ENGINE WAGONS.

To carry 6 tons	...	...	...	£75	
" " 8 "	...	...	...	£85	
If mounted on Springs	...	...	£10 extra.	
Screw Friction Brake	...	...	£5 "	
Spring Draw Bar	...	...	£4 "	

This price list, dating from soon after the company's title became Fodens Ltd in 1901, indicates the range of agricultural traction engines, road locomotives, thrashing machines and 'traction engine wagons' – these last being sturdy trailers designed for steam haulage – on offer. The road locomotives carried equipment making them more suitable for longer journeys, such as extra coal and water capacity and a driver's seat.

almost all of them had diversified into far more types of traction engines and associated equipment than Edwin Foden, who rightly believed that he should build a high quality product with as few variants as possible to meet a known demand.

The price list of that time, includes only four types of agricultural traction engine, four types of road locomotives, two trailers and three thrashing machines. The variants in the traction engine and road locomotive type relate only to engine size, in relation to the trailers, to carrying capacity, and in relation to the thrashing machines, to the specific drum size. Extras are shown separately, as applied to each model.

Note that the £3 extra for a copper top on the chimney, increases to £3 10s for the obviously larger diameter chimney fitted to the 'top of the range' 10 horse power traction engine. The price list is illustrated with examples of the standard range of products offered and the examples reproduced on the following pages show the principal variations to suit customers in operating requirements.

Pages 16 and 17:

The Double Crank Compound Agricultural Engine, No. 455, shown overleaf, is an example of a typical machine as supplied to farmers or farm contractors. It was used as a means of driving thrashing machines or other farm machinery, by belt from the engine flywheel. The gears by which the engine could propel itself (with the thrashing machine on tow or other trailers if required), was put out of mesh while such work continued. Such engines would run almost silently for hours on end on such duty, though there would be a deep humming sound from the thrashing machine. The design of the safety valves, complete with lever allowing them to be tested, mounted on top of the cylinder casing on all these engines is reminiscent of that found on the boilers of LNWR locomotives of the period, suggesting that the design might have been influenced by Edwin Foden's period working under Ramsbottom at Crewe.

The Road Locomotive shown on page 17 was basically similar, but with canopy for the driver – note the railway locomotive-style 'spectacle plate' at the front end – extra water capacity and steam-operated brake. The side cover to the engine hid the rapid to-and-fro movement of the cross-head from frightening passing horses.

Double Crank Compound Agricultural Engine. Mounted on Springs.

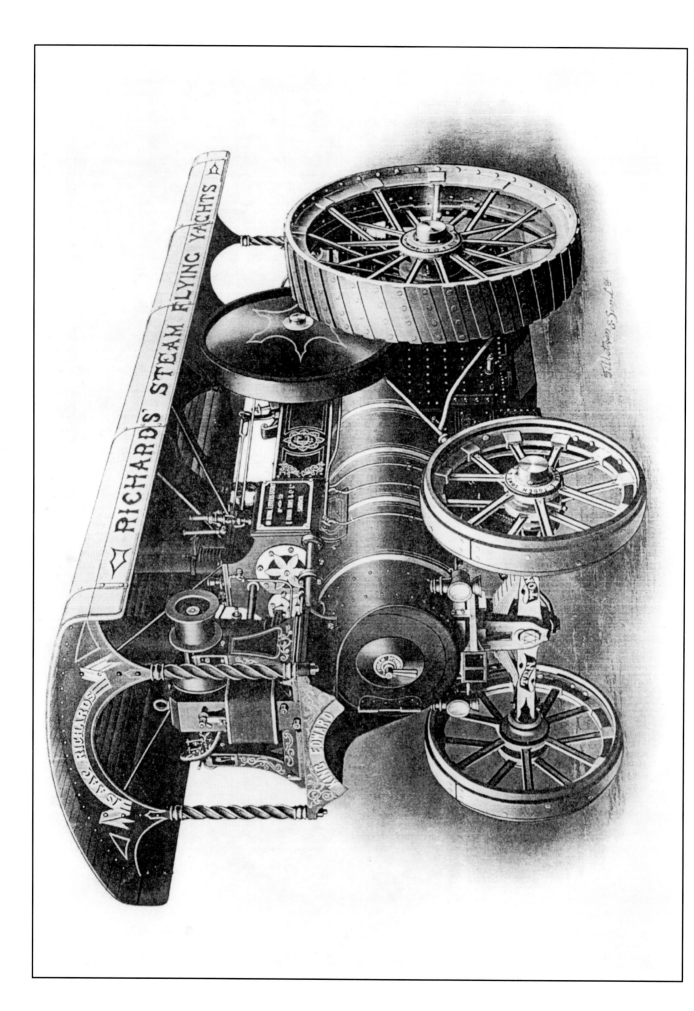

Opposite page: The 8hp Compound Showman's Locomotive shown opposite carried the process of elaboration of the basic engine further, adding a dynamo mounted on a forward extension to the boiler, with pulley for belt drive from the flywheel, and full-length canopy supported by decorative columns. Such a machine formed part of the attraction of the fairground as well as making a dramatic sight as it arrived in town followed by two or more trailers.

Of all the traction engine types produced by the company during this period, there can be no doubt that the Showman's Engines, with their polished brass fittings and highly coloured paint finish were, and in some surviving examples, still are, the most impressive vehicles ever built by Fodens. They were generally maintained in immaculate condition by their respective owners and were indeed an integral part of the showman's presentation, providing transportation for his equipment on the road and mechanical and electrical power for his show on site. Records of the period illustrate the wide variety of applications for the Showman's Engines built at that time:-

Hackney's American Novelty cars
East's Newmarket Hurdle Jumpers
Simon's Electrical Living Pictures
Lord John Sanger's Circus

The 'Locomotives on Highway Act' of 1896 allowed 'Light Locomotives' weighing under 3 tons to travel at speeds up to 12mph without being preceded by a man carrying a red warning flag, a measure still celebrated by the motoring fraternity each year by the London to Brighton Veteran Car Rally.

The repeal of the 'Red Flag Act' also marked the beginning of the end for the railway transport monopoly. In the late 1890s and through the turn of the century, the new motor car manufacturing industry was beginning to spring up in various parts of the country; Daimler, Riley, Standard, Rover, Singer and Hillman in Coventry, Austin, Wolseley and Lanchester in Birmingham and Arrol Johnson in Scotland were all founded during this period and although all were initially concerned only with private passenger transport they had common aims with the road haulage industry in their requirement for an improved road network and the legislative freedom to use it.

The 1896 Act apparently had no gross train weight limitation and therefore, the various steam traction engine manufacturers began to build multi-geared versions of their road locomotives which were designed to operate with several independent trailers as a high payload capacity road train. The road locomotives and trailers were fitted with sold rubber tyres to improve the 'ride' and extra fuel and water stowage to increase their operating radius.

Although Edwin Foden built and sold many road locomotives for operation in road trains and in fact designed and built suitable trailers which were described as 'Steel Traction Wagons', he and

This 8hp Road Locomotive is seen hauling 34 tons of bricks on three trailers for its owner, S. Tompkin of Miles Platting, near Manchester, the gross weight being some 62 tons – the wooden sides of the leading trailer are bulging noticeably under the load of 11 tons or so of bricks. The overall effect was very much of a road equivalent to a railway goods train, and the combined unladen weight of 28 tons was nearly as great as the load. The effect on road surfaces (and tram tracks as evident in this picture) was beginning to cause concern. Solid rubber tyres, as fitted to the trailers and the leading axle of the locomotive greatly reduced noise – the driving wheels have an unusual form of tread, evidently of individual blocks arranged to overlap and give continuous contact, at first glance looking like a giant pneumatic tyre. However this scene, evidently dating from the very early years of the 20th century before registration numbers were introduced, was long before pneumatic tyres capable of dealing with such loads were developed.

Third in a series of prototypes for a Foden Steam Wagon was this vehicle, with small-diameter front wheels and what appears to be a smaller engine than used in later versions, though this was fully exposed rather than being covered as in the fourth prototype seen opposite. When the War Office plans for trials became known, this vehicle was modified to allow tests to be carried out before the fourth prototype was built.

his senior associates were of the opinion that the ideal road transport vehicle would not be in a tractor and load carrying trailer configuration, but more simply and safely as a rigid four-wheel load carrying unit. The decision was eventually taken to build a prototype vehicle and at the outset of the design exercise, only four criteria were firmly established:-

1. It was to be a rigid two-axle, four-wheel vehicle.
2. The payload was to be 3 tons.
3. The power unit was to be the compound engine successfully developed on the range of traction engines.
4. Finally, the wheel dimensions, which could be established by calculation once the unladen weight had been estimated and the wheelbase and payload determined.

During 1898 and 1899, no less than three prototype vehicles were designed, built and tested, the first with an unlikely arrangement of front-wheel drive and rear-wheel steering, before arriving at a fourth and final layout of a horizontal boiler with the two cylinder compound engine mounted on top, rear axle chain drive and a chain steered centre pivot front axle.

Prior to the completion of this fourth design early in 1900 a newly inaugurated 'War Office Committee on Mechanical Transport' declared that they were arranging to carry out a series of trials during the following year to assess the viability of 'Self Propelled Lorries For Military Purposes' as a possible future alternative to the current horse drawn transport'. The phraseology of the announcement made it quite clear that although the Committee had specified that a load of two tons could be carried on a suitable trailer, the main payload of three tons had to be carried on the vehicle. This requirement reduced the competition to some extent because the principal steam traction engine manufacturers had no steam lorry design available. Edwin Foden had no such problem.

The fourth and final design was progressing well and a fourth prototype could now be built to meet the War Office requirements. In actual fact, the third prototype was modified to advance the development and test programme and, when this was satisfactorily concluded, a completely new vehicle was built for entry into the War Office Competition of Self Propelled Lorries for Military

Purposes as it was officially described. The principal variations between the final prototype and the competition vehicle appear, from the two illustrations, to be confined to the cab, body and road wheels.

The trials were arranged to take place over selected roads and cross country tracks in the Alton area of Hampshire where the present Army School of Transport is located.

All vehicles were to arrive on Tuesday, 3rd December, 1901, the trials commenced the following Thursday and were arranged to cover varying routes and road conditions over a period of seven working days. Eleven vehicles entered the competition, two were from the same company, Thornycroft, and five, for one reason or another, did not take part.

The Foden vehicle was handled throughout the trials by Edwin Foden and his eldest son William who, together, had driven their entry the 160 miles from Elworth to Hampshire with no reported problems at all. After the first two days of road trials on Thursday and Friday over varying routes, the competition became virtually a 'two horse race' with the Foden vehicle having a clear lead over Thornycroft in both average speed and fuel consumption.

The competition had now attracted the attention of the National Press and despite their previously universal pro-railway-anti-road transport attitude, they began to report the progress of the trials on a daily basis, thereby providing the leading contestants with unexpected free publicity on a scale that they could normally never afford.

The trials recommenced on Monday and again the Foden vehicle completed the designated route in the shortest time and then repeated the performance on Tuesday. On Wednesday, the Thornycroft vehicle covered a particularly hilly circuit in the shortest time, but in so doing, consumed over twice as much fuel as the Foden. The specific fuel economy runs on Thursday and Friday, December 13th and 14th, were both won by the Foden entry, which also turned in the fastest time on both routes. Over the weekend, newspaper reports were unanimous in their considered opinions that the Foden entry in the competition had proved to be the most successful in the road trials. The final week's trial programme, however, included cross-country routes over soft, swampy ground and under these conditions, the Foden vehicle was

The fourth prototype, Foden No. 524, was built in 1901 to the final design and entered in the War Office trials of self-propelled lorries for military purposes. As on the previous vehicle, the rear axle was mounted in trunnions with the springs outside the wheels in a manner reminiscent of railway practice, but in overall layout the pattern was set for most of the Foden steam wagons built over the next quarter century. Valuable publicity was gained from the prototype Foden's behaviour – like subsequent models of the type, it had left-hand steering.

Below is a selection of quotations from various national newspapers, reproduced in Foden's brochure offering similar vehicles for sale.

The results achieved by our Wagon are amply confirmed by the observations of numerous Newspaper Reporters and Experts, portions of whose reports we give below :

DAILY CHRONICLE, *December 7th, 1901.*

"The Foden Company's Steam Car, which was the first to return on Thursday, was first again yesterday, improving on the previous day's time by about an hour."

WESTMINSTER GAZETTE, *December 10th, 1901.*

"The Foden Steam Wagon, built on the lines of a traction engine, was again first in, for the third time in succession, covering the distance quite easily."

DAILY CHRONICLE, *December 10th, 1901.*

"The Steam Wagon by Foden & Co., Sandbach, came in first, for the third time in succession. A long hill between two and three miles in length, between Odiham and Alton, over a very poor by-road, tested the capabilities of the types severely, but the Foden seemed to make light of the work."

DAILY TELEGRAPH, *December 14th, 1901.*

"The Foden Wagon again completed the journey in five and a half hours, over thirty minutes ahead of the next best, and with 186 lbs. of fuel less."

THE ECHO, LONDON. *December 17th, 1901.*

"Yesterday the tests were made as to which could cover the required distance, 32 miles with the least fuel, the Foden was an easy winner by over 200 lbs. of coal."

THE TIMES, *December 18th, 1901.*

"The Wagon by Messrs. Foden & Sons appears to have been the most successful on the road trials."

DAILY EXPRESS, *February 20th, 1902.*

"The decided superiority of the Foden Wagon soon became manifest, day after day the sturdy little vehicle came through the trying tests streets ahead of the other wagons, and showing consistently, superior economy in working, consuming far less coal and water than any of the other competitors."

Production of steam wagons based on the successful prototype soon got under way – indeed this tipper bears the E. Foden Sons & Co Ltd title on its maker's plate, indicating that it dated from before the change of title to Fodens Ltd. Building a satisfactory design within the weight limit was difficult, and here well under half the frame length was available as load space, though the pivoting of the tipper body so near its centre would have the merit of lightening the task of cranking it up by hand when laden.

not so successful. On the final day, in fact, they had the misfortune to shear a pivot pin in the steering gear, and the combined effect of this misfortune and the final week's wheel adhesion and flotation problems resulted in Thornycroft winning the competition and Fodens being awarded the second prize, a cheque for £250. However, the War Office Committee were so impressed with the overall performance of the Foden entry that they decided to buy the vehicle for further evaluation and in their final statement on the results of the competition, indicated quite clearly that steam road vehicles had adequately proved their worth during the trials and would henceforth, be considered as a viable alternative to horse-drawn military transport.

Edwin Foden and his son William repaired their vehicle and set off on the long journey back to Elworth with the £250 prize money and the sure and certain knowledge that, despite the official result of the competition, they were riding on a winner. Their potential customers would be far more likely to be interested in the new steam vehicle's well publicised road performance, particularly in relation to carrying capacity and fuel economy, rather than any cross-country operational ability. They arrived back home in Elworth late on Christmas Eve 1901 to be welcomed by both family and employees, who have been closely following the progress of the competition in the National Press, almost as local heroes.

There can be no doubt that Foden's successful participation in the War Office trials in 1901 marked a significant turning point in the development of the company. Up to this time, the company had established their reputation mainly as agricultural and associated equipment engineers. Now they were entering the road transport industry and they were destined to take a major part in the expansion and development of this Industry for the next 80 years.

As Edwin Foden returned to his office after the short Christmas break and inquiries began to arrive on his desk concerning the future availability of the new road vehicle, he realised that big changes would be needed at the Elworth factory if the anticipated demand materialised.

His first step was to form a limited company:- Fodens Limited. Cecil Brunner, the Chairman of Brunner Mond, the Chemical Manufacturers at nearby Northwich, was invited to chair the new company, Edwin Foden to be Managing Director, John and Reuben Stubbs from one of the local salt companies, together with the two young Fodens, William and Edwin Richard, were to constitute the remainder of the Board. Edwin Foden's brother-in-law Samuel Twemlow was to be the Company Secretary. It was still very much of a family concern, but nevertheless, the necessary capital was raised in the first year, 1902, to extend the foundry, add new assembly and machine shops and also build a new office block.

The 3-ton steam vehicle design, despite its success at the Military trials, was further modified to improve reliability, simplify maintenance and improve fuel economy still further. This insistence on finalising the design and anticipating service requirements *before* committal to full production, to my mind, illustrates the engineering character of Edwin Foden in its true light. 'Nothing but the best' was good enough for his customers. His original trading policy still rang true.

The new company forged ahead with a full order book and showed a net profit in its first year. The vehicles produced at this time were, of course, all based on the 3 ton capacity military trials vehicle design and the widely reported performance of the Foden vehicle and the eventual results of the trial were extensively used in the sales literature of the period.

Vehicles were individually built to suit the customer's specific requirements, the principal governing factor being the unladen weight which had to remain under 3 tons in order to qualify for the 12 miles per hour speed allowance. If the unladen weight exceeded 3 tons, then the maximum speed was reduced to 4 miles per hour.

This regulation presented the manufacturers with a very real problem, particularly in relation to special purpose vehicles, where the weight of any additional equipment had to be carefully considered, a tipping vehicle being a typical example.

There was no assembly line. Each vehicle was individually

This view of the vehicle assembly shop dates from the period of the early steam wagons with external rear springs, as seen in the background – note also the large-diameter traction engine wheel in the right foreground. The hand power tools used for drilling and riveting were pneumatically driven – the noise of the latter operation was intense but ear defenders were unheard-of in those days and indeed until very recent times. Compressors, pillar drills, sandstones and other fixed machines were belt-driven from overhead shafting, as visible in the left background. The shafting was powered by steam engines in those days but later, when the Company built its own power station, by electric motors. The overhead crane was manually operated. Workshop heating was provided by coke-burning stoves, also used for tea brewing, bread toasting, pie warming and other culinary purposes by the workmen. The shop floor consisted of railway sleepers, later replaced by hardwood blocks.

assembled and fully road tested before final delivery to the customer, and more often than not, the delivery drivers would have to instruct the customer's staff on how to drive and maintain their vehicles. Thus a new classification of drivers came into being. They were the demonstration drivers, as opposed to the normal delivery drivers, a distinction reflected in both status and salary.

Production of the 3-ton steam wagons and company profits continued to increase steadily through 1903 and 1904 and then, early in the following year, 1905, a new 'Heavy Motor Car Order' came into force, which clearly indicated the growing power of the road transport industry in Parliament by increasing the allowable unladen weight of a 'Heavy Motor Car' to 5 tons, the unladen weight of a trailer to 1 ton 10 cwt, the gross laden weight of any one axle to 8 tons and the gross laden weight of a two axle vehicle to 12 tons.

Furthermore, the allowable gross weight of a trailer was increased to 8 tons resulting in a total allowable gross train weight of 20 tons for a vehicle and trailer. Normal speed limits were 8mph, reducing to 5mph when operating with a trailer. However, if solid rubber or pneumatic tyres were fitted and no individual axle load exceeded 6 tons, then the speed limit was increased to 12mph. The introduction of this remarkably wide ranging piece of legislation resulted in an immediate return to the drawing board for all of the steam vehicle manufacturers, who were now presented with a unique opportunity to design and build vehicles with the speed and load carrying capabilities to compete effectively with the railways.

Fodens' initial effort to take advantage of the new constructional regulations resulted in a design based on the successful 3-tonner, but with a modified rear axle suspension system, higher rated axles and wheels and a larger body. Further details of the specification and performance of the new vehicle are outlined in extracts from the sales literature of the period:-

The unladen weight of the vehicle illustrated is shown on the chassis sidemember as 4 tons 18 cwt. 2 qrs, so that although this range of Foden steamers was designated as the '5 Tonner' the maximum legal payload could be much higher, in this particular case, 7 tons 1 cwt 2 qrs, in terms of the 12 tons gross limit, although in this case axle limits added up to 5 cwt less than the latter figure.

Changes in the law made a larger size of steam wagon a practical proposition, and the opportunity was taken to adopt a more conventional arrangement for the rear axle suspension, with the springs on the inner side of the wheels. This example of the 'patent steam wagon' for a Sheffield corn miller could in theory carry just over 6 3/4 tons if the maximum axle weights quoted on the vehicle were taken to the combined limit of 11 tons 15 cwt (this being within the overall legal 12-ton gross laden weight limit), on the basis of its unladen weight of 4 tons 18 cwt 2 qrs. Foden's description of the model, reproduced opposite, says that "the car....is capable of taking a load of 5 tons on itself and 2 tons on a trailer at an average speed of 6 miles per hour".

This was providing, of course, that the designated maximum speed of 8 mph was not exceeded and the vehicle did not operate with a trailer. Overloading and speeding became common offences and the traditional battle between the road user and the law enforcement agencies was augmented accordingly.

The new vehicle range rapidly became popular with operators, not simply because of the overload capacity, but also because of the vehicle's low operational costs due, mainly, to the inherent efficiency of Edwin Foden's compound engine design. The company forged ahead with a full order book and gross profits increased from £11,000 in 1903 to almost £40,000 in 1910. This same year, to suit gradually improving road conditions and increasing competition, the 5-tonner was redesigned to provide improved suspension and braking, and to improve engine efficiency and resultant operating economy still further.

This redesigned 5-tonner proved to be one of the most successful vehicles ever produced by Fodens and its undeniable operating reliability resulted in a continued demand almost for the next decade. Unfortunately, the man who had been primarily responsible for the design and development of this vehicle and in fact, all of its predecessors, did not survive to reap the personal benefits of this success.

On August 31st, 1911 Edwin Foden died.

He had been in failing health for some time, but his death still resulted in a tremendous feeling of shock and loss to the whole of the local community in Elworth and Sandbach, who for so many years had enjoyed the benefits of the company's success and Edwin Foden's personal regard for the welfare of his employees and their families.

He was a Liberal. He was a Methodist. He built scores of houses in the village of Elworth for his employees and their families and he built the Foden Recreation Club to cater for their leisure activities, but to many people, his major personal achievement was to transform the local Elworth village band into the world famous Fodens Motor Works Brass Band. British National Brass Band Champions on

eleven occasions – British Open Brass Band Champions on nine occasions – plus two Royal Command Performances and many International Honours. The full story of the Band and Edwin Foden's major role in its formation and development is told in some detail in a booklet entitled 'By Royal Command' researched and written by a former colleague at Fodens, the late Mr. Don Burgess.

With Edwin Foden's death each and every member of the Band were aware of the fact that they had lost their founder and principal supporter, but, just as the Band played on and continued to maintain the high performance standards established by their founder, so it was with the workers in the factory. There would never be another Edwin Foden, but they would best honour his memory by continuing to work to his standards which had now become theirs: 'Nothing but the Best is Good Enough for Our Customers'. The founder's two sons, William and Edwin Richard Foden, aged 43 and 41 respectively, took over the day-to-day management of the company and, encouraged by increasing customer demand for the redesigned 5 ton range of steam vehicles, they inaugurated an investment programme of new workshops and machine tools, which was to cost the company over £29,000 per year for the following four years.

The investment was quickly justified by an almost immediate increase in production and profitability and then in 1913, a further demand on the company's production capacity became apparent. The War Department anticipating the outcome of the growing tension in Europe, placed an initial order for twenty 5 ton vehicles and at the same time introduced a subsidy scheme whereby hauliers who bought new vehicles from an approved list of manufacturers, could claim a State supported discount amounting to approximately 10% of the list price at the point of purchase, plus an annual maintenance grant; providing that the vehicles were made immediately available to the War Department at the time of general mobilisation. The 'Foden Price List of Steam Motor Vehicles' applicable at this time would indicate that the subsidy applicable to the standard 5 ton vehicle would be around £55.

FODENS LIMITED, Elworth Works, SANDBACH.

Telegraphic Address;
"FODEN, SANDBACH."
Telephone;
No. 7 SANDBACH.

PRICE LIST OF STEAM MOTOR WAGONS.

→ SUBJECT TO ALTERATION WITHOUT NOTICE. ←

5 TON STANDARD WAGON, with flat platform or ordinary side boards. Driving Wheels, 3-ft. 6-in. by 10-in. on face, £550.	Net extra fitted with 12-in. Driving Wheels £10.	Net extra fitted with Brewer's Body, . . "Seabrooke" Type, £15.	Net extra fitted with tipping arrangement £25.	Net extra fitted with Copper Fire-box and Brass Tubes, £30.
6 to 7 TON COLONIAL WAGON, fitted as above, £600.	Net extra fitted with 12-in. or 14-in. Driving Wheels, £10.	Net extra fitted as above, £15.	Net extra fitted as above, £25.	Net extra fitted as above, £40.

This price list dating from the period just before the 1914-18 war, shows that there were effectively two models, the standard 5-ton type and the 'colonial' version of 6 to 7-ton capacity, with options covering broader driving wheels, a brewer's body style – a reflection of its relative popularity – and quite an expensive option of a copper fire-box and brass tubes, doubtless offering longer life before major boiler overhaul became necessary. Note that the word 'motor' was, quite correctly, applied to such products even though usually associated with the internal combustion engine in later years.

When, inevitably, war was declared in August 1914, even the subsidy schedule failed to provide the Services with adequate transport, and additional vehicles were purchased from operators on a compulsory basis at the original purchase price, less 15% for each year in service.

For the duration of the war, Fodens continued to build the 5 ton range of steam road vehicles, primarily, of course, for the War Department, but on occasion for other newly developing sections of the armed forces, such as the Royal Naval Air Service.

In addition to War Department vehicle production, Foden machine shops had sufficient capacity to take on the manufacture of heavy munitions, and for the latter part of the war years, they produced vast quantities of 9.6in shells mainly for the Royal Navy. It was also maintained that not one shell casing was ever rejected by the War Department Inspectorate, but I can personally recall one sectioned example which was normally located in the main reception area for many years. Maybe this one was scrapped *before* inspection?

When eventually the Armistice was declared in November 1918, it was generally considered that the effect of large ex-military fleets of both petrol and steam powered vehicles returned to civilian use would considerably depress the commercial vehicle market, but the Foden order book remained full throughout 1919 and 1920. Further investment in engineering, plant and buildings and also in employee housing, was approved by the Directors and the Engineering Department began to investigate the possible design parameters of a new higher speed 6 ton payload steam vehicle.

The basic 'overtype' engine and boiler layout was maintained, albeit with a larger, higher pressure boiler and improved compound engine design and consequential higher power output, but the new design features included 'Ackerman' steering, three gear ratios, an enclosed cab and improved suspension and braking. Prototypes were road tested by Fodens and selected customers over a period of eighteen months and production commenced in 1922.

Despite increasing competition from petrol engined goods

Among the users of Foden steam wagons in the 1914-18 war was the Royal Naval Air Service, to which these two examples were supplied. At that date, no doubt the Navy would consider steam-driven vehicles had the appeal of familiarity, yet their use to carry aircraft, inevitably powered by petrol engines, seems ironic in hindsight. The frames and bodies were extended to give more internal length for the aircraft wings and fuselages they were to carry.

THE "FODEN" STEAM WAGON.

T HE general design of this Steam Wagon is of a novel and original character. The Boiler, which is of the horizontal multitubular type, forms the front part of the frame work. The sides of the frame are constructed of strong channel steel, tied and braced together in such a manner as to secure great strength in the complete lorry. The platform of the vehicle is 11ft. long by 6ft. 6in. wide. The boiler is fired with coke, coal or wood, and is without doubt the easiest steam maker of any boiler on any motor wagon. The wagon is driven by a compound steam engine fixed on the top of the boiler, so as to be readily accessible, and to work with "dry" steam. The cylinders are 4in. and 6½in. diameter, and are fitted with a patented high-pressure gear, by means of which both cylinders can, in case of emergency, receive live steam from the boiler, and each cylinder exhausts independently into the chimney. The reversing motion is of the ordinary link type, and the whole construction of engine and steering arrangement is so similiar to the "Foden" Traction Engines, that any ordinary traction engine driver can easily handle the wagon. The power is transmitted by a pair of spur wheels acting on a compensating gear by an extra strong roller chain. The gearing is arranged for two speeds—9 to 1 and 24 to 1. The car is mounted on laminated springs, and is capable of taking a load of 5 tons on itself and 2 tons on a trailer at an average speed of 6 miles per hour, and can travel 20 miles without taking up water. It can climb a hill (with slow speed) of 1 in 6 with full load. The travelling wheels are extra large, front wheels 2ft. 9in. by 6in. on face, back wheels 3ft. 6in. diameter by 10in. on the face, and so constructed that frost pins and paddles can be used. The back wheels can be made up to 14in. on face for soft roads.

Foden's own description of its steam wagon, as well as detailing many of its features, conveys an indication of operating conditions of the day, with such factors as the ability of drivers familiar with traction engines to handle the new class of vehicle without specialised instruction and the need for ability to cope with 'soft' roads.

Edwin Foden's standard 5-ton steam wagon was one of the most successful vehicles ever produced by the Company, and a fitting reflection of his skill, surviving as part of the day-to-day scene on British roads long after his death in 1911. Such vehicles, with their distinctive combination of steam locomotive and automobile traditions, were still a familiar sight until the 1930s. This example, on solid rubber tyres, qualified for operation at 12mph if the axle weight was kept below 6 tons. This implied some sacrifice of the type's full potential weight capacity since, although the rear axle was rated as suitable for up to 8 tons, even a 5-ton load seems bound to have resulted in the weight carried by the rear tyres exceeding the 6-ton figure. Note how the cab roof had been extended forward to give some improvement in the degree of shelter offered, and also the addition of mudguards having quite a stylish sweep, although the front pair had to be set back somewhat to allow for the movement of the front wheels on the centrally-pivoted axle when steering.

This train carrying ten steam wagons for the War Department was in the Elworth sidings adjacent to the Foden works and alongside the London & North Western Railway main line linking Manchester to Crewe. Early needs were met by impressed Subsidy vehicles – the Army Service Corps had 104 Foden wagons ready for use in Britain and France by October 1914 – but soon the factory was supplying new wagons, mainly 5-ton, in much larger numbers. Many were supplied to the Roads Department of the Royal Engineers. The increase in output to meet the extra demand resulted in an increase in profits from £100,000 in 1916 to £150,000 in 1918.

By the end of the 1914-18 war, there had been considerable investment in new machine tools and workshop equipment, this view showing the machine shop.

The boiler shop formed a major part of the works in steam days.

The erecting shop was crowded with steam wagon frames when this photograph was taken. There was no assembly line, the frames being mounted on trestles for the axles and other units to be attached.

vehicles and a rapidly developing post war depression, the four wheel 'C' Type initially sold well and was quickly followed by a six wheeler version with double drive rear bogie axles and eventually an articulated unit described at that time as a 'Flexible Six Wheeler'.

The short wheelbase tractor unit was known as a 'D Type Tractor' when built as an independent unit and many have survived to the present day as showmen's tractors.

By the year 1924, the worldwide industrial depression was having a serious effect on transport in general and although a reasonable profit of £33,000 was reported by William Foden at the Annual General Meeting, he also had to report a 'sundry debtors' total of almost £90,000 and the company had only three outstanding orders to fulfil, one of these, an order from King George V for a 5

ton vehicle for use on the Balmoral Estates. This was the second order from the King. There was already a Foden Timber Tractor operating at Sandringham which had been so effectively demonstrated to the King, by one of the Foden senior drivers, that he was awarded a brace of pheasants each shooting season for some years afterwards.

The situation at Fodens remained serious and the general morale was not improved when it was announced that William Foden, the Managing Director, now aged 55, had decided that he would like a change to a less demanding job in a different environment and accordingly sailed off with his family to Australia in November, 1924 to begin a new life as a sheep farmer. Following his departure, the remaining management team, which still included

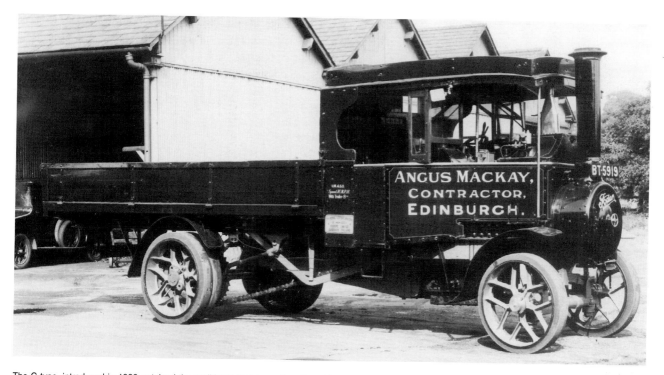

The C-type, introduced in 1922, retained the traditional Foden overtype layout but now had Ackerman steering in place of the centre pivot system, though the front suspension was still of the type with a transverse leaf spring, lending itself to taking the weight of the front of the vehicle under the boiler. The cab was also partly enclosed, with windscreen set back from the front panel – the opening panel in front of the driver, still seated on the nearside, is visible – driving such a vehicle in traffic must have been quite difficult. Unladen weight had increased to 6 tons 5 cwt. This example bearing the name of an Edinburgh concern bore an East Riding of Yorkshire registration number.

A six-wheeled version of the C-type was also introduced, giving a 10 to 12-ton load capacity. This one was in demonstration livery, making prominent use of the Foden name in script form as was to remain familiar for many years. In this case the cab did not have a windscreen, the pillars at the front simply supporting the roof.

Below: This articulated C-type was called the 'Flexible Six-Wheeler'. Note the neat-looking discs on the rear and semi-trailer wheels.

The registration number of this D-type Showman's Tractor indicates that it dates from 1929 and began life with a London based concern. It is seen as preserved in much more recent times, the pneumatic tyres evidently fitted in its later years. Note the dynamo, mounted in much the same fashion as on the old-style showman's road locomotives and the coloured lights under the canopy, typical of many fairground vehicles.

his younger brother, Edwin Richard Foden, decided, somewhat surprisingly, that the successful 'C' type, together with the short wheelbase 'D' type range, should be superseded by a new vehicle range with a vertical boiler and 'undertype' engine configuration similar to the Sentinel steam vehicle design. The only obvious advantages of the undertype layout were the longer body loading space available and the more compact enclosed driver's cab.

The new vehicles, by the usual Foden alphabetical progression, were designated 'E Type' and, by the very nature of their revised engine and boiler locations, could have very little component parts interchangeability with previous models. The boiler, of course, was positioned vertically, and forward of the front axle, the two-cylinder engine and gearbox assembly was located transversely behind the front axle and the drive shaft from gearbox to worm drive rear axle

was offset to the nearside. The boiler fire door was located on the nearside, the driver, quite sensibly, was located on the offside, so that the vehicle required a two man crew.

The designated payload for the four-wheeler model was 6 tons and for the six-wheeler version 12 tons, and although both models achieved their design objectives of higher power and improved handling, not surprisingly, with a completely new design, there were 'teething troubles' and the level of business through the mid 1920s remained low.

In order to maintain a viable level of activity in the works, orders were accepted for special vehicles which, in normal circumstances, would have been rejected immediately. One example was a short wheelbase independent tractor for overseas markets in South Africa and Argentina.

Another example was the Foden 'Agritractor' which was said to operate quite effectively under most difficult ground conditions, but again the resultant production orders were negligible.

A half track, off-road prototype was built to meet the requirements of yet another special inquiry, but, as the vehicle persisted in moving forward in a relatively straight line at all times, no further orders were forthcoming.

During the same period, Fodens designed and built a steam rail coach, using the E type engine and also two short wheelbase shunting engines which were apparently used in the local railway goods yards. In view of the fact that the railways continued to be the favoured mode of goods and passenger transport by successive governments, the decision to build any type of rail vehicle must have been considered at that time to be almost an act of surrender to the opposition.

In the late 1920s, in a final effort to produce a steam powered goods vehicle to compete with the fast developing petrol engined competition, two further models were designed, both based on the E type range. This was the 'O' type range, the four-wheel vehicle designated the 'Speed Six' and the six-wheel, the 'Speed Twelve'. Both models utilised an improved version of the two-cylinder, transversely located, engine, but the gearbox now provided three speeds, the cab was fully enclosed, 40in x 8in pneumatic tyres were fitted all round, singles on the front axle and twins on the rear, and although the speed limit at that time was 20 miles per hour, both models were capable of a comfortable top speed of 45 miles per hour fully laden, and consequently were apt to be operated at speeds not far short of that figure.

The E-type, with its undertype layout, had obvious similarities to the Sentinel, Foden's main rival in the steam wagon business by that time. So radical a change implied heavy investment in a new design of vertical boiler, engine and gearbox arranged for under-frame mounting and shaft drive, yet sales were low, partly because the steam wagon market as a whole was becoming more difficult as competition from petrol-engined vehicles increased, and because Foden, known as an overtype maker, had to convince sceptical users of the virtues of a new product directly competing with the Sentinel and other makes. This six-wheeled version could carry a 12-ton load. Right-hand steering was now a feature.

Above: The Foden Agritractor was a scaled-down version of the steam-driven agricultural engines as built from the 1870s, though using an inclined engine with the motion enclosed, and using wire wheels. Though of more modest size, it could not compete in terms of simplicity of operation with internal-combustion engined tractors, such as the Fordson by then in service in large numbers.

Right: This half-track vehicle for off-road duty used the traditional type of overtype engine. In this test the front wheels were not in contact with the ground, but even when they were, overcoming the tracks' propensity to move straight ahead was a problem.

Right: The Foden shunting engine design married the front-end of a typical overtype Foden steam wagon to a railway underframe. The Foden boiler and chimney looked quite at home in such a situation. Appropriately the two examples are understood to have worked in local goods yards.

The later years of steam vehicle manufacture at Fodens produced a quite wide variety of types. The E-type overseas tractor used the same boiler and undertype engine arrangement as the home-market models but had larger rear wheels. For such a vehicle, the undertype layout had little advantage and indeed required a longer chassis than the overtype. The absence of a covered cab made the chimney almost as prominent as in Victorian designs, contrasting with the enclosed form of the remainder of the design.

There could hardly be a more prestigious owner's name than 'HM The King, Sandringham'. This D-type tractor had been registered by Fodens, receiving the Cheshire number ALG 276 issued at almost the end of 1932, and is understood to have been run for a time as a demonstrator before being supplied to the Sandringham estate, where a Foden timber tractor had been in operation since the early 1920s, in addition to a 5-ton model at Balmoral, as described on page 28. It was thus among the last Foden steam vehicles, even though of the earlier 'overtype' design with engine over the boiler, a layout well suited to tractor duty.

The choice of 'Speed Six' as a model name for the O-type introduced in 1929 had overtones of Le Mans-winning Bentley cars of the period and, even if referring to carrying capacity rather than numbers of cylinders and not quite in the same performance class, it was among the fastest steam wagons produced. Indeed, it was advanced in general design, the shaft drive from the undertype engine being visible in this view of an example being used as a demonstrator. Unfortunately reports of boiler problems had an adverse effect on sales, and in any case the steam wagon market was being adversely affected by legislation and taxation policy.

2 FROM STEAM TO DIESEL

However, despite the considerable improvement in the design and performance of the latest steamers, the internal combustion engined vehicles, now available in increasing numbers, were becoming more popular with operators, due mainly to their lower unladen weight, consequently higher payload capacity, easier starting, cleaner operating conditions and finally, lower price.

The end of the steam road vehicle era was clearly in sight, but the majority of the Foden Board of Directors remained stubbornly opposed to the introduction of an alternative form of power unit.

It was with great reluctance that they eventually agreed in 1930 to allow E. R. Foden and his colleagues in the Engineering Department to investigate the viability of alternative power units, but before any conclusive decision could be attained, this permission was withdrawn and the majority of the Board decided to continue with the steam powered vehicles which had proved so successful in the past. Despite this decision, E. R. Foden continued his investigation, with both petrol and diesel engines and in October

1931 Foden's first diesel-engined road vehicle was completed in the development department.

The specification included a Gardner 5L2 engine, a Daimler bus gearbox and Kirkstall axles. After successful road tests, the vehicle was sold to Jacksons of Wistaston and proved to be a reliable, efficient vehicle in service; in fact, it was still in working condition in 1982, at which time I was entrusted by my new American employers with the task of selling this particular vehicle, together with a 1906 compound steam traction engine and a 1916 vintage 5 ton steam lorry, all previously part of Foden's Vehicle Museum. In March 1982 all three vehicles were purchased by the Science Museum and at the present time are usually located at the Museum's 'outstation' at Wroughton Airfield, near Swindon.

The undoubted success of this first diesel-powered vehicle design made little or no impression on the majority of the Foden Board who were still stubbornly committed to steam. E. R. Foden was, in fact, severely censured for his part in building the vehicle

Foden Diesel No. 1. This was the vehicle, built under the supervision of E. R. Foden and completed in October 1931, despite the withdrawal of the Foden Board's permission, given in 1930, to investigate the possibilities of alternatives to steam power. It had a Gardner 5L2 engine, this being a five-cylinder 7-litre unit of the type which had been introduced in 1929 primarily for marine duty but which had caught the attention of several pioneers of the use of diesel engines in road vehicles. It developed 62bhp at 1,300rpm, very slow by petrol-engine standards, but not so great a problem on a heavy goods model limited to a legal maximum speed of 20mph instead of 30mph as on buses. The Daimler gearbox was, no doubt, of the type used in that company's buses before the Wilson preselective epicyclic type was adopted as standard. This view shows the vehicle as handed over to the Science Museum in 1982 – the cab shown had been fitted, probably in the late 1930s, in an effort to modernise the vehicle. Note that the registration number LG 7186 was earlier than that of the King's steam tractor shown on the opposite page – there were several years of uncertainty before steam vehicle production ceased in 1934 and the Foden Diesel brought the Company a new era of success.

Early Foden diesel models as manufactured for general sale were of the style shown here, eventually known as the R-type, and originally designed to use the Gardner L2-series engine. This one was registered ALG 458 at the beginning of 1933, very soon after the D-type steam tractor was sold to the King, and was evidently in use as a demonstrator when photographed, although the paintwork had the slightly grubby look typical of the unvarnished grey often favoured for prototypes in those days. An interesting detail visible in this view is the positioning of the fuel tank inside the cab, mounted high on the rear panel and thus allowing gravity feed to the engine.

Gardner had introduced its LW series of engines in the Autumn of 1931, retaining the same 4.25in by 6in cylinder dimensions as the L2 range, but of lighter construction and governed at 1,700rpm, being intended specifically for road vehicle duty, and soon tended to displace the L2 for such applications, and production R-types were often so fitted. The 4LW unit, of 5.6-litre capacity, became the usual choice for a lorry intended to work without trailer.

and the Works Manager, who had been involved in the vehicle assembly, was immediately dismissed. He was replaced by a Mr. Wood Whittle, under whose management, the company was destined to verge on complete failure. In the following year, 1932, Foden's annual accounts showed a record trading loss of almost £50,000. E. R. Foden resigned, apparently to enjoy a well-earned retirement in Southport, but within twelve months, he was back in Sandbach to form his own company ERF, together with two of his former colleagues from Fodens, Ernest Sherratt from the Drawing Office and George Faulkner from Works Management. This subsequent personal success with his own company was fully deserved and well overdue.

That same year, 1933, following a government report instigated by the railways which implied that the road haulage industry was increasing its share of the total haulage business at the expense of the railways without adequately subscribing to highway maintenance

E. R. Foden set up his own company in Sandbach and set about building another prototype, this time with Gardner 4LW engine, David Brown gearbox, Kirkstall axles and cab and body by Jennings of Sandbach, in whose former workshop, now rented, it was built. The vehicle was sold to W. F. Gilbert of Leighton Buzzard on 1st September 1933, and registered as MJ 2711 – it is seen here after restoration in 1971. To avoid revealing that it was the first product of the new company, it was given the chassis number 63, allegedly chosen because this was E. R. Foden's age at the time. It bore the new company's full name on the radiator, but subsequently this was changed to ERF. By the end of the year, 31 vehicles had been built and Fodens had a serious competitor on their own doorstep.

The exploration of possible lines of business extended to petrol-engined vehicles and this refuse collector for Runcorn Urban District Council was exhibited at a trade show. It had an engine made by Meadows, in those days building engines for a wide variety of vehicles from private cars, often of sporting character, upwards – in this case the Autovac fuel lift device is visible between the driver's and mate's seats. The unladen weight, 2 tons 18 cwt 2 qrs, was enough to keep it in the 20mph class, the limit for operation of goods vehicles at 30mph then being 2 tons 10 cwt. Note the 'Foden Petrol' title on the radiator, and the foot-operated mechanism allowing dustmen to open the covers on the body.

costs; a revised Road Traffic Act was issued, which imposed a maximum legal limit of 8 tons on any laden axle and heavy taxation on any vehicle with an unladen weight of more than 4 tons. This unladen weight penalty virtually killed off the steam wagon as a viable road haulage vehicle overnight. Several steam vehicle manufacturers went out of business immediately, but Fodens blundered on, building a wide variety of steam tractors and diesel or petrol engined road vehicles to meet the individual requirements of their remaining customers, some of whom retained a commendable confidence in the eventual survival of the company during this difficult period.

With these special vehicle types, production runs were always limited, some were 'one offs' and profits were consequentially low or non-existent. An attempt was made, therefore, to produce a standard, saleable range of diesel engined vehicle utilising the Gardner L2 engine as the initial power unit with Foden transmission and Foden or Kirkstall axles, but unfortunately, this R Type range,

as it was eventually designated, was relatively heavy, the four-wheeler, unladen, weighed almost five tons and the six-wheeler over eight tons.

Under the prevailing market conditions, and without a completely acceptable product range to sell, it was not surprising that the annual balance sheets for the period showed mounting losses. The 1933 trading figures clearly indicated that the survival of the company was questionable and it was obvious that corrective action was needed quickly. It was a group of senior employees at Fodens who, on their own initiative, took the first positive step by sending a telegram to Mr William Foden in Australia requesting his immediate return to save the company. He replied to the effect that although he was quite content to continue his successful sheep farming operations, he had, in fact, already arranged to take a holiday in Europe and would take the opportunity to visit Sandbach and check their reported problems at first hand.

True to his word, he returned to Sandbach during his holiday

The Foden Whitlow diesel timber tractor showed clear affinity to the steam version, its name being derived from those of Wood Whittle, Works Manager and Edwin Twemlow, Chief designer. The transversely-sprung front axle was much as used on C and D type steam models, and the ability to traverse uneven ground is conveyed by the high-mounted front mudguards. The logic of putting the engine weight over the driven axle to improve traction on soft ground led to the Gardner five-cylinder engine being mounted transversely behind the cab. This example with Foden-built timber carriage for Coltman Bros of Claybrooke near Rugby was illustrated in the 1935/6 Jubilee range brochure.

Passenger vehicles also occupied the company's attention, this single-decker, AMA 271, being placed in service in the Spring of 1933, originally to replace the steam-driven band bus known as 'Puffing Billy'. It had strong affinity to the R-type goods models, with full-fronted cab. By the time the photograph was taken, when a more streamlined band coach had come into use, it had been allocated to the role of 'Welfare Coach' and had acquired the style of front hub cap used on later model ranges.

A more ambitious project was the prototype double-decker built later in 1933, the chassis of which conformed to orthodox practice for such vehicles at the time in having a relatively low-loading frame. It is seen here at the bodybuilder, H. V. Burlingham Ltd of Blackpool, with the metal framing for the body in place before panelling – this construction also being in the nature of an experiment, Burlingham continuing with wood framing as standard until the 1950s. It had a Gardner 6LW engine, quite a lengthy unit, and the front bulkhead of the body was set back to accommodate this, resulting in a short first bay in the body structure.

The double-decker, registered AMB 834, was sold to the Ebor Bus Co Ltd of Mansfield, where it is seen in service in company with a Leyland Lion LT2 in June 1938. Fodens decided not to enter the bus market at that time and this vehicle was to remain the only Foden double-deck bus until the introduction of the post-war passenger range in 1946.

the following year and found that the situation was far worse than he could possibly have anticipated. He resolved immediately to accept the invitation of the Chairman, Mr Francis Poole, to rejoin his old company and help to organise a recovery programme, but first of all, of course, he had to return to Australia to arrange an orderly termination of his relatively short, but successful career as a sheep farmer. His youngest son, Ted Foden, had grown tired of farm life in Australia much earlier and had returned to Sandbach in 1929 to work eventually as a salesman for his uncle's company, ERF, but for the remainder of the family, the decision to sell up and return to a questionable future in Sandbach could have raised some doubts and possibly disagreements.

Nevertheless in the spring of 1935 William Foden returned to Sandbach with his family to face up to the daunting task of saving the company his father had founded from complete collapse. The 1934 trading figures available at time of his return indicated quite clearly that the decline of the company had continued with little or no improvement since his initial assessment and immediate remedial action was required. He was co-opted to the Board of Directors and after due appointment as Chairman of an Emergency Management Executive Council, he set about the task of revising the internal accounting systems to clarify the specific financial position more frequently and accurately; also by planning an immediate rationalisation programme to cut out the special vehicle orders and concentrate on designing and building a range of four, six and eight-wheel vehicles with a high degree of component interchangeability, and finally, by reorganising the Sales Department to concentrate on the sale of this rationalised range.

At the Annual General Meeting held in August, 1935, it was announced that William Foden had been offered, and had accepted, the position of Managing Director.

It must have been obvious to shareholders and employees at this time that the company now had a possible chance of survival with proper, well organised management, but the changes would

William Foden.

J. E. Foden.

Ted Johnson, seen on the right of this picture, played a key part in the survival of Fodens Ltd through a difficult period and its subsequent recovery, being the Company's most consistently successful salesman. He is seen here with T. J. Page of Shipstone's, the brewers, of Nottingham. The vehicle was a late example of the R-type with coachbuilt W2 type cab, the registration number BTO 92 being issued in 1935 – by that date some models were being built with conventional wheels as shown here, rather than the rim-fixing type. Ted Johnson's dedication and persistence served the Company well – he had a flair for identifying new and often unique applications for Foden vehicles.

The lightest model in the Jubilee range introduced in 1935 was the OG4/4 model, built to give an unladen weight of under 2 tons 10 cwt and thus qualify for operation at 30mph. It had the newly-introduced Gardner 4LK engine of 3.8-litre capacity, itself of lightweight construction and giving 53bhp at 2,000rpm. The model was designed for a maximum payload of 4 tons – there was also a heavier-duty version to carry 5/6 tons.

take time to become effective. Would the old firm fail before the new rationalised range of vehicles could be built and sold? Prior to the 1935 Commercial Vehicle Show, held at that time at Olympia in November, the company had only three confirmed orders in the Sales Department. The principal representatives on the Foden Stand were William Foden, his son Ted Foden who had resigned from his position at ERF to rejoin his father, and finally Ted Johnson, without doubt Foden's most consistently successful salesman.

During the Show they collectively managed to sell a further 30 vehicles of various types and this was the first real indication that the recovery programme was under way.

At the same time, of course, the design of the new rationalised range of vehicles was progressing rapidly towards completion and early in 1936, the relative details of the new models were outlined in a special sales brochure. By virtue of the fact that the majority of the design work on the new vehicles had been carried out in 1935 which was Jubilee Year, the new range was introduced as the Foden 'Jubilee' range of diesel vehicles and William Foden's message to potential customers included in the introductory sales brochure put the emphasis on a combination of reliability and service. It described the Jubilee range as a practical effort by specialised production, to meet the day-to-day needs of users with a range of standard vehicles.

The new range consisted of two four wheel models of 4 tons and 5/6tons payload capacity fitted with the Gardner 4LK engine,

three heavier four-wheelers of 7.5 tons payload capacity fitted with the Gardner 4, 5 or 6LW engines, two six-wheeler models of 10 and 12 ton payload capacity fitted with the Gardner 5 and 6LW engines respectively and finally the top of the range eight-wheeled model of 15.5 tons payload capacity fitted with the Gardner 6LW engine. The relative unladen weights, annual road tax costs, recommended body lengths, payloads and approximate fuel consumption figures were indicated in the well presented sales literature of 1936.

In addition to the comprehensive range of four, six and eight-wheeler vehicles, two standard trailers were offered mainly for use with the heavier four-wheelers.

One particularly striking feature of the 'Jubilee' standardized vehicle range was the new S Type streamlined cab, designed specifically to fall in line with the 'streamlining' concept which was applied to almost any wheeled vehicle at that time. Unfortunately the wide cab corner pillar resulting from this particular design resulted in some loss of driver visibility and later versions of the S Type cab were less 'streamlined', but more practical.

In all other respects, the S Type range of vehicles achieved their principal design objectives of lower unladen weight, higher payload capacity, maximum interchangeability of major components, mechanical reliability, fuel economy and driver acceptance. The individual vehicle specifications included the full range of Gardner engines, Foden four, five and eight-speed gearboxes, Foden front and worm drive rear axles and frame assembly, Clayton Dewandre vacuum servo braking system, Clayton detachable steel tube

The S-type range of models with Gardner LW-type engines was to be the basis of Foden's renewed success – they were identified by DG type letters. The DG4/7½ had the 4LW unit and, as its designation indicated, could take a 7½-ton payload, increasing to 10 tons with a trailer. A heavier-duty version, the DG6/7, was more specifically intended for use with a trailer carrying up to 6 tons, being fitted with the 6LW engine. The new streamlined cab with its strongly-raked windscreen attracted plenty of attention, in itself important in causing potential users to examine the many practical merits of the chassis. At first, it was combined with a radiator similar to that of the R-type.

This DG5/10 was a six-wheeler with the 5LW engine designed for a 10-ton load and having an 18ft-long platform body – note the use of large-section single tyres on the rear bogie. An alternative version, the DG6/12 had the 6LW and a 12-ton payload capacity, being available with up to 20ft platform length.

The DG6/15 was an eight-wheeler with the 6LW and a maximum load of 15½ tons, with platform length of 23ft 8in. Twin tyres on the bogie were standard and it is notable that this example, BKA 207, supplied to Read Motor Services, transport contractors of Liverpool, in the autumn of 1935, had conventional wheels rather than the detachable rim type still being used on other early DG models.

radiators, Foden cam and roller steering gear and Lucas/CAV electrical equipment.

Engine and gearbox were mounted independently in the chassis with a flexible disc type drive shaft from the rear of the single plate clutch assembly to the forward companion flange on the gearbox. A Hardy Spicer propeller shaft completed the final drive from the gearbox rear companion flange to the rear axle worm drive assembly.

The plan view of this particular model clearly illustrates two of the principal design features of the whole range, the rigid chassis design and the simple driver's controls layout.

There can be little doubt that the new vehicles, although designed and produced in a relatively short period of time, would have attracted customers under almost any market conditions, but at this particular period, the transport industry was becoming aware of the financial advantages of operating diesel engined vehicles when compared with the previously more popular, petrol engined units, due, of course, to the wide variation in fuel costs. It was, therefore, not surprising that when the new vehicles became available, the initial demand was much higher than had been anticipated, resulting in a modest but very welcome return to a trading profit for the financial year ending in April, 1936.

Throughout the remainder of the year and into 1937, the order

Foden continued the practice of making its own trailers, having the advantage of interchangeability of wheels and other parts with the vehicles that were to draw them as well as being capable of being offered as part of a complete lorry-and-trailer outfit to users needing such vehicles. This 6-ton model was illustrated in the Jubilee-range brochure.

book continued to expand; additional machine tools were purchased, more workers were taken on and the factory output increased gradually to provide a trading profit of £46,000 by the end of the financial year.

William Foden's planned recovery programme, assisted, it must be admitted to some extent by changing market conditions, was becoming effective much more rapidly than expected and the resultant expansion programme from 1937 onwards was about to provide me with a worthwhile and interesting job for the whole of my working life.

The S-type models were of rugged construction, even though designed to give a reduced unladen weight compared to their predecessors. Features evident in this view of a single-drive six-wheeler include the separate mounting of the gearbox and overhead-worm rear axle, with generous ribbing to aid cooling of the lubricant. The Clayton Dewandre vacuum brake system was of the triple-servo type with two slave cylinders on the front axle working the front brakes and controlled by the main servo linked to the rear bogie brakes.

3 APPRENTICESHIP YEARS

I left Winsford Verdin Grammar School in July, 1937 and, armed with my Oxford School Certificate with credits in six subjects, some of which would be of little value unless I had ambitions to be a parson or a teacher, three Honours Certificates from the Royal Drawing Society which at least indicated that I could draw, and a letter from my headmaster which tended to confirm my long held belief that he and I had lived in completely separate worlds with little or no chance of gainful communication, I began to look for a job.

My father had a successful grocery business in my home town of Northwich, but although I helped out when called upon, I had no aspirations to become a grocer. For as long as I could remember, I had always had an idea that I would be better suited to a job as an engineering draughtsman, preferably in the automotive industry. This was undoubtedly due to my many relatives in Coventry already involved in the industry. My mother's elder brothers all served engineering apprenticeships at the LMS railway workshops at Crewe – the same workshops where Edwin Foden had spent part of his early career before returning to Elworth and establishing the Foden dynasty. Some stayed on but others, perhaps with more ambition, moved south to Coventry where skilled tradesmen were welcomed in the rapidly expanding motor industry.

As a schoolboy, I regularly spent part of the summer holidays with my relatives in Coventry and I was always interested in the rumoured plans of their employers, who at the time were Humber, Alvis, Singer and Armstrong Siddeley. Occasionally I was able to visit the various workshops with one or other of my uncles or cousins and was always mightily impressed. One was a photographer for a subsidiary of the Iliffe group, which published *The Autocar*, and so I frequently had a preview of new models when visiting his studio. Even at that age I could appreciate the designers' and draughtsmens' skills, and I have no doubt that my ambitions were formulated then.

I was looking for work in mid-Cheshire, an area dominated by the salt and chemical industries, mainly Imperial Chemical Industries, with two huge plants in my home town of Northwich and others in towns nearby. All had mechanical engineering departments, dealing mainly with plant design, but such work did not really appeal to me.

However, as my father had arranged an interview for me with the Chief Mechanical Engineer at ICI Northwich at that time, I was obliged to attend and I was always pleased that I did, because he gave me some excellent advice which I shall always remember. The engineer concerned was Mr. Christopher Hinton, who later became Chief Engineer for the Atomic Energy Authority, and his advice was this:- "Before you enter the Drawing Office, learn all you possibly can concerning the properties and capabilities of materials, machine tools and men. Continue this receptive habit throughout your working life and never be afraid of trying something new".

Some weeks later I was offered an apprenticeship at an ICI subsidiary company in Runcorn, but at that time I had applied and been granted an interview at Fodens with Jack Cowap, the Works Director and Edwin Twemlow, the Chief Designer. Following the interviews, I was taken on a quick tour around the various works departments and then returned to the Works Manager's office where I was offered my first job as an engineering apprentice. It was explained to me that I would be expected to work in certain selected works departments over a period of three to four years and at the termination of this period, subject, of course, to satisfactory progress reports from these departments and the local Technical School, I would be considered for admission to the Drawing Office.

Foden's factory premises at that time were confined to an area on either side of the road connecting the villages of Elworth and Ettiley Heath. A railway branch line ran parallel to the western side of this road and it was in this area between the road and the railway that the original Elworth Foundry and workshops were located. Adjoining the foundry and moulding shop were the pattern shop and press shop or boiler shop, as it was better known, and parallel to the boiler shop and adjacent to the road, the repair shop, service office and service stores. The final block of buildings on this side of the road housed the welding shop, assembly shop, joiners shop, paint shop and finally the timber store. On the other side of the road, directly opposite to the foundry was the main office block, housing, on the ground floor, the Board Room which the Managing Director, William Foden used as his office, the Company Secretary, the Purchase Department and Sales Department. The top floor was occupied by the Cost Accounts Department and the Drawing Office.

Across the office yard was the Time Office where we collected our weekly wage and an office shared by the Works Manager and the Labour Manager. Further down the road on this eastern side was the main six-bay workshop which extended for the full length of the site and included the machine shops, the chassis production line, the raw material and finished parts stores and the tool room. The only other building on this eastern side of the road was the Garage, a huge open structure more commonly known as "King Kong's Kennel", which housed the finished vehicles prior to final test and delivery.

The factory layout was not ideal by any means. Vehicles were built in the Erecting Shop up to a 'chassis only' point and then driven over to the spray booths on the other side of the factory. They were then moved into the Assembly Shop for the fitment of cab, body and electrical equipment, then transferred to the adjoining paint shop for final finishing before being driven back to the Garage for final inspection and delivery.

It was early October, 1937 when I started work in Foden's Assembly Shop under a foreman named Frank Nicholls at a weekly wage of 8/-, a salary destined to be dramatically increased to 10/- two months later following a threatened apprentice strike. The power of collective action was, therefore, demonstrated to me quite early in my working life! I found that my foreman, Frank Nicholls, was a strict disciplinarian, with authority to suspend or sack an employee at a minute's notice, but at the same time helpful, fair in his judgment and an excellent practical tradesman, in his case, coppersmith and sheet metal worker. He led his workmen by example and he always presented an open mind to the use of new materials and production methods, some of which I became personally involved with during my period in his department. Time-served fitters and joiners, who constituted the majority of the work force in the Assembly Shop in 1937, were paid a weekly wage of £3. 6s. 8d. or £3.33p in current monetary terms, for a 47-hour working week.

Working hours were 7.55am to 5.30pm Monday to Friday and 7.55am to 12 noon on Saturdays. We had an hour for lunch between 12.30 and 1.30, there was no works canteen, so the normal procedure as far as I was concerned was a quick sandwich or chip shop lunch in around fifteen minutes and then 45 minutes football in a field behind the timber storage sheds. Assembly and Joiners Shops normally played against Welding and Repair Shops for the simple reason that they were located in the same area of the works.

Rivalry was intense and no quarter was asked for or given. Some of the players who operated machine tools wore wooden soled, metal tipped footwear, more commonly known as 'clogs' by virtue of the fact that normal footwear quickly deteriorated under their particular working conditions. To be tackled by an opponent wearing clogs can be a shattering and painful experience and we learned to play a version of the modern 'two touch' football, simply as a method of self-preservation, long before it became part of standard football coaching procedure.

Nevertheless, I always enjoyed my lunchtime games and the resultant closer acquaintance with my fellow workmates. In fact, after a very short period of time, I came to the conclusion that despite the longer working hours and increased travelling times, working at Fodens was a vastly more rewarding activity than any part of my school career – I never had cause to change that opinion.

Travelling to Elworth was initially somewhat time consuming, but I soon solved that problem, which in any event was a problem shared by almost 50% of the workforce. When I started work at Fodens in 1937 the total number of employees would be around 500, and well over 200 of this number would be travelling daily by bus, bike or train from the adjoining Cheshire towns of Crewe, Congleton, Middlewich or Winsford. Very few workmen had cars. I initially travelled to work by train from Northwich at a cost of ninepence per day, but the train times did not coincide too well with my working hours, so I began to cycle the ten mile journey each way every day and thereby saved a total of four shillings and sixpence per week towards my first car, a 1926 Austin Seven tourer, which I bought in 1938 from the charge-hand electrician in the Assembly Shop for £7 10s. As I recall it, the car required odd mechanical repairs, but, as would be expected from the previous owner, the electrical system was in excellent condition. Much later in my time at Fodens I had the privilege of working, for a short time, alongside the man who was personally involved in the original design of this remarkable model. His name was Stanley Edge, and he had some fascinating tales to tell.

However, to revert to 1937, when I began work at Fodens, the 'S' type rationalised range of vehicles introduced in 1935 had now been operational for a period of two years, and a number of major design improvements had been incorporated, the most immediately obvious modification being the cab design. The original 'Streamline' cab profile with wide section front corner pillars and angled front screen, was superseded by a more practical cab front design, which improved visibility and reduced manufacturing costs. Two versions were introduced, the S.9 for the light four-wheeler 6 ton payload range of vehicles and the S.10 for the heavier four, six and eight-wheelers.

One other later, but easily identifiable change related to the radiator shell assembly on all models which was now curved to match the cab front profiles.

In addition to these relatively cosmetic changes, there was a number of quite comprehensive specification modifications either already in progress or planned for the immediate future.

Firstly, the lightest vehicles in the S Type range were the OG 4/6

The cab design for the S-type models was revised after experience had revealed that the original more extreme 'streamline' version of 1935 created a blind spot for the driver, because of the width of the windscreen pillars at his eye level. This modified S.10 design was introduced, still with a modern profile but also having the advantage of reduced manufacturing cost. At first it continued to be combined with the vertical radiator, as on this example for H. B. Hewitt, haulage contractor, of Manchester.

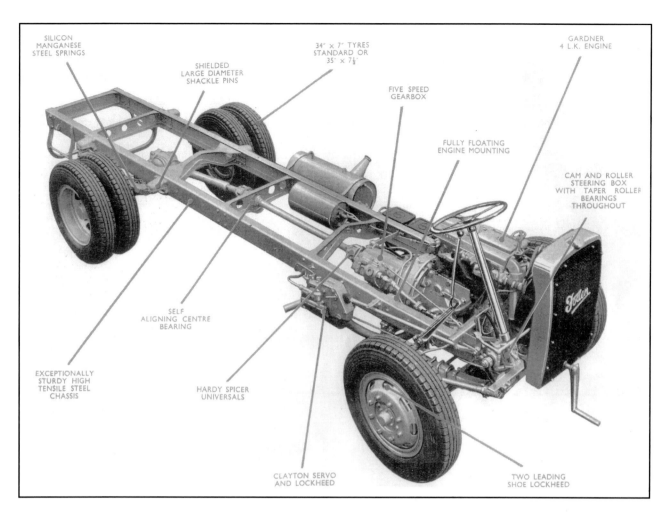

The OG4/6 chassis designed for a 6-ton payload, as being produced from 1937, used the Gardner 4LK engine with Foden-built four-speed gearbox mounted directly behind it, together with vacuum-hydraulic brakes. The radiator was now curved in profile to match that of the cab front. In this form it was marketed at £890. Later a five-speed gearbox was offered, as indicated on this photograph of a chassis with the main features annotated.

four-wheeler models powered by the 53hp 4LK Gardner engine, the latter fitted with Kirkstall 3 ton front and 6 ton worm drive rear axles.

In addition to the redesigned cab, this vehicle specification now included a completely new Foden four speed gearbox mounted directly on to the engine flywheel housing and a hydraulically operated Girling two-leading-shoe braking system. With the new gearbox, the vehicle was now capable of a top speed of 33 mph and a maximum gradient-ability of 1 in 4.25 with a full 6 ton payload. The standard 11ft 3in wheelbase model could be fitted with either a 14ft or 15ft body and in the late 1930s customer demand for this vehicle soon exceeded Fodens' maximum production capabilities which were restricted by the availability of the 4 LK engine from Gardners.

The heavier four-wheel 7½ ton payload model with Foden 4 ton front and 8 ton worm drive rear axles was now offered with a 4, 5 or 6LW Gardner engine and direct mounted four or five-speed Foden gearbox, a common wheelbase of 13ft 7½in to suit a 17ft 6in standard flat body length and three shorter wheelbases of 10ft 3½in, 8ft 7in and 8ft 0¾in to suit tipper and tractor unit applications. The 6LW model with five-speed gearbox could operate with a trailer and carry a total payload of 11 tons.

As the individual vehicle specifications were extended and

improved, more attention was given to the content of the relative sales brochures which now provided far more detailed technical information for the prospective customers.

The two remaining vehicle types which completed the four wheeler range were both short wheelbase tractors, the STG5 Timber Tractor fitted with a 5LW Gardner engine and heavy duty power take off and winch drive, and the longer wheelbase GHT6/ 50 ton General Haulage Tractor fitted with the 6LW Gardner engine.

The standard six-wheeler models were fitted with the Gardner 5 or 6LW engines, Foden five-speed gearbox, Foden 4 ton front axle and 16 ton single or double drive rear bogie axle assembly, providing a payload capacity of 12 tons, with a maximum body length of 22ft 0in. There was also an alternative single drive pivoting arm design rear bogie available with a single wheel at the rear and twin wheels on the leading axle. This arrangement had the desired effect of reducing unladen weight and increasing the payload, but, of course, reduced tractive ability.

Finally, to complete the six-wheeler range, Fodens produced a double front axle vehicle with two 4 ton steering axles and a single drive 8 ton rear axle. The vehicle had a 5LW Gardner engine and Foden 5-speed gearbox, the payload capacity was 10 tons and the maximum body length 20ft 0in. The model was designated the

This plan view of the DG4/7½ type shows the adoption of unit assembly for the engine and gearbox – a noteworthy feature, particularly for a goods model at that period, was the adoption of 'fully floating' engine mounting, claimed to eliminate all vibration from the chassis. The brakes on this model had also changed to the type with vacuum servo acting through a hydraulic system, as widely favoured among British commercial vehicle makers at the time. The provision of servo assistance for the handbrake was an unusual feature – Foden continued to favour the mounting of the handbrake lever to the left of the driver. The standard 6.25 to 1 axle ratio gave 30.5mph in top gear, which meant that the engine was running at an economical 1,100rpm at the legal maximum for this type of vehicle of 20mph.

DFA5/10, but was more generally known, like others of this layout, as "The Chinese Six".

The final vehicle in the S Type range, undoubtedly the most popular with operators, was the 15 ton payload eight-wheeler fitted with the Gardner 6LW engine, Foden five-speed gearbox, twin Foden 4-ton front axles, and a double or single drive Foden 16 ton rear bogie axle assembly. With a mean wheelbase of 13ft 8¼in from second front axle to rear bogie centreline a maximum inside body length of 24ft 0in was attainable for the maximum designed payload of 15 tons.

This double drive eight-wheeler model, together with the double drive six-wheeler was available with shorter wheelbase to suit tipping body applications, the eight-wheeler to suit a 16ft 0in body and the six-wheeler to suit a 14ft 0in body.

This was the range of vehicles destined to support the company for the remainder of the decade, also to constitute the basis of the design for the military vehicles produced during the war years and finally, to meet the immediate requirement for new vehicles after the war was successfully terminated.

The Commercial Vehicle Exhibition held at Earls Court in November 1937 presented the opportunity to show the S Type range at its best and the two eight-wheelers on the Foden stand were considered to be the stars of the Show. All vehicles were finished in the Paint Shop adjacent to the Assembly Shop where I worked and I remember these two vehicles quite well. The customers were Toft Bros and Tomlinson of Darley Dale and L. J. Bassett & Son Ltd of Tittensor.

Orders taken at the Show confirmed the increasing customer demand and this favourable trend was underlined by the company financial statement issued in April 1938 which showed profits for the financial year 1937/38 had increased to £46,000. However, as the orders poured in to the Sales Department, delivery dates became extended to unacceptable levels and it was obvious that there were serious production restrictions which needed immediate attention. The directors realised the need for an experienced Production Engineer, and the eventual successful applicant decided, fortunately for me, to concentrate his first efforts on the cab assembly line where certain clearly definable assembly problems existed. The S.9 and S.10 cabs produced at that time had an ash frame with aluminium panels and they were individually built by joiners and sheet metal workers on the assembly line. The newly appointed Production Engineer, Mr Eric Ingham, had spent his early career with Rolls Royce and Vauxhall Motors, where production rates were far higher than Fodens. He quickly identified the problem and proposed an improved method of assembly which involved the prefabrication of the five major cab elements, front, back, roof and two sides, leaving only a final assembly requirement on the cab line.

I submitted a suggestion through my foreman that an ideal way to illustrate and evaluate the proposal would be to construct two cab models, one using the current method of construction, the other the proposed method. The suggestion was quickly approved and I built two ⅛in scale models in balsa wood which served their intended purpose and also provided me with an influential contact to promote my immediate ambition, which was to move on to other departments to gain further work experience.

In 1938 I was transferred to the Machine Shop, initially on the marking-off bench where components which had no relative jigs or fixtures were individually marked up for machining.

The double front axle or twin-steering six-wheeler had come into favour as a means of catering for an intermediate weight category between the two-axle and conventional three-axle types, the latter normally having twin tyres on both rear axles, making ten tyres in all, whereas this type had eight. It was known as the DFA5/10 in the most usual form, with Gardner 5LW engine, catering for a 10-ton payload, yet weighing under 5 tons unladen. To avoid overloading the rear axle, the rear overhang was quite short. This artist's impression used in sales brochures made the radiator appear narrower than it actually was.

I found that this departmental transfer also involved an automatic football transfer. I was informed by the Machine Shop Storekeeper, a forceful character by the name of Fred Bickerton, more commonly known as "Bicky", that I would now be expected to play for the Machine Shop in the lunchtime games. It should be explained at this point that the Storekeepers in the main departments at Fodens had other unofficial, but traditional duties involving the general welfare of the personnel in their respective departments. They organised cash collections for weddings, funerals, long term sickness and other individual calamities, and also organised all departmental indoor and outdoor sporting events and the usual seasonal orgies. Rivalry between the various departments was generally friendly and well controlled, but between Frank Capper, the Joiners Shop

storekeeper and Fred Bickerton of the Machine Shop there appeared to be a personal vendetta which occasionally culminated in hammers being thrown and the stores door kicked in.

At such times, the respective foreman would intervene, the protagonists would be severely lectured as to their future conduct and confined to their respective stores. The marking-off bench in the Machine Shop was located alongside the Machine Shop Stores so that I was able, on my new job, to observe these occasional altercations at first hand and I eventually formed the opinion that although the two contestants obviously disliked each other, their more violent public conflicts were staged for our benefit.

However, later in that same year, I had another move to the Erecting Shop, where the complete chassis and transmission was

Foden took up the 'streamline' theme of the mid to late 1930s more strongly than any of the other makers in the heavy commercial vehicle business, making its products attractive to operators wanting eye-catching vehicles. This special platform body was built on a DG6/15 eight-wheeler for L. J. Bassett & Son Ltd of Tittensor, Stoke-on-Trent, registered FRF 49, dating from late 1937, when the first Commercial Vehicle Show to be held in the newly-built Earls Court building in London enabled the latest models to be displayed to advantage. It shows how neatly the curved-profile radiator matched the lines of the S.10 cab. This particular vehicle also had a double-bar front bumper, twin fog-lamps and horns, all non-standard items adding to the 'special' look.

The models of that period were popular with both owners and drivers, being sensibly designed, well built from sound materials and thoroughly reliable. By modern standards they were sparsely equipped, there being no cab heaters or noise insulation, and both skill and strength were needed for the crash gearboxes and unassisted steering. Quite apart from the official 20mph speed limit, speed on hills soon dropped with the 6LW engine then giving a maximum 102bhp to move 22 tons gross. Yet the heavy vehicle drivers of those days, often nicknamed 'knights of the road', derived a sense of pride in being given charge of what they soon realised were high-quality machines.

By 1936, the Foden standard timber tractor, type STG5, had evolved as a basically more conventional machine with Gardner 5LW engine driving through a four-speed gearbox to an overhead worm drive rear axle, designed for use with a six-wheeled trailer. Its special features included the three-point suspension arrangement, in principle much as used in steam days, as a means of avoiding stress when traversing rough ground, and a 30-ton winch, with land anchor device, which could move timber or the loaded trailer even when normal haulage would have been impossible.

assembled. Some of the vehicles passing through the Erecting Shop at that time were destined for the Scottish Motor Traders Show held at the Kelvin Hall, Glasgow in November and the picture below from the *Foden News* of the period indicates the growing popularity of the various Foden vehicle types with Scottish operators.

In 1939 I had a further work experience move to the Tool Room, initially as a fitter and machinist, producing jigs and fixtures for new vehicle components, a job that I found very much to my liking because each job presented different fitting problems and involved the use of various machine tools. We had specialist machine tool operators in the Tool Room, but we also had individual machines that the fitters were allowed to use and my liking for this type of work probably resulted in my next and final move in the Works.

In mid 1939 Fodens had managed, with some difficulty, to

import a new Hauser jig borer from Switzerland, and following the installation of this highly efficient new machine in a temperature regulated glasshouse in the Tool Room, I was offered the job of operating the machine on a shift basis together with one of the older foreman machinists, a man named Albert Barker, but more commonly known in the Tool Room as "Patsy" Barker. He was an admirable mate to work with, and we had an effective basic working relationship whereby I handled the occasional machine set-ups where a certain amount of trigonometry was required and Albert maintained the range of boring tools in prime condition at all times.

The Scottish Show, held biennially in Glasgow, acted as the main exhibition for commercial vehicles in years when there was no London Show, and that of November 1938 was destined to be the last public commercial vehicle display until 1948. The display was a good cross-section of the Foden range of the time, with the latest version of the light 6-ton OG4/6 model with Gardner 4LK engine in the foreground, a double front axle six-wheeler behind it and an eight-wheeler to the right. This view also conveys the difference in appearance between the S.9 cab used on the OG-series models and the S.10 used on the heavier models, the former more upright in appearance largely because of being built to a shorter length made possible by the smaller engine and thus allowing maximum load space. The unladen weight, as recorded for registration purposes, of this model had now been reduced to the 2 tons 10 cwt figure hitherto confined to the 4-ton OG4/4 model, which was no longer offered. Note that all three exhibits had a style of deep single-piece front bumper and twin fog-lamps, the latter more than mere decoration in an era when industrial smog was frequently met in many parts of the country.

A view of our Exhibits showing three latest type Diesel Commercial vehicles, including one four one six and one eight wheeler. The fourwheeler is the new 6 tonner, under 50 cwt. registration weight, supplied to the order of Messrs. Cowan & Co. General Carriers, Glasgow, making their 36th repeat order. Judging from the enquiries and the number of orders received up-to-date this vehicle is going to revolutionise this class of Road Transport.

Messrs. David Barrie Ltd., of Dundee have further increased their fleet of Fodens by the purchase of an eight-wheeled vehicle, as shown above. The double front axle 6 wheeler in the photograph is the third Foden Diesel in service of Messrs. Brysons Motors Ltd., Glasgow.

NEW 6 TON FODEN DIESEL—REGISTRATION WEIGHT UNDER 50 CWTS

4 THE WAR YEARS, 1939-45

When War was declared in September, 1939 we were already working a 72-hour week on alternate, twelve-hour day and night shifts, one week of days, one week of nights, mainly on jigs and fixtures, not solely for our own military vehicle programme, but also for the Rolls Royce and Ford Motor companies, who were both tooling up for the production of the Merlin engine destined for the Spitfire fighter aircraft. Early in 1940 we were informed that Fodens had joined a consortium of companies whose prime objective was to build armoured fighting vehicles for the Ministry of Supply and within a very short time we began to receive orders and drawings for the relative jigs and fixtures required to manufacture this type of vehicle, which was in fact the 'Crusader' cruiser tank. To meet this additional production responsibility, additional labour was urgently required throughout the company and I have no doubt that under normal circumstances I would have had the opportunity to work in several other works departments before being considered for the Drawing Office. However, these were hardly normal circumstances and there was apparently an immediate vacancy in the jig and tool section of the Drawing Office. I was duly interviewed by Mr. Edwin Twemlow, the Chief Designer, and eventually offered the job at a weekly wage of three pounds ten shillings. I had to wait for some time while a replacement was trained to take my job on the jig borer and I eventually entered the Drawing Office in June or July of 1940.

I found the new job interesting, but not too demanding because I was really drawing out jigs and fixtures similar to those which I had previously been making, and when Jack Mills, the Chassis Design Section Leader asked if I would like to work for him on the

Foden received orders for General Service vehicles for use by the army, beginning in 1940. The designs were derived from the civilian S-type DG-series models, and the initial versions had standard 36in x 8in tyres, with twins at the rear, as shown in this drawing of what was described as the '14ft W.D. Wagon'. This two-axle model was basically similar to the civilian DG5/7½ as built up to that time, but with typical military canvas tilt body, the spare wheel relocated behind the cab and various other changes, such as the forward extension of the frame with crash bar protecting the radiator and gas detector plate in front of the nearside windscreen.

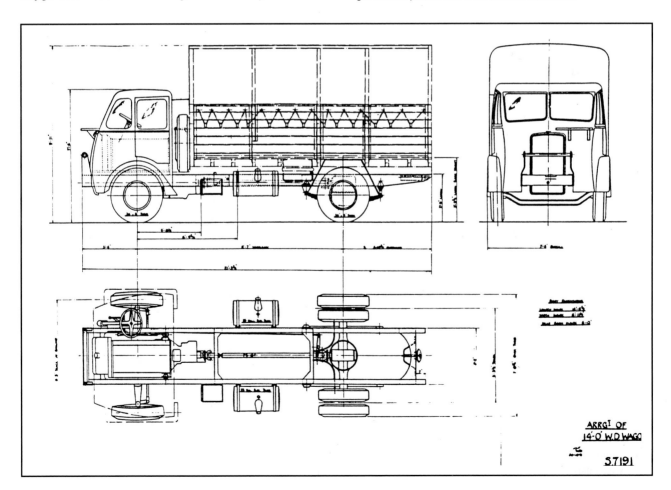

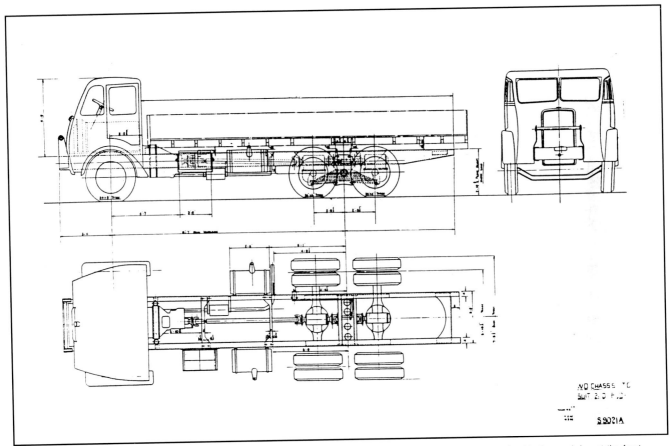

This early version of the military six-wheeler with dropside body differed only slightly from the civilian DG6/12, most noticeably the crash bar at the front.

military vehicles, I accepted the offer immediately and never had cause to regret it. I had no way of knowing at that time that I would be working almost continuously under his direction and guidance for the next 32 years at which point in 1972, he had achieved the position of Engineering Director and I was the Design Department Manager. At that time, the Design Department staff totalled approximately sixty, but when I started work in the Drawing Office in 1940, the total was exactly fourteen, including the Chief Designer, Chief Draughtsman, seven draughtsmen of varying ages and abilities from design draughtsmen to juniors such as myself, two racers, one technical clerk, one secretary and a junior in the print room. In such a small department, a high degree of co-operation and team spirit was always essential to achieve any degree of efficiency and fortunately, although the original staff total increased dramatically in the later years, this commendable ability to work together was retained and even extended outside working hours with the formation of the Drawing Office Sports and Social Club, which eventually had Cricket and Football teams capable of competing effectively with any of the more extensively staffed works departments. However, in July 1940 all of this future was uncertain. The French armed forces had capitulated, the British Army was in process of reforming after Dunkirk, the German air offensive was about to start, and I had been instructed by my new boss to revise the spare wheel carrier design on the six wheeler Army vehicles.

Fodens had received extensive orders for four and six-wheeler General Service Vehicles in 1940. The respective vehicle specifications were based on the four and six-wheeler 'S' type DG range, with 5 and 6LW Gardner engines, Foden 5 speed gearboxes,

Foden 4 ton front and 8 ton worm-drive rear axles with an S type double-drive two-spring rear bogie axle assembly on the six wheeler. Original tyre equipment size was 36in x 8in all round, with twin tyres on the rear driving axles, but as the Desert War developed in North Africa, single 13.50in x 20in single tyres were fitted to improve flotation. Unfortunately, no power steering or suitable steering linkage damping device was available and it was subsequently implied that the Foden drivers could be easily identified from their more fortunate colleagues, by their damaged hands. The wood framed, aluminium panelled S10 cab was modified to enable the top section from the waistrail to be removed to facilitate shipment, and an observation hatch with machine gun mounting ring was fitted into the cab roof on the mate's side.

Heavy duty pulling jaws and a radiator protection bar were incorporated in the extended front end of the main chassis frame and a cast pulling jaw was fitted to the rear crossmember. The wooden bodies were made with a canvas tilt cover over a tubular steel framework and could be dismantled in sections, again to assist shipment. During the war period a total of 1,750 vehicles of this type were delivered to the Army, the majority being six wheelers. The four wheelers were used mainly in the UK, the six wheelers initially in North Africa, then Greece and Italy, and finally France, Belgium, Holland and Germany. All of the Foden vehicles operating in the Greek sector had to be destroyed before and during the evacuation in May, 1941.

In the Autumn of 1942 we were ordered to prepare waterproof instruction manuals for the Foden six wheeler vehicles and it immediately became obvious that at last the tide was turning and an

The military version of the Foden six-wheeler evolved into this form, with single 13.5in x 20in tyres, the body then requiring to be modified to allow for the upward movement of these larger-diameter tyres allowed by the degree of articulation available with the Foden rear bogie, this latter an important asset when traversing uneven ground. Wartime needs meant elimination of peacetime 'frills' but the Foden remained instantly recognisable, notably by the shape of the S.10 cab, even though it had been modified to allow the top to be removed for shipping.

Allied landing on some section of the European coast was imminent. I was allocated the job of checking the vehicles' wading capabilities and preparing the required waterproofing kit with appropriate fitting instructions, and it proved to be quite an interesting assignment. The vehicles had to be made capable of operating during the landing operation in a sea depth of 48in plus an intermittent wave depth of 18in and the waterproofing kits had to be made capable of fitment in three stages within a specific time scale as follows:-

Stage 1	At Concentration Areas 200 miles from Embarkation Points.	50 man hours.
Stage 2	At Marshalling Areas 20 miles from Embarkation Points	4½ man hours.
Stage 3	During loading or on the Landing Craft.	30 Minutes.

We found from static tests in our own tank wash pit that the most vulnerable areas on the Foden vehicles were the Gardner engine crankshaft front end oil return sleeve, which, of course, tended to induce water into the engine crankcase when fully immersed, the engine fuel pumps and the Bendix Cowdrey brakes.

The crankshaft was sealed by means of some circular felt seals enclosed in a detachable clamp type housing, the fuel pumps were waterproofed by the application of a plastic compound and the brake problems were dealt with by a series of specific instructions to the driver after landing and then further workshop attention to the brakes at the first opportunity after landing. The principal problem with the brakes related to the long term corrosive effect of sea water on aluminium alloy components used in the brake

actuator assembly and was hardly likely to affect the vehicle's performance during, or immediately after the landing operation.

There were other, less important areas of necessary attention, but, after we had carried out a series of successful embarkation and landing trials on the Instow and Westward Ho beaches of North Devon, we were better prepared to complete the waterproofing instructions handbook with some degree of confidence.

The trials not only involved embarking and disembarking from landing craft in various sea conditions, but also rounding a series of buoys moored at the maximum depth parallel to the shore line. Some of the vehicles became waterlogged during this test and had to be towed in, but the Foden six-wheeler completed the exercise without any apparent problem. The waterproofing manual was eventually completed and submitted to the appropriate military authority, together with the necessary waterproofing material and parts kits and our fervent hope for fair weather landings. Eventually, long after the European War ended, we learned that the waterproofing exercise had been successful.

In the North African, Sicilian and Italian beach landings only 0.15% of 'B' type General Service vehicles were lost due to waterproofing failure or inefficient driving.

The Foden four and six-wheeler General Service vehicles performed reasonably well under wartime operating conditions, considering that they were, in fact, simply modified civilian goods vehicles, but they were far inferior in design and operational ability to the equivalent German military vehicles for a very good reason, which we only completely discovered some time after the war when we began to export crane carriers and other specialised vehicles to Germany and had the opportunity to meet and talk to German automotive engineers. Apparently in 1933, long before the invasion of Poland and the start point of World War II, an edict was

A convoy of standard Foden six-wheel General Service vehicles ready for delivery after final test.

issued by the Nazi dominated German Government to the German automotive industry to rationalise the complete range of vehicles then being produced, and to concentrate future production on certain specific models suitable for conversion to military use. This measure was known as the "Von Schell Standardisation Programme" and was most effectively implemented. Private car models were reduced from 52 to 19, commercial vehicles, more significantly, from 113 to 30 models in four separate weight categories. Similar stringent rationalisation measures were imposed on engine, gearbox, axle and other basic automotive unit manufacturers resulting in overall automotive production industry readiness that we could never match.

In addition to the 1,750 General Service vehicles built for the Armed Forces during the War, Fodens produced 770 Crusader and Centaur cruiser tanks, plus several cruiser tank conversion projects to meet specific operational requirements in the latter stages of the War in Europe and finally part of the 'Whale' and 'Shark' sections of the Mulberry Harbour used to land non-amphibious transport for the Normandy invasion of Europe in June 1944. These departures from the normal pattern of Foden products are worthy of a more detailed account.

Typical of British tank designs at the beginning of the 1939–45 war was the Matilda, seen here in Mark II form, quite heavily armoured but slow moving and with a 2-pdr gun which was to prove ineffective against more powerful German weapons.

The cruiser tank saga is a story worth recounting because without the forethought of a few individuals and in particular, one man, William Morris, founder of the car manufacturing business bearing his name, and later Lord Nuffield, we may not have had a viable cruiser tank production facility at all. The tank had been designed and developed by British engineers during the latter stages of World War I, specifically as an infantry support weapon for attacks on fixed defensive positions. Two typical examples of this type of heavily armoured, slow moving tank in service at the commencement of World War II in 1939 were the 'Valentine' and 'Matilda', both designed and built by Vickers.

Despite repeated pressure from both retired and serving senior military personnel, very little progress had been made in tank design in the 1920s and early 1930s, and Morris had been made aware of the Army's requirement for a lighter, faster and more manoeuvrable armoured fighting vehicle following a visit to the Soviet Union by Field Marshall Wavell and General Martel in 1935, when they had an opportunity to witness the performance of the Russian high speed, medium weight cruiser tank. One of the major new design features of the Soviet tank was the track suspension, which they found, to their surprise, had been designed by an American engineer named Walter Christie. (Basically, each solid rubber tyred track suspension wheel was independently mounted on spring loaded arms). This arrangement allowed considerably higher track speeds and was much more reliable than the leaf spring mounted pulley design used previously.

In 1936 Nuffield sent one of his senior automotive engineers to the States and eventually discovered that Christie had already submitted designs and actually built prototype high speed tanks for the American Army with little result. He immediately decided to purchase one of the prototypes, arranged shipment to the U.K. disguised as an agricultural tractor and subsequently invited Christie himself to the U.K. in the spring of 1937. The prototype tank was successfully demonstrated to the appropriate British Military Authority at speeds up to 50 mph and Nuffield immediately decided to design his own version of the tank, at that time without any official backing. However, by the end of 1937, with the backing of General Martel, by this time promoted to the position of Assistant

Left: The first British tank with Christie suspension was this A13 cruiser tank, given the name Covenanter, still with 2-pdr gun, but capable of higher cross-country speeds.

Right: The Crusader, type A19, was the development of the cruiser tank that was entrusted to Fodens to put into production. When the Author joined the Drawing Office in 1940, almost the whole staff were involved in jig and tool design for its manufacture. The early versions again had the 2-pdr gun, but later this was replaced with the 6-pdr, as seen here.

Foot of page: Among the tests required to be carried out on the Crusader tanks were checks that water did not enter the hull and that the electrical circuits were not affected by immersion. This tank wash pit was used for this purpose, as seen here with an early Crusader with the 2-pdr gun. This tank was also used in the development of waterproofing for military versions of Foden wheeled vehicles, as described in the text of an earlier page.

Director of Mechanisation, the Nuffield group of companies became tank manufacturers, and a new company entitled Nuffield Mechanisation and Aero Ltd was established, initially based in workshops adjacent to the Wolseley car plant in Birmingham. Staffed primarily by personnel from Morris Commercial who had some experience of Ministry requirements, the new company, during 1938 and 1939, designed and produced the first cruiser tank models with Christie suspension. This first model was known as the "Covenanter" and the first two were delivered to the Army early in 1939. By December of that year the total had grown to 67, but the country was now at war, and tank production required a dramatic and immediate boost.

Nuffield Mechanisation was accordingly appointed as the 'Parent' unit of a group of selected manufacturers under the overall guidance of Sir Miles Thomas, Lord Nuffield's appointed second in command, with the specific objective of building cruiser tanks in ever-increasing numbers. The selected group included Fodens, Ruston Bucyrus, Clayton Dewandre, West's Gas, and later the MG Car Company.

In 1940 when I moved into the Drawing Office at Fodens, almost the whole of the staff were engaged in jig and tool design to prepare for the manufacture of the latest version of the cruiser Tank by this time redesigned and renamed Crusader.

The power unit was a modified twelve-cylinder 'Liberty' engine originally designed in 1918 for airship propulsion, gearboxes were supplied by Nuffield, brakes and controls by Clayton Dewandre. The main hull and turret were originally fabricated from $^5/_8$ in section armour plate, later substantially increased in thickness and reinforced in critical areas. Each Crusader tank comprised

The Centaur was a further development from the Crusader, with 6pdr gun as main armament from the beginning as well as a redesigned turret.

6,200 parts and required 60,000 individual machining and assembly operations. Two of the main jigs and fixtures designed at Fodens to fabricate and machine the hull and turret were considered to be more effective than those in use, and were accordingly adopted for the complete group, who were now made more aware of the fact that Fodens had an effective engineering department. The first Foden built Crusader was delivered to Farnborough in October 1940. By the end of the war the total was 770 and the design had changed considerably.

The first change involved the two pounder main armament which, although apparently adequate against the Italian forces in North Africa, proved to be less than adequate when facing the heavier German Panzer tanks and the German 88mm anti tank weapons. A six-pounder gun replaced the original two pounder, other changes increased the armour plate thickness in the main hull and the turret design was completely modified to house the heavier armament. The original Mark I Crusaders eventually became obsolete and these later versions of the cruiser tank were renamed 'Centaur'.

The engineering capability of Fodens had apparently now been recognised by the Group and we were accordingly entrusted with the design and prototype build of two conversions of the obsolete Mark I Crusaders.

The declared objective of the first Crusader conversion was to provide an armoured towing vehicle and gun crew carrier for the newly designed 17-pounder anti tank gun. In addition to the normal kit and weapon stowage requirements of the eight man crew, sufficient rounds of ammunition had to be carried to ensure that the gun could be brought into effective action in the event of any delay in the arrival of the supporting ammunition carriers. The new gun had been designed to at least equate to the performance of the German 88mm dual purpose weapon and was already in production

The Crusader is seen here as converted to a towing vehicle for a 17-pdr gun. The driver and commander were seated facing forward in the normal offside and nearside control positions. Seating space for the six-man gun crew was also provided, three on each side, facing inwards to the emergency ammunition rack. Rifles, rations, radio and medical equipment were stored on the rear bulkhead, toolboxes and fuel on the track guards. Spare track links were stowed in racks on the front armour plate. The angle-iron fabrication on the engine cover at the rear was a carrier for a spare wheel for the 17-pdr gun.

when we received the order for the prototype towing vehicles, so we had little time to spare. In order to provide the required stowage space inside the tank hull, it was necessary to remove the turret and turret mounting plates completely and then cut out all the internal bulkheads between the engine compartment and the main frontal armour plates. Into this space we had to fit the gun crew, their weapons, ammunition, medical and communication requirement and personal kit, plus the 17-pounder shells and finally, the driver and commander.

We designed, built and demonstrated a prototype in seven weeks, the final demonstration taking place on Horse Guards Parade. As the draughtsman allocated to this particular project, I was allowed to travel down to London with our leading tank test driver on the Diamond-T tank transporter, and it proved to be quite an interesting trip. There were two RASC drivers in charge of the transporter, but the cab seated only three, with the result that one of us had to travel on the ballast box. Fortunately the weather was fine. The journey from Sandbach to London lasted almost two days, our overnight stop being the Army Barracks in Weedon. We were met in St. Albans by a Metropolitan Police escort and guided with impressive priority through the London traffic to the St. James's Park entrance of the Horse Guards Parade where we off-loaded the converted Crusader and prepared for the following day's inspection and demonstration.

On this and subsequent trips to London on similar projects, we were accommodated overnight at the Great Central Hotel in Baker Street, which during the War served as the headquarters for the RASC and also the Special Operations Organisation. The accommodation was first class, we had our meals in the Sergeants' Mess and transport was always available. The inspection and demonstration of the converted Crusader the following day appeared to meet the requirements of the various Military and Ministry personnel who attended, and in the early evening I was on my way back to Sandbach by train with instructions to complete a further three pre-production conversions. The same small team of pattern makers, fitters and welders who had carried out the prototype conversion in the Experimental Department at Fodens built a further three pre-production units before transferring all drawings, templates and other conversion data over to our Group colleagues, Ruston Bucyrus, the crane and excavator manufacturers at Lincoln, who apparently had capacity available for full production. The transfer involved several meetings with our opposite numbers at Rustons and I recall they were particularly impressed with our photographic method of recording each stage of the conversion sequence and the general standard of our team's workmanship.

We had no way of knowing it at that time, but the favourable impression created by our personnel was to serve our company well in the future when Rustons became one of our principal customers for truck mounted crane chassis. Ruston Bucyrus converted almost 200 Crusaders into gun towing vehicles and according to Group records, they were operational through to the successful termination of the European War in 1945.

The second project we were called upon to implement involved the conversion of obsolete Crusader tanks into armoured bulldozers prior to the Allied invasion of Europe in 1944. This was to prove a much more difficult exercise than the gun towing conversion by virtue of the fact that the new operational requirements as an armoured bulldozer differed in so many respects from the original design parameters as a Cruiser tank. For example, the Crusader transmission arrangement was in no way suitable for normal earthmover application. However, it was pointed out to us that the main military purposes of the armoured bulldozer were to assist in the clearance of defended road blocks, and to doze and level damaged roads in forward areas. Effectively reassured, we obtained a suitable width bulldozer blade from Alldays and Onions and designed a frame assembly supported by cast outriggers from the main tank hull and upon which we mounted the blade thrust arms and pivots, together with guide rollers to withstand any side loading.

We removed the tank turret and internal bulkheads, welded a small jib structure on the forward armour plate and used the hydraulic turret rotation drive motor as a winch drive unit to raise and lower the blade with a wire rope via guide pulleys located in the jib and the hull top plate. The bulldozer crew consisted of a driver and commander only, so that we had no equipment stowage problems with this particular conversion. In the transit condition, the bulldozer blade and thrust arm assembly had to be located high enough for the driver and commander to view the road under the blade; hence the necessity for the height of the jib on the forward armour plate. In the operational condition, when bulldozing at normal road level the crew had a clear view over the top of the blade. We had received an initial order from the Ministry for five prototype conversions; I was again the draughtsman allocated to the job, and we had utilised virtually the same selected work crew who had carried out the successful gun towing conversion programme. These men, all first class tradesmen, pattern makers, fitters and

When the Crusader tanks became obsolete under the fierce competitive conditions of war, it was decided to convert numbers of the type into armoured bulldozers to allow rapid clearance of road blocks or levelling of damaged roads in forward areas under possible enemy sniper fire. Foden was entrusted with the design work and the conversion of five prototypes and, as with the gun towing conversion, the author was the draughtsman allocated to the project, working with a small team of craftsmen, the leading hands involved all being destined to become departmental heads in later years.

welders performed minor miracles on a regular basis to enable us to complete our projects successfully and on time. The leading hands were Tom Lowe (welder), Les Bostock (fitter) and Bill Burrows (pattern maker). All were destined in later years to become heads of their own departments at Fodens.

Following the delivery of the first prototype to the Department of Tank Design at Chobham, our Chief Designer, Edwin Twemlow, travelled down to observe the initial field trials and on his return expressed his doubts regarding the reliability of the converted tank under the working conditions he had witnessed. There can be no doubt that the Army personnel entrusted with the task of carrying out the first 100 hour reliability trials with the prototype Crusader Bulldozer were setting about their task with some considerable energy and enthusiasm.

A detailed report of the problems encountered with track failures, clutch plate wear and thrust bearing failures, etc is included in a recently published booklet entitled *Muck Shifting for King George or the Bulldozer Goes to War* compiled by Mr. Maurice Sanders, one of the service personnel involved in the trials; but at no point in the narrative is there any indication of any major modifications requested or implemented during or following the presumably successful completion of the reliability trial programme.

Certainly in the Drawing Office at Fodens we received no instructions for any significant modifications, the field trials continued, and we delivered the remaining four prototypes as scheduled. Foden's tank assembly lines were fully committed to the production of the latest Centaur Tank at this time and it was decided that another member of the Nuffield Group, MG Cars at Abingdon, who obviously had production capacity available, should complete the conversion programme on both Crusader and Centaur tanks.

We accordingly transferred all drawings and other necessary conversion data to MG and although I have no knowledge of the total number of tanks eventually modified, I have recently discovered from Mr John Marchant of Milton Keynes, who owns and occasionally operates a surviving Centaur bulldozer, that the first units were delivered to the Army in Belgium early in 1945 and were subsequently and successfully used in accordance with their designed objectives until the final German surrender in May 1945. In the latter stages of the War in Europe, shortly after the Rhine crossings, the Nuffield Organisation apparently received a commendation from the Ministry of Supply which read 'Your effort on Centaur bulldozers has been absolutely magnificent and fully justifies the waving of the flag. The reports we have on Centaur bulldozers after crossing the Rhine have been first class and indicate the effort was well worthwhile.'

In the cleaning up of German cities, wrecked by RAF bombing and British artillery fire, the armoured Centaurs with their bulldozer blades swept thousands of tons of rubble aside to make way for tanks and transport vehicles. Protected from fanatical German snipers who remained suicidally in battered buildings, the Centaur crews, behind thick armour, were often the spearhead of 'mopping up parties'. To my knowledge, no copy of this commendation was ever received by Fodens.

Fodens contribution to the War effort was not solely confined to the production of 770 Crusader and Centaur Tanks and 1,750 four and six-wheeler General Service Vehicles. A special department, set up in the Machine Shop, staffed almost exclusively by female labour working three eight hour shifts per day, and supervised by some of my ex-colleagues from the Tool Room, produced vast quantities of 20mm cannon shells for the Spitfire and Hurricane fighter aircraft. From an initial production rate of 6,000 shells per week in 1941, the rate increased rapidly to 60,000 per week and the total output by the end of the War was 7,500,000.

During the War years Foden's welding department had been considerably expanded to meet the increased production requirements of the military vehicle and Cruiser tank building programmes. Welding standards had been improved to satisfy the exacting standards continually monitored by Ministry inspectors, and the receipt of an order from yet another Government Department for a batch of large structural sub-assemblies early in 1944 evoked no special interest in the welding shops.

The structures were code-named 'Whale' and 'Shark' but even this unusual nomenclature gave no clue to their eventual purpose, and it was not until some time after the Normandy landings in June that it was finally appreciated that the sections so recently fabricated at Fodens were, in fact, part of the 'Mulberry' harbour structure

Mass production was something quite new to Foden, but from 1941, 20mm cannon shells for Spitfire and Hurricane fighter aircraft were produced in a special department in the machine shop, and within a few months 60,000 per week were being produced by an almost exclusively female labour force, with three shifts each working an 8-hour day. Here an automatic lathe is seen (left) being used to turn, bore and tap the shell and (right) the dimensions are being checked.

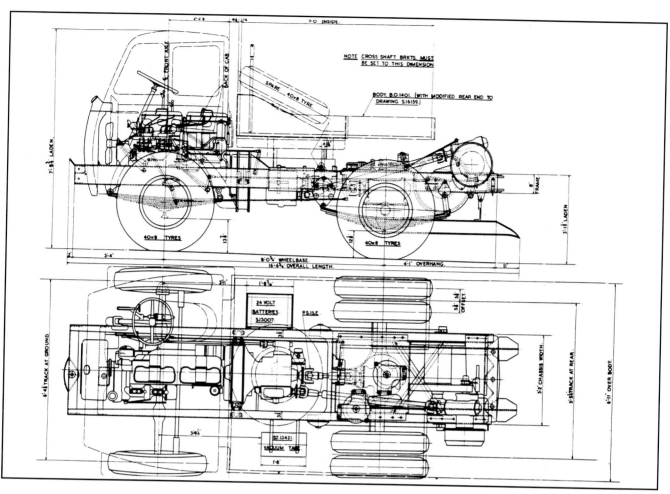

The STG6 tractor was chosen for a wartime contract from the Forestry Commission. This was basically the standard product as originally introduced in 1937, modified to suit the Commission's requirements.

which provided such a vital element in the first weeks of the operation until more conventional landing methods via a serviceable harbour were made available.

One other major Government Contract completed during the War years involved the production of 50 timber tractors for the Forestry Commission.

This model had originally been designed in 1937 with a 5LW Gardner engine, five-speed Foden gearbox and power take off, double reduction rear hubs, Foden worm drive winch with brake and anchor lift mechanism and an extremely short wheelbase of 8ft 0¾in to ensure maximum manoeuvrability. Guide pulleys were located to facilitate winching to front or rear. 40in x 8in tyres were fitted to increase ground clearance,

I recall that we did try at this time to introduce a spooling device to guide the wire rope on to the winch drum without overlapping, but it was not successful and, as the Forestry Commission had not specifically requested this feature, we proceeded no further with the idea. In service, the tractors proved to be highly efficient and after the War, we received regular orders from timber operators in the UK for this model, our only real competitor in this field as far as I can remember being the Latil tractor, a much lighter and less powerful vehicle.

The War in Europe ended with the surrender of the German armed forces on 4th May 1945 and this long awaited and momentous victory was suitably celebrated on VE Day four days later. It was a

day when Fodens' Band would normally have played loud and long in Elworth, but at that time, they were engaged on a 2,000 mile ENSA tour of France, Holland and Belgium, and on VE night they were in Brussels and scheduled to give a performance at the Brussels Opera House. Their predecessors, The Sandbach Volunteer Brass Band, 45 years previously, on the occasion of the Relief of Mafeking, had failed to turn up for their scheduled performance in Elworth and so provided the reason for the formation of an independent band, eventually to become Fodens. The band of 1945 gave a stirring performance in accordance with their published programme and left their own celebrating until later.

Two months later, on 14th July, Japan capitulated and World War II was thankfully at an end. It was time to welcome back the 349 Foden personnel who had served in the armed forces and to remember the thirteen who would not be returning. It was time to stand down S Company, 11th B/N Cheshire Home Guard which comprised exclusively Foden employees, and also to disband the various Fire Brigades, First Aid and Heavy Rescue Squads, similarly staffed by Foden personnel.

They had fortunately sustained no casualties during the War years, nor had the factory been damaged. Not so fortunate were our near neighbours, Rolls Royce at Crewe which had eighteen employees killed during a daylight raid on the afternoon of 29th December 1940.

The return to peacetime conditions made it appropriate to reassess the changes introduced in the road transport industry, particularly relating to haulage, during the war years and, more specifically, Foden's future role in relation to it.

During the last three years of the war civilian road transport was controlled by a 'National road transport organisation' introduced by the wartime coalition Government in 1942 as a measure to meet the emergency conditions of the time. Oil supplies, all imported in those days and subject to intensive attack by German submarines, had to be conserved, and yet road transport was vital to the war effort as well as essential civilian needs. Even so, it was widely predicted at the time that it could prove to be a first step towards the eventual nationalisation of the industry if a Labour Government was elected after the War.

In pre-war days, the Foden business had been based on designing and building vehicles to suit the varied needs of individual private haulage operators as well as many 'own-account' users of Foden vehicles to carry the products they made, the future of this latter activity also being threatened under some of the proposals then being discussed. Hence the nature of the specific details of proposals for nationalisation and the consequential effects on Fodens were matters of great concern to the Company. This became acute when, in the General Election of July 1945, a Labour Government with a substantial working majority was indeed elected on a platform which included a clearly-stated intention to nationalise all long-distance road haulage in the United Kingdom.

Yet this was by no means the only potential post-war problem facing the Company. There was no shortage of orders, for very few new vehicles of any make had been available for most of the war period, but the supply of raw materials was limited amidst the immense pressures for post-war reconstruction and renewals of all kinds.

In common with many other companies which had been engaged on military contracts during the War years, Foden's manufacturing capability had increased dramatically between 1939 and 1945 and, if this capacity was to be fully utilised, then drastic changes would need to be made to the former manufacturing and purchasing programmes. One particular area of concern was Gardner's ability to meet our future engine requirements and it was this factor primarily which resulted in Foden's decision to design and build its own engine. Alternative engines had been considered in the past. In fact, in 1938 a 'Nemesis' four-cylinder oil engine with the same bore and stroke as the Gardner 4LW had been fitted experimentally, but had been found to compare unfavourably with the Gardner 4LW in relation to fuel consumption, starting capability and noise emission.

The specific decision to design and build a diesel engine at Fodens had been made during the war years and was, of course, subject to the approval of the Ministries of Supply and Defence which controlled the activity of the factory at that time. The two men primarily concerned with the initial design study, once the necessary Ministry clearance had been granted, were the company's Chief Designer, Edwin Twemlow and the Chief Draughtsman, Jack Mills. With commendable initiative, they decided to develop a range of high speed diesel engines utilising the two stroke combustion cycle and incorporating the Kadenacy principle of air charging via a rotor type blower. Early testing was carried out on a single cylinder engine in a workshop near to the Drawing Office.

The building had originally housed the Service Stores, but was now redesignated the Experimental Department and was initially staffed by three fitters, two from the Maintenance Department, Harry Mason and Norman Williamson, together with Bob Johnstone, who had previously worked for Edwin Twemlow as a mechanic during his successful Motor Cycle Tourist Trophy racing exploits in the Isle of Man. He won the Lightweight TT in 1924 and 1925. With an unconventional design, production and performance problems were not unexpected and it was not until 1945 that a four-cylinder version of the Foden engine was completed and tested.

(Continued on page 58)

The initial experimental work on the Foden two-stroke diesel engine was done during the latter part of the war, using a single-cylinder engine seen here on test.

The immediate post-war Foden DG-series goods models looked generally very similar in outline to those being built in 1939. At that stage, all continued to be Gardner-engined, though the demand on that concern's engines far outstripped supply and even though Foden had been a regular and large-scale Gardner user since its diesel lorry production began, the uncertainty about whether enough engines would be available was the main reason for Foden developing its own diesel engine in the post-war years. Various minor changes had been introduced to the chassis, as can be seen in these views. A new and very distinctive style of large chromium hub cap was now standard, those for front wheels shaped to fit over the retaining nuts while at the rear the effect was more akin to contemporary car styles. The driver's windscreen was now of single-panel type, though still hinged at the top to allow it to be opened. The steering wheel, previously quite high-set, had been lowered slightly, though the column angle was still rather greater than that of most competitors' models. A starting handle was fitted and the smaller decompression lever alongside the radiator prevented the valves closing until the engine was turning fast enough to fire. This allowed hand starting, though swinging even a 5.6litre 4LW was no easy task, so it was rarely used.

The four-wheeler shown above was supplied to Shipstones, the Nottingham brewers, being registered HTV 790 in the autumn of 1946 – an earlier delivery to this concern is seen on page 37. At that date, brewers were still delivering beer in heavy wooden barrels and the chains were a convenient way of retaining them in position while allowing rapid unloading on arrival at public houses.

The DG6-15 shown below was supplied to G. A. Seal Ltd, transport contractors of Tamworth, Staffs and registered LRF 484 in the summer of 1946. At that date the Gardner 6LW engine was still developing the same 102bhp at 1,700rpm and torque rating of 348 lb.ft at 1,100rpm as when introduced in 1931, so the five-speed superlow gearbox was helpful in allowing steep gradients to be climbed even though the speed then reached at maximum revs was only 2.2mph. The standard gearing gave 30.4mph in top gear.

Work on the design of the Foden two-stroke engine was in hand in the immediate post-war years, even though no announcement was made until just before the 1948 Commercial Motor Show. This view shows a production example of the FD4 Mk1 four-cylinder version, of which the first prototype was completed and tested in 1945. It was of only 2.72-litre capacity, yet developed 84bhp at 2,000rpm. The Kadenacy principle allowed a low-pressure blower, visible below the fuel injection pump, to deliver air to ports in the cylinder walls designed to give it a high degree of swirl, aiding combustion. Exhaust was by conventional push-rod operated valves, there being two per cylinder. Largely aluminium construction helped to keep weight down, and this engine was used in an 8-ton model with unladen weight of 3 tons 15 cwt, but that was not introduced until the early 1950s, as described in the next chapter – early production examples, offered from 1948, used the FD6 six-cylinder 4-litre engine of similar design.

Maximum torque developed at 1,500 rpm was 235 lbs/ft and fuel consumption was under 0.4 lbs/bhp/hour over a wide speed and load range. The six cylinder version developed 120 bhp at 2,000 rpm, 350 lbs/ft torque at 1,500 rpm, and weighed under 1,200 lbs with starter and dynamo fitted. The equivalent engine in the Gardner range, the 6LW developed 112 bhp at 1,700 rpm and 358 lbs/ft torque at 1,300 rpm but had an installed weight some 350 lbs higher than the Foden FD6. The Gardner range of engines, however, had the advantage of a long established reputation for reliability and in this respect, the new Foden engines had still to build customer confidence. Nevertheless, the Company's prime objective of introducing a viable alternative engine supply source had been attained in time for announcement at the 1948 Commercial Show.

Engine assembly and test facilities were duly established adjacent to the Experimental Department, additional supervisory staff were appointed; Ted Gibson, Martin Britain and Rod East, all destined to make an important contribution to the development and application of this latest Elworth product and the Foden Engine Saga was under way. The full story of the design, development, and subsequent varied applications of the Foden range of engines, very often in operational areas far removed from the primary requirements of the original automotive application, would constitute a complete publication in itself, but needs the detailed knowledge of an author more closely involved in this development than I was in my time at Fodens.

With the successful introduction of the Foden engine as an alternative to the Gardner range of engines, one potential post war supply problem was solved for Fodens, who were now able to offer a range of vehicles with all major units produced at Elworth. There were, however, far more serious problems on the horizon which were destined to affect the whole of the road transport industry. When the war ended in 1945 the existing Coalition Government was dissolved, a General Election followed, and a new Labour Government was elected with an effective working majority and a

By this time, the design had been finalised to incorporate a cast aluminium alloy crankcase and cylinder block with cast iron wet liners, a nickel steel crankshaft with five steel-backed white metal main bearings, cast iron pistons and cast iron cylinder heads. All timing gears were profile ground and unlike the Gardner engine were located at the rear or flywheel end of the engine. All bearing assemblies were fitted in detachable housings to aid servicing and the fuel pump, complete with hydraulic governor, fuel lift pump and filter was mounted as an integral unit in an accessible position on top of the blower. The lubricating oil pump, together with the centrifugal water pump were driven by the same power take off source at the front of the engine. Finally, the fan drive, the only major engine feature that I was personally involved with, was taken directly off the front end of the camshaft and spring loaded horizontally to reduce the torsional effect of the fan assembly on the drive shaft when starting or stopping the engine.

The most remarkable feature of the Foden two-stroke engine was, of course, the power to weight ratio, a most important factor in commercial vehicle design where any reduction in unladen weight results in a corresponding increase in payload and earning capacity.

The Foden four cylinder engine developed 84 bhp at 2,000 rpm and weighed less than 1,000 lbs with starter and dynamo fitted.

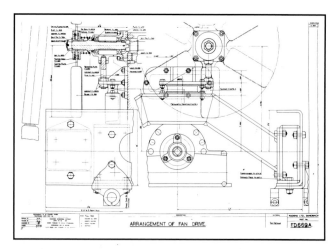

The author's contribution to the Foden two-stroke engine design concerned the fan drive and this drawing passed on 27th October 1946 bears his initials as draughtsman.

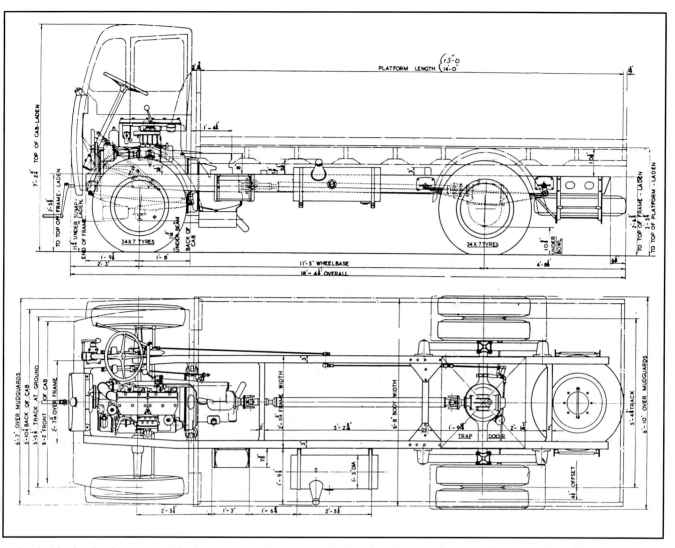

A series of reduced scale arrangement drawings was prepared to accompany the data sheets for use by the sales staff in the immediate post-war period. This one shows the light OG4-6 model with Gardner 4LK engine, Foden four-speed gearbox, Kirkstall axles and 11ft 5in wheelbase. It was designed for a 14ft platform length as shown, but also available with 15ft body on the same wheelbase. The unladen weight limit for operation at 30mph had been increased to 3 tons, so the specification could include a starter with larger-capacity battery to suit and other items which would have pushed the weight over the pre-war limit.

clearly stated intention, despite widespread objections from operators and manufacturers alike, to nationalise all long distance road transport in the U.K. This comprehensive transfer of control from private ownership was fortunately destined to take a considerable time, and, in the immediate post war period, there was, of course, no shortage of orders for new vehicles, particularly for the home market, where almost all vehicles were over five-years-old and, unlike the situation after the first world war, very few ex-army vehicles were offered for sale. The odd vehicles that were made available brought very high prices in the second hand market. An ex-WD Foden four wheeler for example, was sold at auction for £3,000, a price far in excess of the list price for a new vehicle of similar type at that time. There was also a severe shortage of the basic materials needed to build the vehicles at this time, which resulted in the introduction of a Ministry controlled rationing system with a proviso that supply priorities would be given to materials required for export products. In fact all manufacturers had to sell 60% of their total production to overseas markets in order to qualify for raw material supplies.

Fodens had traditionally negotiated and delivered export orders to all parts of the world for both steam and diesel engined vehicles and had established dealerships accordingly, but the greater concentration of export business had always been located in Australia and Southern Africa, and it was in these two specific areas that Foden's Sales Director, Ted Foden, considered that the required additional post war overseas sales would be achieved.

Although new vehicle designs were in their final stages in the Drawing Office at this time and prototype vehicles were in progress, all the production vehicles built and sold in the 1945-1946 period were simply derivatives of the pre-war DG range, and these were the vehicles, with little or no modification to suit widely varying climatic and operational conditions, that our overseas dealers were called upon to sell in order to maintain the required degree of profitable activity at the Sandbach factory. Despite the lack of special overseas features in the vehicle specifications, the required sales levels were eventually achieved due to the combined efforts of the dealers and our overseas sales staff, headed by Ted Foden, who, in the immediate post war years, was obliged to spend almost all of his time recreating Fodens overseas markets.

In the Drawing Office at this time, we were heavily committed to new design projects involving single and double-deck passenger chassis and a new standardised range of goods vehicles, using a high proportion of common components, plus, of course, the new Foden two stroke engines; and, in order to encourage our UK field

1946 MODELS. GENERAL TECHNICAL DATA.

	MODEL	STANDARD OG 4-6	END TIP OG 4-6	TRACTOR OGTU4-7	STANDARD DG 4-7½	T.W.T. DG 4-7½	TRACTOR DGTU4-10	STANDARD DG 5-7½	T.W.T. DG 5-7½	TRACTOR DGTU5-15	STANDARD DG 6-7½
	STANDARD DRG. No.	21091	21124	22 026	S.12 156.	S.13080.	S.12199.	S.12116.	S.13080.	S.12183.	S.12104.
	PAYLOAD	6 TONS	6 TONS	—	7½ TONS	7½ TONS	—	7½ TONS	7½ TONS	—	7½ TONS
*	UNLADEN WEIGHT WITH STANDARD CAB & BODY	2T-12C-0Q	2T-13C-0Q	2T-7C-2Q	3T-19C-2Q	4T-12C-0Q	3T-10C-0Q	4T-2C-0Q	4T-15C-0Q	3T-12C-0Q	4T-4C-0Q
	WHEELBASE	11'-5"	8'-0"	8'-0"	13'-7½"	10'-3¼"	8'-0¾"	13'-7½"	10'-3¼"	8'-0¾"	13'-7½"
	OVERALL LENGTH	18'-4⅛"	13'-6⅞"	12'-6½"	23'-0⅞"	16'-8⅛"	13'-7"	23'-0⅞"	16'-8⅛"	13'-7"	23'-0⅞"
	BODY DIMENSIONS	14'-0" X 6'-4½"	9'-0" X 6'-6"	—	17'-6" X 7'-2"	11'-0" X 6'-10½"	—	17'-6" X 7'-2"	11'-0" X 6'-10½"	—	17'-6" X 7'-2"
	TURNING CIRCLE	42 FT	31 FT.	31 FT.	52 FT.	42FT.	35 FT.	52 FT.	42FT.	35 FT.	52 FT.
ENGINE DETAILS	TYPE	4 L.K	4 LK.	4 LK.	4 L.W.	4 L.W.	4 L.W.	5 L.W.	5 L.W.	5 L.W.	6 L.W.
	BORE & STROKE	3¾" X 5¼"	3¾" X 5¼"	3¾" X 5¼"	4¼" X 6"	4¼" X 6"	4¼" X 6"	4¼" X 6"	4¼" X 6"	4¼" X 6"	4¼" X 6"
	CAPACITY C.C.	3800	3800	3800	5600	5600	5600	7000	7000	7000	8400
	B.H.P.	53 AT 2000 R.P.M.	53 AT 2000 R.P.M.	53 AT 2000 R.P.M.	68 AT 1700 R.P.M.	68 AT 1700 R.P.M.	68 AT 1700 R.P.M.	85 AT 1700 R.P.M.	85 AT 1700 R.P.M.	85 AT 1700 R.P.M.	102 AT 1700 R.P.M.
	MAX. TORQUE	147 LBS. FT. 1200 R.P.M.	147 LBS. FT 1200 R.P.M.	147 LBS. FT 1200 R.P.M.	232 LBS. FT. 1100 R.P.M.	232 LBS. FT. 1100 R.P.M.	232 LBS. FT. 1100 R.P.M.	285 LBS. FT. 1100 R.P.M.	285 LBS. FT. 1100 R.P.M.	285 LBS. FT. 1100 R.P.M.	348 LBS. FT. 1100 R.P.M.
CLUTCH	DIAMETER	12"	12"	12"	15½" O/DIA X 10" BORE	15½" O/DIA X 10" BORE	15½" O/DIA X 10" BORE	15½" O/DIA X 10" BORE	15½" O/DIA X 10" BORE	15½" O/DIA X 10" BORE	15½" O/DIA X 10" BORE
	AREA	344 SQ INS	344 SQ INS	344 SQ INS	220.2 SQ IN	220.2 SQ. IN	220.2 SQ. IN	220.2 SQ. IN	220.2 SQ. IN	220.2 SQ. IN	220.2 SQ. IN
GEARBOX RATIOS	4TH	1-1	1-1	1-1	1-1	1-1	1-1	1-1	1-1	1-1	1-1
	3RD	1.64-1	1.64-1	1.64-1	1.635-1	1.635-1	1.635-1	1.635-1	1.635-1	1.635-1	1.635-1
	2ND	3.3-1	3.3-1	3.3-1	3.037-1	3.037-1	3.037-1	3.037-1	3.037-1	3.037-1	3.037-1
	1ST	6.8-1	6.8-1	6.8-1	6.15-1	6.15-1	6.15-1	6.15-1	6.15-1	6.15-1	6.15-1
	REVERSE	10.6-1	10.6-1	10.6-1	6.15-1	6.15-1	6.15-1	6.15-1	6.15-1	6.15-1	6.15-1
	SUPERLOW WHEN FITTED	NONE FITTED	NONE FITTED	NONE FITTED	13.6-1	13.6-1	13.6-1	13.6-1	13.6-1	13.6-1	13.6-1
	REAR AXLE RATIO	6-1	6-1	6-1	6.25-1	6.25-1	6.25-1	6.25-1	6.25-1	6.25-1	6.25-1
MAX. ROAD SPEEDS	4TH	35.5 M.P.H.	35.5 M.P.H.	35.5 M.P.H.	30.4 M.P.H.	30.4 M.P.H.	30.4 M.P.H.	30.4 M.P.H.	30.4 M.P.H.	30.4 M.P.H.	30.4 M.P.H.
	3RD	21.7 M.P.H	21.7 M.P.H.	21.7 M.P.H	18.6 M.P.H	18.6 M.P.H.	18.6 M.P.H	18.6 M.P.H.	18.6 M.P.H.	18.6 M.P.H	18.6 M.P.H.
	2ND	10.7 M.P.H	10.7 M.P.H.	10.7 M.P.H.	10.0 M.P.H.	10.0 M.P.H.	10.0 M.P.H	10.0 M.P.H	10.0 M.P.H.	10.0 M.P.H.	10.0 M.P.H.
	1ST	5.3 M.P.H	5.3 M.P.H.	5.3 M.P.H.	4.95 M.P.H	4.95 M.P.H	4.95 M.P.H	4.95 M.P.H	4.95 M.P.H	4.95 M.P.H.	4.95 M.P.H.
	REVERSE	3.3 M	3.3 M.P.H	3.3 M.P.H.	4.95 M.P.H.	4.95 M.P.H.	4.95 M.P.H	4.95 M.P.H.	4.95 M.P.H.	4.95 M.P.H.	4.95 M.P.H.
	SUPERLOW	NONE FITTED	NONE FITTED	NONE FITTED	2.2 M.P.H.	2.2 M.P.H	2.2 M.P.H.	2.2 M.P.H.	22 M.P.H.	2.2 M.P.H.	2.2 M.P.H.
TYRES	SIZE	34" X 7"	34" X 7"	34" X 7"	36" X 8"	36" X 8"	36" X 8"	36" X 8"	36" X 8"	36" X 8"	36" X 8"
	MAX. TOTAL RATING	8T-10C	8T.-10C	8T-10C.	12 TONS	12 TONS	12 TONS	12 TONS	12 TONS	12 TONS	12 TONS
BRAKES	TYPE	2 LEADING SHOE	2 LEADING SHOE	2 LEADING SHOE	COWDREY	COWDREY	COWDREY	COWDREY	COWDREY	COWDREY	COWDREY
	SIZE FRONTS	16" X 2½"	16" X 2½"	16" X 2½"	16½" X 3½"	16½" X 3½"	16½" X 3½"	16½" X 3½"	16½" X 3½"	16½" X 3½"	16½" X 3½"
	SIZE REAR	16" X 3½"	16" X 3½"	16" X 3½"	16½" X 6"	16½" X 6"	16½" X 6"	16½" X 6"	16½" X 6"	16½" X 6"	16½" X 6"
	BRAKE APPLIC N	REAR WHEELS	REAR WHEELS	REAR WHEELS	REAR WHEELS	REAR WHEELS	REAR WHEELS	REAR WHEELS	REAR WHEELS	REAR WHEELS	REAR WHEELS
	…GS FRONT No.-…TH-THICKNESS	12-2½" X 5/16"	12-2½" X 5/16"	12-2½" X 5/16"	11-3" X 3/8"	11-3" X 3/8"	11-3" X 3/8"	11-3" X 3/8"	11-3" X 3/8"	11-3" X 3/8"	11-3" X 3/8"
	…GS REAR …TH-THICKNESS	12-3" X 7/16"	12-3" X 7/16"	12-3" X 7/16"	9-3½" X 9/16"	9-3½" X 9/16"	9-3½" X 9/16"	9-3½" X 9/16"	9-3½" X 9/16"	9-3½" X 9/16"	9-3½" X 9/16"
	STEERING	CAM ROLLER	CAM ROLLER	CAM ROLLER	WRM & SCTR 20.5-1	WRM & SCTR 20.5-1	WRM & SCTR 20.5-1	WRM & SCTR 20.5-1	WRM & SCTR 20.5-1	WRM & SCTR 20.5-1	WRM & SCTR 20.5-1
	FUEL TANK CAPACITY	15 GALLS.	15 GALLS.	15 GALLS.	32 GALLS.	32 GALLS.	32 GALLS.	32 GALLS.	32 GALLS.	32 GALLS.	32 GALLS.

	MODEL	T.W.T. DG 6-7½	TRACTOR DGTU6-20	STANDARD DG 5-11	STANDARD DG 5-12	T.W.T. DG 5-12	STANDARD DG 6-12	T.W.T. DG 6-12	STANDARD DG 6-15	END TIP DG 6-15
	STANDARD DRG. No.	S.13080.	S.13130	S.12103.	S.12195.	S.13108.	S.12179.	S.13108.	S.12115.	S.13110.
	PAYLOAD	7½ TONS	—	11 TONS	12 TONS	12 TONS	12 TONS	12 TONS	15 TONS	15 TONS
*	UNLADEN WEIGHT WITH STANDARD CAB & BODY	4T-17C-0Q	3T-14C-0Q	4T-18C-1Q	5T-12C-0Q	6T-12C-0Q	5T-15C-0Q	6T-16C-0Q	6T-12C-0Q	7T-15C-0Q
	WHEELBASE	10'-3¼"	8'-7"	MEAN 13'-1¼"	MEAN 16'-5¼"	MEAN 11'-1¼"	MEAN 16'-5¼"	MEAN 11'-1¼"	MEAN 13'-8¼"	MEAN 9'-9¼"
	OVERALL LENGTH	16'-8⅛"	14'-1¼"	25'-6⅝"	27'-7⅛"	20'-5½"	27'-7⅛"	20'-5½"	29'-8⅜"	21'-10"
	BODY DIMENSIONS	11'-0" X 6'-10½"	—	20'-0" X 7'-2"	22'-0" X 7'-2"	14'-0" X 6'-10½"	22'-0" X 7'-2"	14'-0" X 6'-10½"	24'-0" X 7'-2"	16'-0" X 6'-10½"
	TURNING CIRCLE	42FT.	37FT.	50 FT.	65 FT.	46FT.	65 FT.	46FT.	76FT.	57FT.
ENGINE DETAILS	TYPE	6 L.W.	6 L.W.	5 L.W.	5 L.W.	5 L.W.	6 L.W.	6 L.W.	6 L.W.	6 L.W.
	BORE & STROKE	4¼" X 6"	4¼" X 6"	4¼" X 6"	4¼" X 6"	4¼" X 6"	4¼" X 6"	4¼" X 6"	4¼" X 6"	4¼" X 6"
	CAPACITY C.C.	8400	8400	7000	7000	7000	8400	8400	8400	8400
	B.H.P.	102 AT 1700 R.P.M.	102 AT 1700 R.P.M.	85 AT 1700 R.P.M.	85 AT 1700 R.P.M.	85 AT 1700 R.P.M.	102 AT 1700 R.P.M.	102 AT 1700 R.P.M.	102 AT 1700 R.P.M.	102 AT 1700 R.P.M.
	MAX. TORQUE	348 LBS. FT. 1100 R.P.M.	348 LBS. FT. 1100 R.P.M.	285 LBS. FT. 1100 R.P.M.	285 LBS. FT. 1100 R.P.M.	285 LBS. FT. 1100 R.P.M.	348 LBS. FT. 1100 R.P.M.	348 LBS. FT. 1100 R.P.M.	348 LBS. FT. 1100 R.P.M.	348 LBS. FT. 1100 R.P.M.
CLUTCH	DIAMETER	15½" O/DIA X 10" BORE	15½" O/DIA X 10" BORE	15½" O/DIA X 10" BORE	15½" O/DIA X 10" BORE	15½" O/DIA X 10" BORE	15½" O/DIA X 10" BORE	15½" O/DIA X 10" BORE	15½" O/DIA X 10" BORE	15½" O/DIA X 10" BORE
	AREA	220.2 SQ. IN	220.2 SQ. IN	220.2 SQ. IN	220.2 SQ. IN	220.2 SQ. IN	220.2 SQ. IN	220.2 SQ. IN	220.2 SQ. IN	220.2 SQ. IN
GEARBOX RATIOS	4TH	1-1	1-1	1-1	1-1	1-1	1-1	1-1	1-1	1-1
	3RD	1.635-1	1.635-1	1.635-1	1.635-1	1.635-1	1.635-1	1.635-1	1.635-1	1.635-1
	2ND	3.037-1	3.037-1	3.037-1	3.037-1	3.037-1	3.037-1	3.037-1	3.037-1	3.037-1
	1ST	6.15-1	6.15-1	6.15-1	6.15-1	6.15-1	6.15-1	6.15-1	6.15-1	6.15-1
	REVERSE	6.15-1	6.15-1	6.15-1	6.15-1	6.15-1	6.15-1	6.15-1	6.15-1	6.15-1
	SUPERLOW WHEN FITTED	13.6-1	13.6-1	13.6-1	13.6-1	13.6-1	13.6-1	13.6-1	13.6-1	13.6-1
	REAR AXLE RATIO	6.25 -	6.25-1	6.25-1	6.25-1	6.25-1	6.25-1	6.25-1	6.25-1	6.25-1
MAX. ROAD SPEEDS	4TH	30.4 M.P.H.	30.4 M.P.H.	30.4 M.P.H.	30.4 M.P.H.	30.4 M.P.H.	30.4 M.P.H.	30.4 M.P.H.	30.4 M.P.H.	30.4 M.P.H.
	3RD	18.6 M.P.H.	18.6 M.P.H	18.6 M.P.H	18.6 M.P.H	18.6 M.P.H	18.6 M.P.H	18.6 M.P.H	18.6 M.P.H	18.6 M.P.H.
	2ND	10.0 M.P.H.	10.0 M.P.H	10.0 M.P.H	10.0 M.P.H	10.0 M.P.H	10.0 M.P.H.	10.0 M.P.H.	10.0 M.P.H	10.0 M.P.H
	1ST	4.95 M.P.H	4.95 M.P.H.	4.95 M.P.H.	4.95 M.P.H.	4.95 M.P.H	4.95 M.P.H.	4.95 M.P.H	4.95 M.P.H	4.95 M.P.H
	REVERSE	4.95 M.P.H	4.95 M.P.H	4.95 M.P.H	4.95 M.P.H.	4.95 M.P.H	4.95 M.P.H	4.95 M.P.H	4.95 M.P.H.	4.95 M.P.H
	SUPERLOW	2.2 M.P.H	2.2 M.P.H	2.2 M.P.H	2.2 M.P.H.	2.2 M.P.H	2.2 M.P.H.	2.2 M.P.H	2.2 M.P.H	2.2 M.P.H
TYRES	SIZE	36" X 8"	36" X 8"	36" X 8"	36" X 8"	36" X 8"	36" X 8"	36" X 8"	36" X 8"	36" X 8"
	MAX. TOTAL RATING	12 TONS	12 TONS	16 TONS	20 TONS	20 TONS	20 TONS	20 TONS	24 TONS	24 TONS
BRAKES	TYPE	COWDREY	COWDREY	COWDREY	COWDREY	COWDREY	COWDREY	COWDREY	COWDREY	COWDREY
	SIZE FRONTS	16½" X 3½"	16½" X 3½"	16½" X 3½"	16½" X 3½"	16½" X 3½"	16½" X 3½"	16½" X 3½"	16½" X 3½"	16½" X 3½"
	SIZE REAR	16½" X 6"	16½" X 6"	16½" X 6"	16½" X 6"	16½" X 6"	16½" X 6"	16½" X 6"	16½" X 6"	16½" X 6"
	BRAKE APPLIC N	REAR WHEELS	REAR WHEELS	ALL REAR WHEELS	ALL REAR WHEELS	ALL REAR WHEELS	ALL REAR WHEELS	ALL REAR WHEELS	ALL REAR WHEELS	ALL REAR WHEELS
	…GS FRONT No.-…TH-THICKNESS	11-3" X 3/8"	11-3" X 3/8"	11-3" X 3/8"	11-3" X 3/8"	11-3" X 3/8"	11-3" X 3/8"	11-3" X 3/8"	11-3" X 3/8"	11-3" X 3/8"
	…GS REAR …TH-THICKNESS	9-3½" X 9/16"	9-3½" X 9/16"	8-3½" X 9/16"	20-4½" X 7/16"	15-S4938	20-4½" X 7/16"	15-S.4938	20-4½" X 7/16"	15-S.4938
	STEERING	WRM & SCTR 20.5-1	WRM & SCTR 20.5-1	WRM & SCTR 20.5-1	WRM & SCTR 20.5-1	WRM & SCTR 20.5-1	WRM & SCTR 20.5-1	WRM & SCTR 20.5-1	WRM & SCTR 30-1	WRM & SCTR 30-1
	FUEL TANK CAPACITY	32 GALLS.	32 GALLS.	50 GALLS.	50 GALLS.	32 GALLS.	50 GALLS.	32 GALLS.	50 GALLS.	25 GALLS.

* UNLADEN WEIGHTS ARE GIVEN FOR STANDARD MODELS WITH NO EXTRAS. FOR TRACTOR UNITS CHASSIS & CAB ONLY. FOR BUS CHASSIS ENGINE CASING ONLY

This chart shows the range of goods models being offered in 1946. At that stage, all models had Gardner engines, the Foden two-stroke units still being in course of development for production.

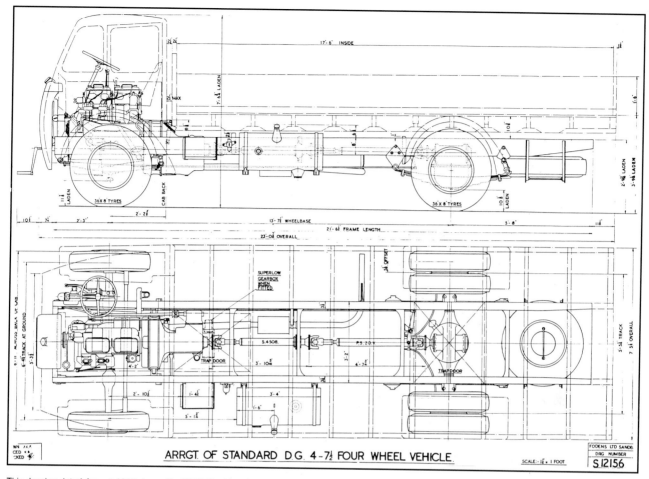

ARRGT. OF STANDARD D.G. 4-7½ FOUR WHEEL VEHICLE.

SCALE :- 1½" = 1 FOOT

FODENS LTD SANDB
DRG NUMBER
S 12156

This drawing dated August 1945 shows the DG4-7½ with 13ft 7½in wheelbase. The same cab and front-end layout was used for the whole DG range, the front of the engine being set in the same position for all models, so there was about 1ft of vacant space behind the cylinder block of the 4LW engine in this case.

sales staff to concentrate their efforts on the sale of standard vehicle types included in the existing DG range, we produced a series of data sheets and reduced scale arrangement drawings for their guidance. Our attempt by this method to introduce a degree of sales rationalisation at that time was only partially successful, but surviving copies of these data sheets and drawings do serve to illustrate this important range of Foden vehicles in a far more comprehensive manner than any amount of photographs, and, in later years, when we began to introduce Sales Data publications from the Drawing Office on a regular basis, this was the general method of presentation that we adopted.

Models are listed in ascending order by payload category. Each category generally includes three basic types; long wheelbase flat platform body vehicles, medium wheelbase tipping vehicles and short wheelbase tractor units. The relative unladen weights and maximum payloads, together with the complete vehicle specifications and performance data for each model are included, and for the guidance of the respective body builders and trailer manufacturers, the general arrangement drawing number for each vehicle type is also shown. Very few original Foden assembly drawings relating to the DG range of vehicles have survived to the present day, but fortunately, my former chief at Fodens, Jack Mills, managed to retain his own personal copies of the reduced scale arrangement drawings and relative data sheets, and it is from this source that we are able to illustrate the DG range of vehicles produced and sold in the years immediately after the war, in some detail. The lowest payload vehicle in the post war range was the OG

4/6 model which still retained the same basic specification as the pre-war model with 4LK Gardner engine, Kirkstall axles and Foden 4 speed gearbox, but now had a maximum unladen weight allowance of 3 tons.

This increase of 10 cwt on the pre-war limit of 2 tons 10 cwt resulted in a much more comprehensive vehicle specification which could now include a starter motor, higher capacity batteries, and other ancillary equipment. Two standard wheelbase models were offered for standard flat platform bodies, tipping bodies and articulated trailer applications, but despite our efforts in the Drawing Office to retain some degree of rationalisation by arranging for two basic models to cover all three applications, the records show that other variants were built to suit specific customers' requirements. The following arrangement drawings relate to the three standard models included on the Technical Data Sheet.

In the post war period there was a considerable demand for the OG4/6 range of Foden vehicles generally for short haul local distribution work, but production was limited by the restricted availability of the Gardner 4LK engine and rarely exceeded a rate of three to four units per week.

The major proportion of models in the heavier DG range were, however, fitted with four, five or six-cylinder Gardner LW type engines, but, as so many other vehicle manufacturers, including our near neighbours, ERF, fitted these same engines, supplies were similarly limited and our requirement for an alternative engine supply source was emphasised accordingly. The 1946 General Technical Data Sheet includes no less than 18 different models

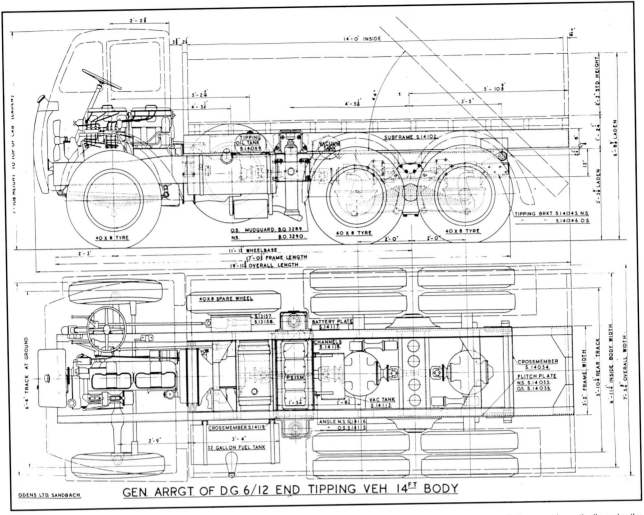

GEN. ARRGT. OF D.G. 6/12 END TIPPING VEH. 14^FT BODY

This DG6-12 end tipper had 40 x 8 tyres on 22in rims, of larger diameter than standard, and there was just enough space to fit the spare in vertically under the front offside of the body. The rear end of the lengthy 6LW engine protruded slightly through the rear face of the cab. The model was also available as a three-way tipper with a shorter wheelbase and relocated tipping gear, the side tipping function being used in road building and maintenance before the advent of Barber Green asphalt spreaders.

fitted with the Gardner 4, 5 or 6LW engine, but all vehicle specifications included the Foden five speed gearbox, Foden 4 ton rated front axles and 8 ton rated worm drive rear axles in single or double drive configuration. Bendix-Cowdrey brakes were fitted with Lockheed hydraulic actuation. The accompanying arrangement drawings illustrate typical examples.

The 1946 Technical Data Sheet indicated the high degree of major unit commonality in the DG range of vehicles and one of the principal common features was the five speed Foden gearbox fitted as standard to all of the 16 Gardner LW engine vehicles in the range.

Designed and introduced in 1937 with straight spur gears, four evenly spaced ratios from direct drive top gear to 6.14 : 1 bottom gear and a superlow ratio of 13.28 : 1 both forward and reverse gears, the gearbox had provision for power take off drives on both

The long-wheelbase six-wheeler with standard tyres is represented by this example supplied to the New Cheshire Salt Works Ltd in the author's home town of Northwich – the registration number KLG 972 dates it at the beginning of 1948. This model was available with either 5LW or 6LW engine and was rated at 12 tons payload capacity but there was also a DG5-11 model with single tyres on the rearmost (non-driving axle) and in this case the rear axle was suspended on a frame-mounted swivel arm attached to the rear of the driving axle springs. It gave reduced unladen weight but few were sold.

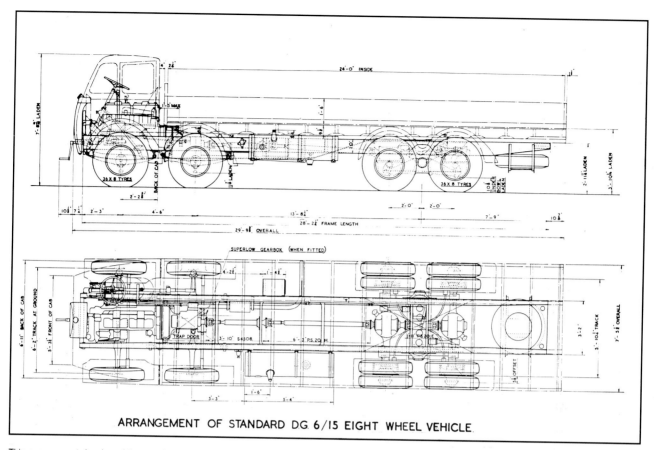

ARRANGEMENT OF STANDARD D.G. 6/15 EIGHT WHEEL VEHICLE.

This arrangement drawing of the standard DG6/15 eight-wheeler was passed in March 1945, ready for the resumption of postwar production, and there was strong demand for the type, still largely as designed in 1936 but built in sizeable numbers in 1946 and 1947, while the drawing office was busy on the next generation of models.

offside and nearside which continued to be fitted on the post war range of DG vehicles until December, 1947.

The gearbox casing was originally designed and produced in aluminium alloy, but during the war years and for some time after the war, due to material shortages, the casing was made in cast iron.

Gearwheels were originally produced in a 5% nickel steel, later superseded by a nickel chrome molybdenum alloy known as 'Fox's 540'.

There were many other major common elements in the DG range which had the effect of reducing purchasing problems,

The super-low five-speed gearbox as had been built since 1937 helped to solve the problem of gearing a vehicle with Gardner engine, tightly governed to 1,700rpm, so as to give economical running in top gear and yet adequate climbing ability to tackle steep gradients when the need arose. The extra gear was provided in an extra assembly at the rear of the main box, bringing in two extra stages of gearing, but had the advantage over the overdrive type of gearbox that these were only in use when a steep gradient was encountered.

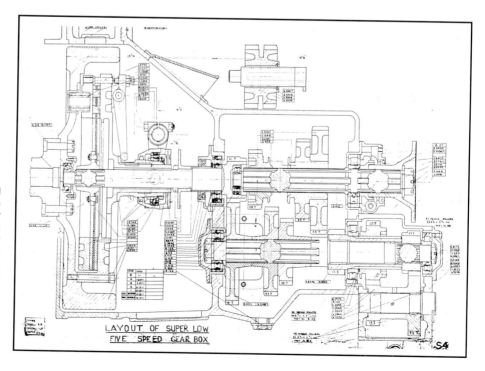

LAYOUT OF SUPER LOW FIVE SPEED GEAR BOX

When details of the Foden passenger range were announced in September 1945, a photograph of a Willowbrook-bodied Barton Transport Leyland TD7 double-decker dating from 1940 was extensively retouched as shown to convey the appearance that had been decided upon. This caused a sensation, for the full-width bonnet and concealed radiator broke new ground, the only previous application of a similar idea at that stage being a prototype built for its own use by the Midland Red concern. Foden was the first manufacturer to offer vehicles of this style for general sale. A prototype double-decker was being bodied by Willowbrook, appearing in November 1945, but this was based on a modified wartime utility design and doubtless the bodybuilder provided this picture to give an idea of how the bus would look with more stylish bodywork, though in fact no bus of this style was actually built.

improving assembly times and reducing service and spares costs, but the basic vehicle design had remained virtually unchanged from the mid-1930s and a new model range with new design features was long overdue.

In the Drawing Office, during the final stages of the war, new vehicle designs were continuously under review, and the Foden engine design and development programme was already in progress. Eventually, and somewhat surprisingly, it was decided that the first new post-war Foden vehicle to be introduced would be a bus chassis suitable for single or double-deck bodies.

Fodens had built several passenger vehicles at times when orders for standard goods vehicles were limited, but most were simply goods vehicle chassis fitted with a bus body. Only the 1933 double-decker had been designed specifically as a passenger vehicle. The new bus chassis would be powered by both Gardner and Foden engines and unladen weight and a low centre of gravity would be

This general arrangement drawing dating from June 1946 shows the PVSC5 single-deck chassis with Gardner 5LW engine. The front-end design with this power unit was quite compact, and other noteworthy features were the cross-braced frame and the use of one-piece side-members with the low-level rear end to support the luggage boot on a coach model formed as an integral part of the pressing. At that stage, the Foden engine option was yet to be announced, not being offered until 1948.

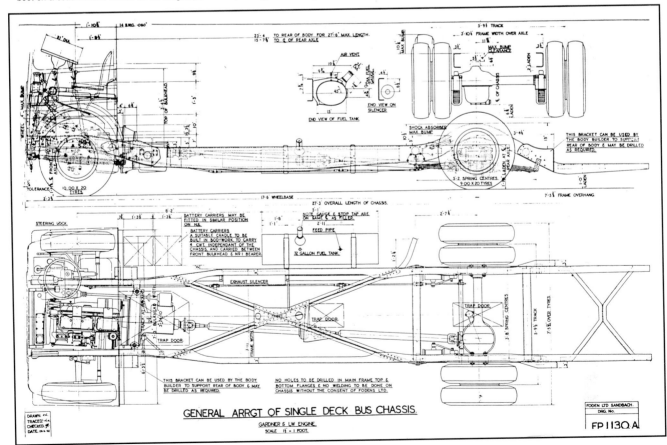

GENERAL ARRGT OF SINGLE DECK BUS CHASSIS.

GARDNER 6 LW ENGINE.
SCALE 1½ = 1 FOOT.

FP1130.A

The first prototype post-war Foden bus chassis, 23000, received a Willowbrook body at the end of 1945. In 1948 this body was transferred to a new chassis, 27222, registered KMA 570, and after further use by Foden this vehicle was sold to W. A. Cawthorne of Barugh and then passed in 1951 to the Yorkshire Traction Co Ltd, as seen here in service in 1952. The chassis type was PVD and a Foden two-stroke engine was fitted. The lowbridge body was based on framing similar to the wartime design built by Willowbrook; the lack of taper at the front of the upper deck caused it to overhang the cab side slightly, though in this case some rounding of the outline had been made.

important design criteria, particularly in relation to the double-deck chassis. My own first assignment on the new bus chassis was the completion of the initial frame arrangement.

To decide on the most suitable frame design three scale models had been made by my old foreman, Frank Nicholls, in the Assembly Shop. All the sidemembers were identical, but one model had conventional pressed channel section crossmembers, the second model had tubular crossmembers and the third a combination of a central cross bracing assembly and tubular crossmembers.

The three alternatives were thoroughly tested, the combination of cross bracing with tubular crossmembers proved to be the most satisfactory, and was accordingly adopted. One other feature which had been finalised was the transmission drive line from the gearbox

to the rear axle which was to be completely in line to eliminate any possible propshaft vibration problems. To achieve this objective, the engine/gearbox assembly was inclined and the worm drive assembly in the rear axle was offset and tilted to suit. To complicate the geometry further, a rubber mounted intermediate bearing assembly had to be incorporated into the frame cross bracing at the point where the intermediate and main propshafts were connected. It was a difficult assembly to design, equally difficult to make, but completely successful in achieving the required performance objectives in service.

The allowable gross weight of this single-deck model was 9 tons 10 cwt, the chassis weight was 4 tons, leaving a body and passenger load allowance of 5 tons 10 cwt This same chassis was

Warrington Corporation was to prove the biggest operator of Foden double-deck bus chassis, building up a total fleet of fifteen, all PVD6 models with Gardner 6LW engines, out of the total of 59 of the type built. Seen here are Warrington's first seven, of which five, including that nearest the camera, had bodywork by East Lancashire Coachbuilders but two (second and fourth from the right) received second-hand Metro-Cammell/Crossley bodywork from pre-war Crossley chassis. Number 36, second from the right, had chassis number 23000, which had been the original prototype for post-war bus production, rebuilt from PVD to PVD6 specification before delivery to Warrington.

Much thought was put into the design of the Foden passenger range, which included several innovations from accepted practice in bus design of the time. The frame was the author's first assignment and the diagonal crossbracing, chosen after experiments with model frame assemblies, gave greater rigidity than the usual reliance on mainly tubular crossmembers, even though it was quite complex to design and make.

also built with the 6 LW Gardner engine and a slightly reduced body and passenger load allowance of 5 tons 8 cwt. I found that general arrangement drawings for passenger vehicles needed far more

Almost all existing passenger models made by other makers at that time suffered from continual vibration of the steering column on any but the smoothest roads, conveyed to the driver's hands on the steering wheel. The Foden design used a large-diameter aluminium housing to reduce this and an ingenious design made it possible to house the speedometer in the centre, an exclusive Foden feature. From a driver's viewpoint, perhaps the most interesting feature was the brake system, with engine-driven hydraulic pump, similar in principle to that adopted later on the London Routemaster buses, but many operators took a conservative view on such matters, still favouring the vacuum servo.

information for the body builder than standard goods vehicles, for the simple reason that most bus bodies totally enclose the chassis and all access to necessary servicing points had to be clearly defined. It was about this period during the development of the bus chassis that I began to maintain a more comprehensive record of the work that I was personally involved with, and from these records I note that my next jobs on the original bus chassis were the front and rear road springs, both with reverse camber in the laden condition, followed by the shoe return springs for the newly designed two leading shoe brake assembly introduced on the bus chassis and later applied to the whole of the new FG range of goods vehicles which was destined to follow the passenger vehicle range.

To be a member of Fodens Drawing Office staff during this formative period after the war, when so many completely new designs were introduced, was undoubtedly a privilege which we probably did not fully appreciate at the time. On the range of passenger vehicles for example, in addition to the unique chassis frame and transmission arrangement already described, a completely new braking system was introduced incorporating many original features. The hydraulically operated front and rear wheel brakes were designed with two leading shoe type actuation and automatic adjustment. The 16.5-in inside diameter front and rear brake drums were designed with helical ribs to aid heat dissipation and at the same time add strength to the drum section without a corresponding increase in weight. The most remarkable feature of the braking system, however, was the footbrake boost arrangement which consisted of a completely independent hydraulic circuit, powered by an engine driven gear pump and generating pressures up to 1,200 psi, which could be proportionately applied to the normal footbrake hydraulic circuit via the brake pedal.

The handbrake incorporated a variable leverage design to provide a lighter and more progressive application and a compensating linkage was utilised at the rear axle to equalise the braking effort applied to each rear wheel.

One other additional safety device fitted to all Foden bus chassis at this time was the Lockheed 'Hill Holder' valve which simplified restarting on hills by effectively 'locking on' the hydraulic foot brake pressure until the clutch was released to engage the transmission.

The single plate clutch and four or five speed gearboxes offered on the early bus chassis were fairly conventional derivatives of the standard goods vehicle gearboxes in production at that time, though second and third gears now had the benefit of helical gears for quiet running. In conjunction with the flexible engine mounting, the Foden was among the quietest of bus models having Gardner engines in which to ride, even on the PVSC5 using the 5LW engine. An option offered for some time was a fluid coupling, but this was later withdrawn, presumably due to lack of demand.

The passenger vehicle front axle was similarly conventional in design, but the rear axle, with offset transmission line and underslung worm gear provided to ensure a constant body floor height, was a completely new design based on a one piece steel alloy drop forging.

Final drive from the differential assembly to the rear wheel hubs was transmitted via 2in diameter 100 tons tensile axle shafts with a dog toothed flange coupling arrangement.

Design improvements introduced on the new passenger vehicle range were not confined solely to the basic mechanical elements of the vehicle. The driver's environment received a good deal of

The PVSC5, with Gardner 5LW engine, tended to be the Foden model most favoured for single-deck bus duties, although sales in this category were limited. The most popular choice of body make was Saunders, producing 23 of the total of 55 of this model built. This example, No.11 in the fleet of Caerphilly Urban District Council, was one of four supplied to that undertaking in 1947; it remained in service there until 1963. A larger batch of similar vehicles was supplied to Crown Coaches, an amalgamation of independent operators in Durham and Northumberland.

The primary bus sales targets were the major city bus undertakings but the nearest approach to success in this direction was the delivery of five PVD6 double-deckers to the 160-vehicle bus and trolleybus fleet of Derby Corporation in January 1952. They had Brush bodywork to the rather plain style favoured by that undertaking at the time. Although the Gardner engine was already well-established in the fleet, subsequent Derby bus orders continued to go to Daimler, favoured since pre-war days.

Lancashire United Transport Ltd, in those days one of the country's largest companies not belonging to any of the major combines, also took five PVD6 models, delivered in 1951. In this case, Northern Counties bodywork was chosen, of a curvaceous style which matched the Foden bonnet design quite effectively. Here again the Gardner 6LW engine was already the standard choice for double-deckers, but the Guy Arab was emerging as the preferred choice of chassis make.

attention and improvements introduced involved the provision of fully adjustable seating, centralised electrical controls and a novel instrument panel located in the centre of the steering wheel.

The steering gear was designed as a completely integral unit mounted on the offside chassis sidemember. The original design embodied a conventional worm and sector reduction gear, but this was later superseded by a recirculatory ball unit in which all moving surfaces were in rolling contact, thereby considerably reducing steering effort.

With so many completely new features embodied in the range of passenger vehicles introduced at this time, it was decided that a separate passenger vehicle sales organisation should be formed to market the new Foden product. Ted Johnson was accordingly appointed as Passenger Vehicle Sales Manager and, with very little assistance other than an office based clerk and typist, he set about the new job with his customary enthusiasm, concentrating initially on the sale of the double-deck chassis to the various major municipalities. He was only partially successful in attaining this first sales objective.

The local City of Chester and the Borough of Warrington purchased fleets of Foden double-deck bus chassis and these initial orders were later followed by orders from Derby and Merthyr Tydfil, but his primary sales targets were the major city bus undertakings of Manchester, Liverpool, Birmingham, and Glasgow and these proved to be unattainable with a newly designed product from a relatively new bus chassis manufacturer.

By far the most successful of Foden's passenger range was the PVSC6, the single-deck model with Gardner 6LW engine, of which 316 were built, largely between 1946 and 1950, the majority being placed in service by independent operators and having coach bodywork, although 60 were exported. There was remarkable variety among the builders of the coach bodies, the early post-war years being a time when the demand encouraged many new or hitherto little-known firms to enter this market. Among the latter was Wadham Bros, of Waterlooville, Hants, which built fourteen coaches on the PVSC6 chassis, including this 1948 example, KMB 95, of H. Coppenhall, based in the Foden home town of Sandbach. The 6LW engine required a longer bonnet, but the sloping-pillar styling fashionable at the time helped to disguise the way the bulkhead was set back slightly behind the front mudguards.

The single-deck chassis, however, proved to be a much more popular model with a wide range of bus and coach operators, and it was the continuous flow of orders from this particular sector of the market that eventually justified Fodens' decision to design and build the range of passenger vehicle chassis. The single-deck bus or coach chassis was fitted with many different types of bodies to suit customers' individual requirements.

As sales and service reports from an ever increasing number of satisfied operators of Foden coaches and buses were studied at Sandbach, it became clear that, despite the simultaneous introduction of many completely new design features in the new product, the traditional high standard of Foden reliability had been maintained.

This favourable information served to confirm Fodens' decision to embody many of the new bus features in a completely new range of goods vehicles to supersede the now somewhat 'dated' DG range introduced before the war.

The new range was designated FG for the Gardner engined vehicles and FE when fitted with the alternative Foden engines, and was destined for a long and eventful production run. According to my records, the first detail drawings I produced on the new vehicle range related to the front suspension on the single and double front axle models, together with the brake linkage arrangements.

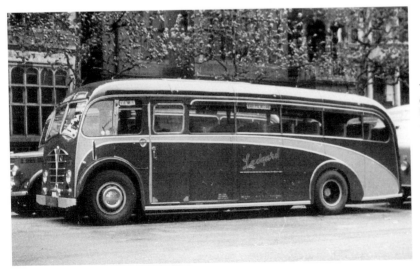

The most popular bodybuilder on Foden passenger chassis was Plaxton, producing a total of exactly 100 bodies, of which 81 were on the PVSC6 chassis. From about 1949, there was increasing interest in full-fronted coach bodywork and the Foden design lent itself particularly well to this, quite a number of the Plaxton output on the PVSC6 chassis being of this type. This example, MUA 866, was supplied to Samuel Ledgard of Armley, Leeds in August 1949 and is seen two months later parked near the Albert Hall in London on the occasion of a national brass band contest, having carried the Black Dyke Mills Band. The latter was a great rival of the Foden Motor Works Band, and one can imagine what the Foden players might have thought if they saw its transport on that day.

The new FG goods range, on which most of the design work took place during 1946, adopted many of the new features first seen on the passenger models, and this new S.18 cab adopted the same type of front grille panel. The cab was of traditional ash-framed construction but the pillars were now encased in aluminium panelling and the window outlines had become more rounded in conformity to contemporary styling trends. The distinctive ribbed Foden bumper and large hub cap suited the new design well.

Features common to both the FP passenger vehicle and the FG and FE goods vehicle range included the two leading shoe hydraulic brake system, the engine suspension arrangement, the driver's controls and instrumentation and the front axle assembly.

For the FG/FE vehicle range a completely new flush front cab was introduced with an easily identifiable front grill panel based on the bus front panel design. The cab was designed and built in the traditional style with an ash frame and aluminium panels, but all the previously exposed wood door and corner pillars were now protected with an aluminium skin and the overall exterior and interior cab finish was significantly improved. The traditional passenger vehicle standard of finish was now effectively applied to the goods vehicle range.

One other major feature introduced on the six and eight-wheel vehicles in the FG range, was the four spring articulated rear bogie axle assembly, designed by Jack Mills and destined to outlast, in production terms, any other Foden manufactured unit in my time.

Originally designed for a laden weight of 15 tons and later uprated for the 24 ton gross weight eight-wheeler, to 16 tons, it was light, reliable and, with the advent of automatic lubrication, easily maintained. It was not effectively superseded as a standard Foden production unit until the introduction of the various rubber suspension systems some twenty years later.

The worm gear final drive units incorporated in the new

articulated bogie axle assembly had originally been designed for the 'R' type range of vehicles in 1932, at which time they were fitted in the heavy forged axle casings of that period. In the new four spring bogie they were fitted to the much lighter, pressed steel,

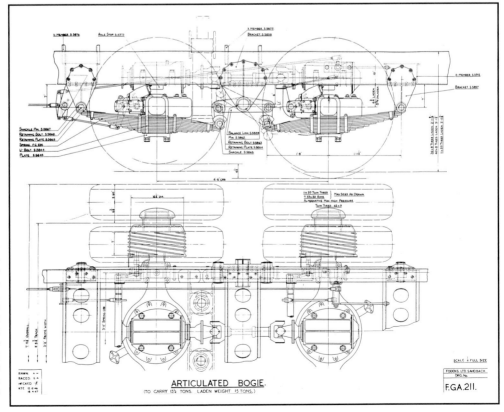

The four-spring bogie, with balance links connecting the springs of the two axles, was designed by Jack Mills for the new FG range during 1946, remaining in production for 20 years. The design of the overhead worm-drive units dated back to the R-type of 1932, but were now incorporated in lighter welded pressed-steel casings. Note the spiral ribs on the brake drums, designed to help in cooling as well as stiffness.

ARTICULATED BOGIE.
(TO CARRY 13½ TONS. LADEN WEIGHT 15 TONS.)

F.G.A.211.

welded axle casing which in service proved equally reliable.

Most of the finalised design, assembly, and detailed component drawings, together with jigs, tools and fixture drawings for the new FG vehicle range were produced in the Drawing Office during 1946 so that this particular year marked a busy and memorable period for the whole of our department. For me, this was particularly true because I had planned to be married in June of that year and, as Fodens did not pay particularly high wages at that time, I considered it necessary, at least as a temporary measure, to supplement my income. The only saleable talent I possessed outside normal work was experience gained in car repairs, mainly on my own cars. By 1946 I had progressed from my initial 1926 Austin Seven to a 1937 Ford 10 two-door saloon, known in the trade as the 'turtleback'.

A budding local entrepreneur had built up a stock of pre-war cars during the war years but had no idea how to get them to saleable condition. With two former workmates from the light platers section, I set out to earn a little extra cash on our Sundays off. I handled the mechanical repairs whilst my mates attended to the bodywork. This continued for some months when, my mates suitably rewarded, I had built up funds for my marital expenses and gained a number of satisfied customers.

By the end of 1946 with all detail work on the new range of vehicles virtually completed, the final General Arrangement

Drawings of each model were being prepared and production of the first prototypes was under way.

This first Arrangement Drawing FGA 1 relates to the long wheelbase FG four-wheeler with 17ft 6in flat platform body, 4LW Gardner engine, 4 ton Foden front axle, 8 ton Foden worm drive rear axle and Foden 5 speed gearbox. The payload was 7½ tons, the legal maximum gross vehicle weight 12 tons, so that the maximum unladen weight would be 4½ tons.

The initials at the foot of the drawing indicate that I was the draughtsman, Marjory Armstrong, the tracer, and Jim Pringle, a senior draughtsman, the checker. The drawing was dated January 31st, 1947.

The FG range of vehicles was similar to the superseded DG range in relation to the availability of alternative wheelbases for tractor unit, tipper, and flat platform applications, and was, of course, identical to the DG range in relation to the alternative fitment of 4, 5 and 6LW Gardner engines.

Produced with a 13ft 7¼in wheelbase to suit a 24ft 6in body length and a maximum overall length limit at that time of 30ft 0in, the FG eight-wheeler model was undoubtedly the most popular unit in the complete range.

The standard specification included the 6LW Gardner engine, five-speed Foden gearbox and Foden 16 ton double-drive four-spring rear bogie. The two Foden front axles were each rated at 4

The first arrangement drawing for the new FG goods range was this one, drawn by the author and dated 31st January 1947. The new cab was slightly shorter and the drawing indicates that the space between it and the headboard of the body needed to be increased from the normal 2.25in to 4.5in to allow for the protrusion of the rear of the 6LW engine's cylinder block, when that engine was fitted.

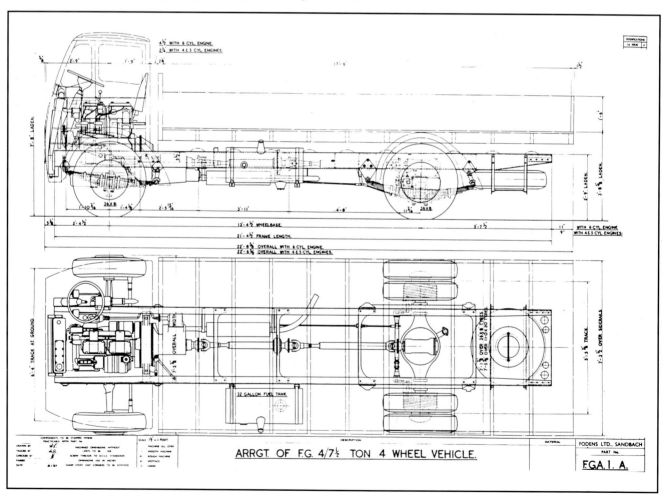

ARRGT. OF F.G. 4/7½ TON 4 WHEEL VEHICLE.

FODENS LTD., SANDBACH

F.G.A. 1. A.

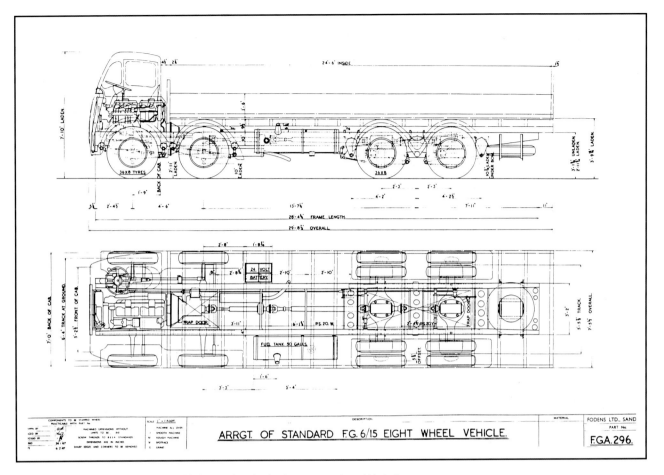

ARRGT. OF STANDARD F.G. 6/15 EIGHT WHEEL VEHICLE.

F.GA. 296.

The standard eight-wheeler, now of type FG6/15, continued to be the most popular vehicle in the range.

tons, resulting in a total gross vehicle rating of 24 tons, the legal maximum for an eight-wheeler in that period. Foden's main competition in the eight-wheeler market was Leyland Motors, who, by virtue of their much higher production rate, could generally offer their standard vehicles at a considerably lower price than Fodens and although it was not, specifically, our responsibility in the Drawing Office, we regularly carried out cost reductions investigations together with the Production and Purchase departments on selected elements of the vehicle specification in order to reduce this adverse selling factor.

Very often, we would find that 'buying out' would result in a lower cost than 'in-house' manufacture, indicating even then a possible change in our future company policy. However, it was now 1947, we were about to introduce a completely new range of vehicles on to the home market and almost at the same time, the Government, despite objections from operators and manufacturers alike, introduced a new Transport Act which effectively brought all UK long distance road transport under the control of a newly created body entitled the British Transport Commission. This organisation was invested with the authority to take over the control of all road transport companies whose operations extended beyond a 40 mile radius from their home base and to transfer their business to the Road Haulage Executive controlled from eight divisional centres in various parts of the country. The only exemptions from this Nationalisation programme were manufacturers who employed their own transport fleets to distribute their own specific products, heavy indivisible load haulage, bulk liquid transport, furniture removals and, of course, operators who confined their transport

business within a 40 mile radius of their home base.

Although Fodens were fortunate in having many customers who were operating within the exempt classifications and could, therefore, continue to operate independently and retain their right to purchase the vehicles of their choice, it was rightly considered by Fodens' management that the Government Nationalisation measure would seriously restrict home market sales, at least temporarily, if not permanently.

To offset this possible reduction in demand, it was decided to increase our sales effort in the continually expanding overseas markets and, in order to stimulate sales in a wider world market, we were asked to design left hand drive versions of the FG vehicle range. Taking the eight-wheeler model as an example, although the standard maximum payload of 15 tons was not increased, the channel frame section was increased from 10in to 12in and the tyre size from 36in x 8in to 11in x 22in in anticipation of more demanding operating conditions overseas and of course, left hand drive controls were a necessary option.

As I recall it, our left hand drive control arrangement was designed to limit the required number of new parts to an absolute minimum.

For example, the left hand change speed linkage was achieved with standard right hand components plus a cross-shaft assembly at the gearbox end of the linkage. With this arrangement, the standard right hand gearbox and selector mechanism could also be utilised on left hand drive vehicles. Our Overseas Sales Department was never happy with this arrangement which they implied was the one section of the overseas vehicle specification which did not

This prototype dump truck conversion was produced for Hughes Bros of Buxton in 1947-8, based on an existing vehicle. Although not directly successful in providing the basis for follow-up business, it aroused considerable interest and demonstrated that there was considerable scope for heavy-duty off-highway tippers.

compare favourably with our competitors. However, in service, the arrangement gave no trouble, and certainly had no identifiable effect on the volume of sales which continued to expand in all areas.

This favourable trend was most noticeable in Australia, South Africa and Rhodesia where our Sales Director, Ted Foden, spent almost nine months of 1947 seeking new sales opportunities for Foden vehicles and checking the service performance of existing customers' vehicles.

Fodens' material supply permits in the UK continued to depend to a large extent on the value of overseas sales which accordingly retained a high priority at this time.

There were, of course, bound to be service problems with certain overseas vehicle applications, where the combination of adverse climate and operational conditions far exceeded the designed limitations, but fortunately these problems were infrequent and could usually be corrected within acceptable limits of time and cost.

One notable exception was the S.18 home market cab; built basically with an ash frame and aluminium panels, and having a perfectly satisfactory service life under UK operational conditions. However, when subjected to the combined effect of a tropical climate and unmade roads, the wood framework of the cab needed continual attention and the decision was made to design an all metal, completely interchangeable replacement. This new cab was fabricated from a variety of steel sections, panels were pop-riveted to the framework and a double skin roof was incorporated to provide additional heat insulation.

In overseas service the new all metal cab proved to be far superior to its wooden counterpart and was frequently utilised for heavy duty home market applications, where the resultant increase in unladen weight was not a critical factor.

One of the earliest home market applications for the all steel cab was destined to test its capabilities to the full. It was at this time in the 1947/48 period that we began to develop Fodens' first off-road site vehicle, the forerunner of the comprehensive range of contractors' plant, later to constitute a significant proportion of the company's total output. The first request for this type of vehicle came from an old established Foden customer, Messrs Hughes Brothers of Buxton who owned limestone quarries in that area and had used Foden vehicles to deliver their products for many years. In

the quarries, the limestone was handled by small Muir-Hill, four wheel, forward dump trucks, which were proving to be inadequate under their particular operating conditions and it was to replace these vehicles that Fodens were asked to design a higher payload four wheeler with power tip gear and dual-controls to enable the vehicle to operate as a forward or end tipper. It was not a job that Fodens had any particular need to take on at that time, with the production rate limited by the availability of basic materials and a full order book, but Hughes Brothers were valuable customers, the Foden salesman involved was Ted Johnson, a most persistent personality, and the customer had offered to provide an old four-wheeler standard tipper as a basis for a prototype vehicle. I was the unfortunate draughtsman to be allocated for this particular job, for which I had no particular enthusiasm from the outset. However, the conversion, when completed, achieved the three principal requirements of hydraulic powered tipping gear, reversible driving position and above all, increased payload capacity.

In service, however, the converted vehicle showed no significant improvement on the customer's existing vehicles other than payload capacity and no further vehicles of this type were built. Nevertheless, from the interest shown in the project, it became obvious that there was a market for a heavy duty off-highway tipping vehicle and Fodens were not slow to respond to this need.

The initial vehicle design produced was virtually a heavy duty version of the standard overseas six-wheel end tipper with a 12in channel section flitched frame, all steel cab, 14in x 20in tyre equipment, and a steel scow end body.

Vehicles built to this design operated initially with some success on waste disposal duties for the Steel Company of Wales and Guest Keen Iron and Steel, but were not constructed to the specification required for heavy duty, continuous, off-road work as exemplified by an open cast coal extraction site. This fact became abundantly clear when our somewhat over-confident Sales Department sold a fleet of six-wheeler end tippers with dumper bodies to contractors who were extracting coal for the NCB from an open-cast site near Whitley Bay.

Reports of repetitive service problems resulted in a request for assistance from our Service Department and I was ordered up to Whitley Bay to check the situation at first hand. The Foden vehicles, together with six-wheel Aveling Barfords and four-wheel ex-US

The initial production design adopted for a heavy-duty off-highway tipper was based on the overseas-specification six-wheeler, with a 12-in flitched frame, the all-steel cab and 14.00-20 tyres, with a steel scow-end dumper body. This DG5/12 was built for Holloway Bros (London) Ltd.

Army Euclids, were hauling overburden from a deep coal seam up very steep, poorly maintained access roads on a 24 hour round-the-clock basis. Maintenance varied from poor to non-existent and all the vehicles on the site were in trouble in one way or another. I spent a full week with the NCB and contractor's engineering staff and became more aware of the exacting requirements of a true off-road contractor's plant vehicle.

It was from the field information gathered at this, and many other similar applications both home and overseas that we subsequently finalised our dump truck design to include a much heavier range of frames, axles, transmissions, bodies and cabs to provide a safer working environment for the operator, easier access for servicing and an extended working life for the vehicle.

Throughout the years, from the founding of the company in 1856, Fodens had established an enviable reputation for innovative engineering in the design of their various products, and it had been the custom to introduce these new features to customers and the general public at the various agricultural and automotive exhibitions held annually in various parts of the country.

The two principal automotive exhibitions had been established over the years in London and Glasgow by the Society of Motor Manufacturers and Traders and the Scottish Motor Traders Association respectively, and in 1948 the Commercial Motor Transport Exhibition, as it was then known, was due to be held at Earls Court in London during the first two weeks in October.

This was the commercial vehicle manufacturers' first opportunity to show their products collectively for ten years

and a great deal of interest was generated, both within the industry and its wide range of customers and also with the general public. This interest was reflected in the record total attendance of 147,000 which included a party of 400 Foden employees, all eager to see how their own Sandbach-built vehicles measured up to the opposition.

From both customer and press reaction during the Show, they had every reason to be proud of the Foden exhibits which included two passenger vehicles; one a long 17ft 6in wheelbase chassis, suitable for a single-deck or touring coach body, the other a 16ft 3in wheelbase, complete double-deck city bus for Chester Corporation, both powered with the Gardner 6LW engine and Foden four-speed gearbox; a Gardner engined 12 ton payload six-wheeler; a Foden engined 15 ton payload eight-wheeler, a left hand drive Gardner powered four-wheel tractor unit, plus a four-wheel three way tipper and an eight-wheeler van.

Vehicle design features highlighted included the recirculatory ball steering box, two leading shoe hydraulically boosted braking system and the double leverage handbrake, but the real star feature of the Foden stand and indeed of the whole show, was the Foden six-cylinder two stroke engine with its remarkable fuel economy

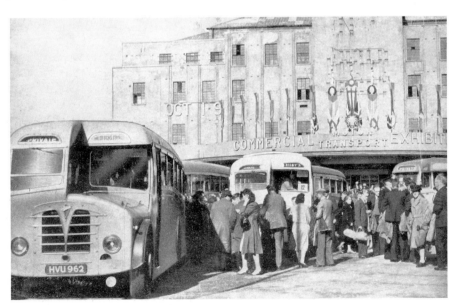

A fleet of Foden coaches was hired from various operators based in the north-west to take a party of 400 Foden employees to the first post-war Commercial Motor Transport Exhibition, held at Earls Court, London, in October 1948.

and power to weight ratio. Technical Press reports, normally diffident with a completely new design, were highly complimentary:- 'So far as power units are concerned, the new Foden certainly ranks as an outstanding example of British enterprise' and 'With the two stroke engine, of which there has been so much talk, Fodens may be said to have stolen the show'.

It was indeed a fabulous Show for Fodens. The stand was the centre of attention for the whole of the Show period and a record number of orders were taken. It must have been particularly gratifying for William Foden, our Managing Director, who had given up his home and business in Australia fourteen years previously to return and guide the company back to prosperity from the brink of a disastrous failure. He attended the Show each day, having celebrated his 80th birthday the previous week with a party and concert in the Works Recreation Club at Sandbach. The Drawing Office staff were allowed only a two-day visit to Earls Court at that time, but even during that limited period we had the opportunity to view and evaluate all of our main competitors' products at first hand and compare them, and alternative proprietary items with our own efforts and choice.

I was always interested in the various techniques employed by individual salesmen to sell their product, not least on our own stand, and I very soon came to the conclusion that the Foden sales staff would benefit from a wider and more detailed knowledge of the specification and performance capabilities of the particular vehicle they were offering to their various customers. At that time, any suggestion of this nature from a relatively junior member of the Drawing Office staff would have received little serious attention, so I kept my thoughts to myself and concentrated my attention on my own, far more interesting job.

During the following year, 1949, with a full order book as a result of a successful Show and a continuing shortage of basic materials, it might have been considered at least prudent, if not absolutely essential, to adopt a rationalised production policy and build only standard vehicles with a guaranteed profit margin, but this was never the Foden way, there was always a new and promising application for a Foden vehicle to be considered, and 1949 was no exception. Thomas Smith, the Crane and Excavator

Manufacturer from Leeds, had received enquiries from McAlpines and ICI Alkali Division for two truck mounted cranes and had passed on the inquiry for the two special chassis to Fodens. The decision was taken to proceed with the necessary design work and relative quotation and, after several meetings with Jim Upex, Smith's crane design engineer, we submitted a special eight-wheeler layout with a 14in steel joist section main frame incorporating fabricated box section crossmembers to house the four stabilizer beams, a jib rest assembly behind the cab to support and locate the jib in transit, and a solid beam rear bogie axle assembly to provide increased stability when lifting in the 'free on tyres' condition. To allow sufficient inter-axle movement in the rear bogie to retain tyre adhesion in transit, the suspension beam eye ends were fitted with rubber 'Spheralastik' bushes at their fixed ends and a trunnion arrangement at the shackle ends.

After completion of the prototype vehicle I attended several field trials at Smiths, during which we very soon decided that a proposed excavator application resulted in unacceptable degrees of instability and that all future applications should be confined to crane duties. It proved to be a sound decision, made at the right time.

Fortunately, the first two prototype vehicles for ICI and McAlpines were required for crane duties only and subsequent field service reports indicated that both units were operating efficiently. We were particularly fortunate with the ICI prototype which was operating locally with Alkali Division in Northwich and therefore, subject to regular inspection in service. Smiths reported numerous inquiries for the new product and within a month, we received a further order for six vehicles mainly for major Public Works Contractors.

This initial order from Smiths marked Foden's entry into yet another branch of the contractors' plant industry which was eventually destined to involve many of the world's leading crane and excavator manufacturers including Ruston Bucyrus, our wartime associates from Lincoln, Jones Cranes of Letchworth, Neals of Grantham, Coles of Sunderland, Priestman of Hull, Demag and Wilhag of West Germany, Fiorontini of Italy and Pauley and Harnischfeger of the USA.

However, all this was part of the future.

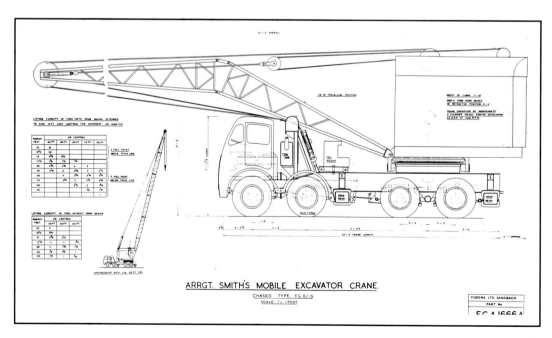

ARRGT. SMITH'S MOBILE EXCAVATOR CRANE.
CHASSIS TYPE. FG 6/15
SCALE: ¼' = 1 FOOT

The mobile crane for Thomas Smith of Rodley, Leeds was an initial venture into what was to prove an important line of business for Foden. Its design was based on the FG6/15 eight-wheeler, but with a steel joist frame and modified suspension. The arrangement used when travelling is shown in the main view, with the jib, reduced to its minimum length by removal of the detachable extension sections, resting on a bolster mounted on the frame behind the cab. Even so, the overall length in this form was 41ft 9in.

6 THE 'FIFTIES

Fodens announced a record turnover of £200,000 for the 1948/49 Financial Year and in the Drawing Office we were preparing to introduce yet another sensational automotive debutante for the forthcoming Commercial Vehicle Exhibition due to be held at Earls Court in September, 1950. This time, it was a completely new passenger vehicle project.

Fodens' entry into the passenger vehicle market immediately after the war had been viewed with a certain degree of scepticism by the traditional UK bus manufacturers and their attitude was, to some extent, justified by Fodens' subsequent inability to establish their vehicles in any significant numbers in major city corporation fleets. In relation to the touring coach chassis application, however, the Foden product had proved to be highly successful and in conjunction with leading body builders, had won several major design awards and commendations in London, Paris, Nice and New York. This was the commercial background which resulted in Fodens' decision to design the rear engined coach chassis, which, yet again, served to emphasise the company's continuing policy of engineering enterprise. Previous efforts to introduce this type of power unit and transmission layout on both goods and passenger vehicles had barely progressed beyond the prototype stage in the UK, although the alternative underfloor engine layout had been adopted by several manufacturers in the period up to 1950.

The arrangement introduced on the new Foden bus chassis involved mounting the engine, the flywheel housing and the clutch assembly transversely across the rear of the chassis frame, and the embodiment of a right angle spiral bevel drive assembly to align the gearbox and transmission with the standard offset worm drive rear axle.

This rear engine and transmission arrangement had several advantages when compared with the normal forward engine layout from both maintenance and operational aspects. Great emphasis was put on accessibility, the power unit and transmission assembly being on a subframe readily removed for major overhauls which also provided suitable access for all servicing. The layout helped in insulating passengers from noise, and the weight carried by each tyre was more evenly matched on the basis of a twin-tyred rear axle. Probably most important to the operator, virtually the whole length of the vehicle, newly increased to 30ft for home-market passenger models with two axles, was free for passenger space.

With such a major departure from conventional passenger vehicle design there were bound to be certain problem areas encountered during the development of the new vehicle, but as I

The rear-engined layout for bus or coach models seems commonplace today but Foden's 1950 design was the first to be marketed for general sale in Britain. This was the PVRF6 version, with Foden FD6 six-cylinder two-stroke engine, the compact dimensions and light weight of which made it well suited to the concept. Despite the unfamiliar layout, some of the main units and various smaller items were common to the front-engined chassis. The weight distribution, with more weight at the rear, gave more even loading of the tyres, enabling the same size to be used for the singles at the front and the twins at the rear.

Something of the originality of thought and high engineering quality to be found in the rear-engined coach chassis is conveyed in this cutaway view showing the spiral bevel angle-drive unit and gearbox assembly mounted under the rear offside of the frame. The drive was taken from the transversely-mounted engine through the angle-drive and then via the gearbox and the flange on the right of the picture forwards to the rear axle. The large gear-driven fan drew air through this side-mounted radiator. Note the use of helical gears within the gearbox.

FD6 two-stroke developing 126bhp at 2,000rpm or the Gardner 6LW, which had just been uprated to give 112bhp, still at 1,700rpm. The gearbox was available in either four-speed or five-speed, the latter being of the superlow type with a spread of ratios extending from the direct 1:1 top gear to the super-low ratio of 9.97:1.

The new Foden vehicle was shown to the public for the first time in September 1950 at the Earls Court Commercial Show. There were two chassis exhibited on the Foden stand, one with a Gardner 6LW engine, the other with the FD6 Foden engine, and there was also a complete rear engine coach with a Whitson body, later destined to win two major awards at the Paris Show for the premier vehicle in its class and also the most elegant coach in the whole of the Show. Fodens' position in the passenger vehicle industry at that time was illustrated by the fact that five of the principal coach body builders at Earls Court were exhibiting their products on Foden chassis – Messrs Windover, James Whitson, Plaxton's, Thomas Harrington and Churchill Constructors.

Fodens other exhibits on Stand No. 69 at the 1950 Show included a 7½ ton payload four-wheeler fitted with a 4LW Gardner engine and van body, and a 15 ton payload eight-wheeler tanker fitted with the 6LW Gardner engine, both fairly standard vehicles, with four speed Foden gearboxes.

The sixth and final vehicle on the Stand, however, was a completely new unit designated FG 8/15 and designed specifically for heavy duty operation in Fodens' rapidly expanding overseas markets in South Africa, Rhodesia and Australia. The power unit was the new Gardner 8LW engine developing 150bhp at 1,700rpm and 478 lbs ft maximum torque at 1,300rpm with an equally new Foden epicyclic auxiliary gearbox with overall reduction ratios exceeding 20:1; fitted behind the standard four-speed main gearbox.

Fodens' exports to South Africa had now increased to a level which justified more direct sales and service representation in the country and a new subsidiary company was accordingly founded entitled Fodens (South Africa) Ltd with headquarters in Johannesburg.

1950 had been a significant, progressive year for Fodens and this favourable trend was reflected in the October Annual Report and Accounts which indicated a record Gross Trading Profit. The following year, 1951 was declared 'Festival of Britain' year and Fodens were invited to submit a rear-engine coach chassis and a Foden two-stroke diesel engine for inclusion in the Transport

recall it, they were quickly and successfully identified and solved. One example was the possible engine oil and water coolant problem resulting from the unorthodox radiator location at the rear offside of the vehicle.

A special, high capacity combined still tube and block element radiator was accordingly designed, together with a close cowled, six blade, 21in diameter fan driven at 1½ times engine speed from the bevel drive transmission gearbox and, as a result of these corrective features, the required oil and water temperature control was accordingly maintained.

The remote location of the engine, clutch and gearbox meant that there were some problems in avoiding the action of the accelerator, clutch pedal and gear lever being too heavy. At first a hydraulic accelerator was used, but later a special cable proved as effective and cheaper. Properly-designed mechanical linkage worked well for the clutch and gear-change, though an automatic lubricator for the latter's linkage was provided, worked by the clutch pedal.

As with the front-engined Foden coach and bus chassis, the rear-engined model was offered with a choice of engines, the Foden

This plan view shows a Gardner-engined PVRG6 model in export form, with 19ft 6in wheelbase for a chassis overall length of 32ft 6in – with body, the intended overall length was 33ft. The home versions complied with the newly-introduced 30ft limit and had a 16ft 6in wheelbase. The recommended 4.4 to 1 rear axle ratio with the Gardner engine gave a governed road speed of 45.5mph. On the PVRF6, with the Foden two-stroke engine, the recommended ratio was 5.0 to 1, giving 47mph. In practice, because the Foden engine fired on every downward stroke, it sounded much faster-revving than it was and was not unlike a racing car engine in aural effect.

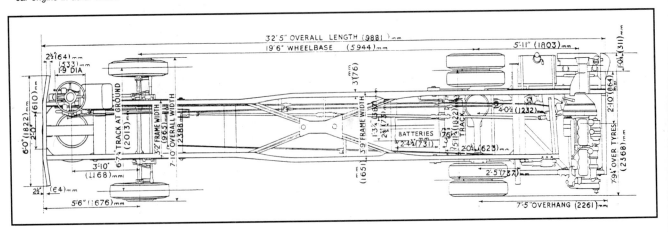

The rear-engined Foden gave the bodybuilder freedom to pursue the 'streamline' styles in favour at the time. Bellhouse Hartwell Ltd, of Westhoughton, Lancs, was one of the firms which built up quite a following for a time, having built 21 bodies on front-engined Foden coach chassis (eleven PVSC6 and ten of the Foden-engined PVFE6, the latter being the largest number by any bodybuilder on that model, of which 52 were built in all). This 1951 example of its work was one of nine on the rear-engined model (five PVRF6 with Foden engine and four PVRG6 with the Gardner 6LW), and went to Taylor of Leigh, Lancashire.

Pavilion at the South Bank Exhibition. More significant, however, from Fodens' long term viewpoint, was the receipt of a substantial contract from the Admiralty for the supply of the Foden engine for a wide variety of service applications.

The contract had been finally awarded to Fodens following an extensive programme of evaluation and testing over a period of many months and the extent of the Admiralty requirements would necessitate a considerable increase in Fodens' manufacturing, assembly, and testing capabilities. Meanwhile, the demand for the FG range of vehicles for both the home and overseas markets continued to increase, and to meet the specific needs of the Dutch market where Fodens had a particularly active dealer, it was decided to supply the required vehicles in kit form and allow the dealer's staff, under Foden supervision, to assemble the vehicles in Holland.

In May 1951, changes to the management structure of the company were announced whereby Mr. William Foden became Governing Director and his two sons and nephew, Mr Reg Foden, Mr Ted Foden and Mr. Edwin Twemlow, became Joint Managing Directors. One month later, on 1st June, my own department head, Jack Mills, was appointed Chief Designer, and soon afterwards, among other departmental moves, I was appointed Chief Draughtsman. One of the first jobs undertaken following my promotion, was the design of an 8 ton payload, 12 ton gross vehicle weight four-wheeler, designated the FE4/8.

The specification requirements listed by our Sales Department included an eight ton payload and a three man cab, this latter feature to suit brewery delivery requirements. In the early 1950s all draught beer was delivered in heavy wooden barrels with a much higher

capacity than the alloy kegs used at the present time, so that, with no suitable power assisted loading equipment available, a three man crew was essential. The maximum allowable gross vehicle weight for a two-axle four-wheeler goods vehicle at that time was 12 tons, and therefore, to achieve the required payload of 8 tons, the

The marine version of the Foden six-cylinder two-stroke diesel engine opened up a new market for the company.

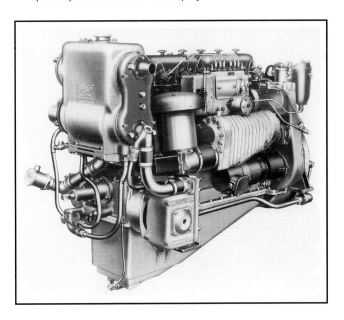

The 8-ton FE4/8, introduced in 1952, was the first Foden vehicle type to use the four-cylinder version of the two-stroke engine which, though of only 2.73-litre capacity, developed 84bhp. Its compact size allowed the cab to be arranged to accommodate a crew of three, particularly useful in certain trades, and the opportunity was taken to produce a completely new cab. This was entirely designed and produced by Foden's own facilities, although its styling was such as to cause some to believe that it had been the product of an 'outside' concern. A demonstrator with flat platform body on the 13ft-whelbase chassis is seen.

maximum unladen weight of the new model was limited to four tons, a factor which precluded the inclusion of standard FG vehicle range components in the specification. The most suitable engine available was undoubtedly the Foden 2.73-litre four-cylinder two-stroke, developing 84bhp at 2000rpm with a torque peak of 235 lbs ft at 1500rpm.

Three alternative Foden gearboxes were offered, with four, five or eight ratios available from 0.78 : 1 overdrive down to 6.18 : 1 bottom gear, the eight speed gearbox incorporating a novel electric gear shift mechanism.

Axles were supplied by Kirkstall, the front, a conventional forged I beam unit rated at 4 tons, the rear a hypoid spiral bevel drive unit rated at 8 tons, both fitted with two leading shoe brakes actuated by the Foden hydraulic boosted braking system.

The four models built were priced to compete effectively in a market somewhat new to Fodens at that time and I recall that each specification was carefully checked for possible cost reductions before finalisation. One example of effective cost reduction was the purchase of all electrical equipment from the same source as the fuel injection equipment, namely CAV, at a special unit kit price per vehicle. The FE4/8 range of vehicles was introduced to the public in September of 1952 at the Earls Court Commercial Vehicle Show and proved to be an effective competitor for several years.

One other major new Foden product introduced at the 1952 Earls Court Show was the twelve-speed epicyclic gearbox, a further development of the successful eight-speed epicyclic gearbox first produced in 1950. The new gearbox extended the range of available ratios from 0.77 : 1 in overdrive top to 20.8 : 1 in underdrive first and, when utilised with suitable rear axle ratios and double reduction rear hubs was capable of dealing with gross vehicle train weights up to 80 tons.

The two principal applications for the new gearbox were the six-wheel eight cubic yard dump truck, powered by a 6LW Gardner or FD6 Foden engine, and the six-wheel 80 ton gross train weight haulage tractor fitted with an 8LW Gardner engine. Examples of both vehicle types were exhibited on the Foden stand and created considerable interest.

This early dump truck design was little more than a converted six-wheeler road vehicle fitted with low pressure tyre equipment, an overseas pattern steel cab and scow end body with cab protection canopy, a flitch frame, and high speed tip gear.

However, as a heavy duty, off-highway tipping vehicle it performed well enough and provided a sound basis for our subsequent development of the Foden dump truck range.

The other application of the new twelve-speed gearbox on the 80 ton haulage tractor served to enhance the specification and

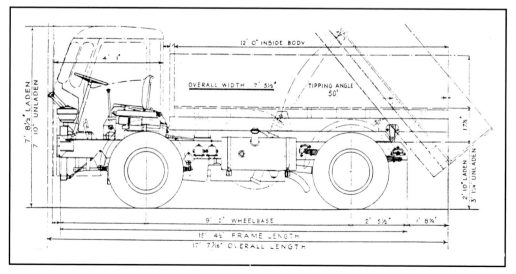

The layout of the FE4/8 is conveyed by this drawing of a tipper on the 9ft 2in wheelbase version of the chassis. There were also two tractor versions, including one for use with Scammell automatic coupling gear.

The cab interior of the FE4/8 model. The compact engine not only allowed ample room for three within the cab but also allowed the driver to enter and leave the cab by the nearside door, a useful feature when used for the delivery of items in areas where traffic was heavy.

coaches were exhibited on bodybuilders' stands or in the demonstration park. A 3,000-mile test of a Foden-engined example of the rear-engined coach, which included many of the more difficult Alpine passes, resulted in a fuel consumption figure of 10.2 miles per gallon. A general increase in demand for the widening range of Foden models and a further increase in pre-tax profits was reported.

Fodens' export business had now expanded and diversified to an extent whereby a temporary import restriction in a particular area had little effect on the overall volume of vehicles delivered. In addition to the Australian, South African and Rhodesian prime market areas developed immediately after the war, there was an increasing demand for Foden vehicles in Holland, Spain, Portugal, Greece, Yugoslavia and many other countries which, at that time, had no heavy vehicle manufacturing facility of their own. Vehicles of this size were normally stowed as deck cargo and required anti-corrosive treatment in vulnerable exposed areas.

Eventually, of course, in principal export areas, where Fodens had a company owned subsidiary, a typical example being South Africa, a complete vehicle assembly facility was established, and the vehicles were exported in component kit form from the factory, thereby reducing transportation costs considerably and finding employment for additional local labour in the customer's own country. In the post war years, during, and even after, the British transport nationalisation period, Fodens received only limited orders from the British Transport Commission or British Road Services so that a viable export market and a degree of specialisation in its range of products was an absolute necessity if it was to retain a major position in the British commercial vehicle industry.

The fact that the company did successfully diversify into the manufacture of diesel engines, passenger vehicles, dump trucks, crane carriers, military vehicles and many other specialised transport vehicles for so long showed, to my mind, a highly commendable attitude on the part of the Company's Directors and of course, made our working life in the Design Department so much more interesting.

The value of this widening of Fodens' manufacturing capacity, particularly in relation to the two stroke engine, became increasingly evident in 1953, some five years after the introduction of the engine in a purely automotive application as an alternative to the Gardner engine. At the Engineering and Marine Exhibition held at Olympia in September of that year, Fodens were able to exhibit a complete

performance of a model already in continual demand for both home and overseas markets, the limiting production factor, as in the past, being the availability of the Gardner engine.

Fodens' increasing representation in the UK passenger vehicle market was illustrated at the 1952 Show by two rear-engined vehicles on the Stand, the Foden powered model in chassis form, and the Gardner engined version, complete with a 41-seater luxury coach body by James Whitson. In addition, five other Foden

The twelve-speed gearbox was a combination of the standard Foden four-speed constant-mesh unit with an epicyclic unit giving overspeed, direct or a low range. The epicyclic unit was controlled by a separate lever but engagement had a preselective effect, the actual change not being made until the clutch pedal was used, either when making a change in the main gearbox or separately.

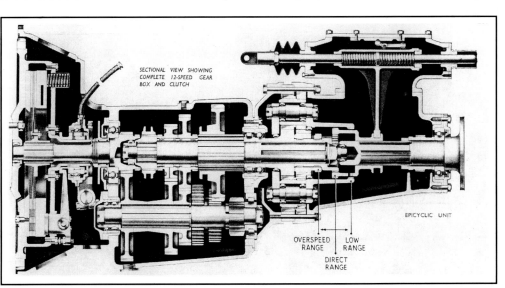

SECTIONAL VIEW SHOWING
COMPLETE 12-SPEED GEAR
BOX AND CLUTCH

EPICYCLIC UNIT

OVERSPEED RANGE | LOW RANGE

DIRECT RANGE

The 8 cubic yard dump truck was one of the two main applications for the twelve-speed gearbox, which was designed for working continuously in low ratio in conditions such as those shown here – the vehicle was a demonstrator.

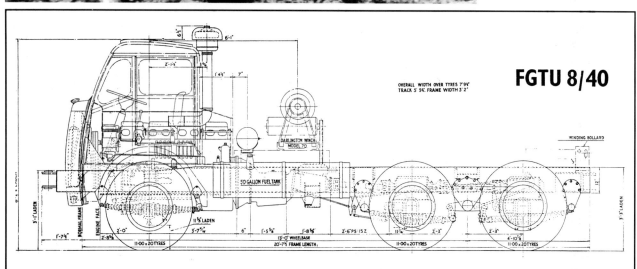

FGTU 8/40

OVERALL WIDTH OVER TYRES 7'9".
TRACK 5' 9". FRAME WIDTH 3' 2"

Above: The heavy-duty tractor, of which the FGTU8/40 version for use with semi-trailers is shown here, was the other main application for the 12-speed gearbox. The alternative FGHT8/40 version designed for haulage of separate trailers weighing up to 80 tons carried ballast weights. Both used the Gardner 8LW in-line straight-eight engine, the length of which required a 1ft 4.5in protrusion behind the cab – at the time, it was the only Gardner unit capable of developing 150bhp.

Left: The typical Foden to be seen on the road continued to be the eight-wheeler, this example having been registered in London in late 1952. A minor modification to the cab introduced by that time was the shaping of the windscreen framing to give a slight vee effect – this example has the driver's windscreen open a little in the way often used to give extra ventilation in warm weather.

range of marine propulsion units based on the four and six-cylinder engines, and a completely new, twelve cylinder, twin crankshaft propulsion unit with a continuous rating of 210bhp at 1800 rpm.

Also exhibited were 35 KW and 60 KW self-contained generator sets, powered by four and six cylinder Foden engines.

Notable applications for the Foden marine products at this time were the twin FD four-cylinder marine propulsion units fitted to the Admiral's Barges for the Royal Yacht Britannia and the FD six-cylinder 60 KW power pack for emergency power requirements on the same vessel.

During this same year, 1953, I recall that our hydraulic brake boost system on the passenger vehicle range was modified to ensure that the system remained fully operative in the event of an engine or boost pump failure. To overcome this problem, we fitted an additional, electrically powered, hydraulic pump which was automatically activated by falling engine oil pressure.

Two other notable events of this particular year, 1953, were the achievement of Fodens' Band in winning the National Brass Band Championship for the tenth time before an audience of 10,000 at Earls Court, and on a much lower level, the achievement of Fodens' Drawing Office cricket team in reaching the final of Fodens' inter-department cricket knock-out competition for the first time.

Although the total Drawing Office staff of draughtsmen, technical clerks, typists, tracers and print room operatives never totalled more than 40 personnel at this time, we had an active sports and social organisation, with cricket and football teams well able to compete with all of the larger works and office departments in the company. Consequently, departmental morale was usually good, but, when it was announced in the 1954 New Year's Honours List that our Departmental Head and Chief Designer, Jack Mills, had been awarded the MBE for 'The important part he has played in the design and development of the Foden Two Stroke Engine in its application for Service needs', our morale was boosted sky-high.

We were all immensely proud of his personal achievement, which he richly deserved, and more than pleased with the reflected credit gained by our department.

This particular year in Fodens' history, which commenced so dramatically with the award to Jack Mills for his part in the design and development of the Foden engine, was followed by a particularly adventurous application of the engine which resulted in a substantial

The FD12 twelve-cylinder twin-crankshaft marine propulsion unit was the equivalent of two of the FD6 units geared together, providing a compact package with a continuous rating of 210bhp at 1,800rpm and was supplied complete with 2;1 reduction and reverse gearbox.

amount of free publicity for the relatively new Foden product and a convincing demonstration of its reliability.

In January 1953 a senior ex-Naval Officer had contacted Fodens' Marine Sales Department with a proposal to attempt a double crossing of the Atlantic with a small power craft, a feat apparently unattained at that time. The plan went ahead, and two Foden six-cylinder marine engines were fitted in 'Aries', a former lifeboat. It was equipped to carry a crew of five, one of whom was David Foden, then 18 years old and on leave from the Army.

She left Dartmouth for the Atlantic and hopefully, New York, at 8.25 am on 26th May. Despite a favourable weather forecast, the North Atlantic was unseasonably rough and the 45 ton 'Aries', only 61ft-long with a beam of 15ft, took some severe punishment, as did her crew. Nevertheless, by 4th June , they had reached the Azores and after refuelling at Ponta Delago, set off for Bermuda which, after problems with seaweed fouling the propellers, they reached on 19th June, before continuing to New York. The return journey began on 16th July.

The weather during the homeward crossing was, in the words of the skipper in a subsequent BBC broadcast, "unspeakably filthy", but on 7th August the Aries finally reached Dartmouth and claimed the record for the first double crossing of the Atlantic by a

'Aries', a converted lifeboat powered by two Foden two-stroke marine engines, is seen in the Thames after the double crossing of the Atlantic made in 1953. A total distance of almost 9,000 miles had been covered and the engines had been running for 1,500 hours, behaving faultlessly throughout.

The PVD6 double-decker with Gardner 6LW engine continued to be built, even though only in small numbers; in 1954 three were supplied to Warrington Corporation and one of these was displayed at the Commercial Motor Show that year. They were unusual in having bodywork built by Crossley, a concern which had been a major builder of bus chassis but whose production had ceased in 1952 though the bodybuilding department continued several years to produce bodies for other makes of chassis. This was the last time a Foden passenger model with engine at the front appeared at Earls Court, and manufacture of the PVD6 ceased with a final batch for Warrington in 1956, these having East Lancashire bodywork.

small power craft. The westward journey from Dartmouth to New York had taken 28 days and during the first 22 days from Dartmouth to Bermuda, the Foden engines were operating continuously. The return journey from New York to Dartmouth was completed in nineteen days and again the Foden engines continued their faultless performance.

This performance had been maintained over a total operational period of 1,500 hours and a total distance of almost 9,000 miles, a remarkable achievement which resulted in a good deal of justifiable praise for the crew and of course, a massive publicity boost for the Foden engine.

Later in the year, our publicity department noted that over 30 British shipyards were now installing Foden marine engines and at the 1954 Earls Court Commercial Vehicle Show in September, three of the six vehicles on the stand were fitted with Foden engines, one, a four-cylinder installation in a completely new model which I had been working on earlier in the year, a four-wheel dumper. A viable market for this particular vehicle had been evident for a considerable time. In fact, our first enquiry and subsequent prototype had been a four-wheeler design, but once the six-wheeler model was introduced, the resultant extensive orders from the Steel Company of Wales, Guest Keen Iron and Steel and other large operators had totally absorbed our production capacity for this type of vehicle at that time. Now, by selectively sub-contracting a proportion of our steel fabrication work we were able to introduce the new model to an expectant market, which we correctly assumed would be much more competitive and cost conscious than the particular section of the extraction industry where our range of higher payload six-wheel Dump Trucks were operating so successfully.

Cost was, therefore, a prime factor in our design study and I well remember that the 6 cubic yard capacity scow end body had a cost price limit of £170. The prototype body, according to my notes at the time, was built for £157.

The new vehicle was offered with the choice of Foden four-cylinder or Gardner 5LW engine, eight-speed epicyclic gearbox, standard Foden front and worm-drive rear axles, fitted with 11.00 x 22 front tyre equipment and 15.00 x 20 single rears. Two completely new features included in the design were the transmission handbrake and the all steel half cab. The transmission brake was fitted on the rear end of the rear-axle worm-drive casing and provided a completely independent brake in a location less liable to mud contamination than the conventional wheel brakes which were initially hydraulically operated and later air pressure operated.

The all-steel half cab provided additional protection for the driver and at the same time improved access to the nearside of the engine for servicing purposes, and the short 8ft 3in wheelbase ensured a high degree of manoeuvrability, an important factor in the smaller quarries, where the new vehicle would be expected to

The four-wheel 6 cubic yard dump truck introduced in 1954 – one of these, with Foden four-cylinder engine, was also exhibited at the Show that year.

The specification of the six-wheel 9 cubic yard dump truck included a bulldozer blade, as seen here, together with other features developed for the four-wheel version. The half cab had come into favour for such work just as it was disappearing from Foden passenger vehicle output and the prominent display of the Foden name in script form on the radiator stoneguard also had echoes of earlier practice. The resulting overall appearance was in keeping with the rugged duties of such vehicles.

operate. Selective double reduction rear hubs, which, when engaged, reduced the road speed and the transmission stresses by half, were offered as an extra feature at this time, but later, as payloads and engine horsepower increased, they became a standard fitment.

The six-wheel 9 cubic yard capacity dumper was now offered with the choice of Foden or Gardner six-cylinder engine, eight-speed epicyclic gearbox, double-drive four-spring rear bogie axles with double reduction hub option and, of course, the all steel half-cab and transmission handbrake.

Fodens could now offer a complete range of four and six-wheeler off-highway dump trucks which would ensure their future profitable involvement in the extraction industry and they were about to enter the new and equally profitable market of the truck-mounted concrete mixer.

It all started when Gibsons Readymix Concrete, of Gosforth, a well established Foden customer, asked if we would investigate the practicality of a power take off drive for their truck mixers as an alternative to the normal separate donkey engine drive, in order to reduce the vehicle unladen weight and increase the maximum payload and resultant earning capacity. The estimated payload advantage was around 6 cwt, not a great increase per delivery, but, when calculated over a period of multiple short haul work, the increase in earning capacity was considerable.

Our initial drive arrangement incorporating a gearbox power take off mounted Twiflex clutch assembly was not successful because the drive was momentarily interrupted at each gear change, but we eventually developed a hydraulic drive arrangement with the power source derived from the Gardner engine crankshaft front end, or alternatively, the Foden camshaft rear end.

As both these power sources were constant, and not affected by gear changes in the transit condition, our major problem was solved and we began to sell our specially modified four, six and eight-wheeler chassis, not only to individual contractors, but also direct to the mixer manufacturers at a rapidly increasing rate. Ransome and Rapier, Stothert & Pitt and Winget were our principal U.K. customers, together with Thompson-Stetter and Ritemixer/Mulder in the wider European market.

About this same period in the mid 1950s Foden's readiness to

The ready-mix concrete business provided another outlet for a Foden heavy-duty six-wheel chassis with half-cab layout, although in this case designed for road use. Here a continuously-running source of power was taken from the front of the Gardner engine crankshaft, driving the Ransome and Rapier 4.5 cubic yard mixer hydraulically.

83

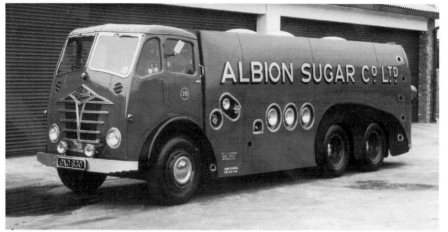

As conveyed in the pictures on this page, Foden built up extensive business in vehicles for specialised bulk transport from the mid-1950s, the willingness to adapt its products to individual needs giving an advantage against larger but less flexible makers. This multi-compartment liquid sugar tanker supplied in 1954 to the Albion Sugar Co Ltd, Albion Wharf, Woolwich, also had the virtue of stylish appearance, the body neatly matching the lines of the standard cab. Its registration number, OXO 630, might have been appropriate to a quite different food product. Unladen weight of such vehicles could be considerable – in this case 9 tons 4cwt 1qr 14lb.

Below left: Reliable means of heating was essential for liquid chocolate, as carried in this tanker supplied to Cadbury of Bourneville, Birmingham, in 1954.

adapt its range of standard vehicles to suit new applications was rewarded by many substantial orders from manufacturers who now required their particular product to be delivered in bulk, rather than bagged or packaged. Typical examples were sugar, flour, cement and of course, the local product, salt. Then there were the more unusual products:– liquid sugar, liquid ethylene and even liquid chocolate.

Each one of these presented varying problems of loading, transporting and discharge, but with the wide range of power take off drives available from the Foden gearbox, we were able to provide the necessary auxiliary power required for almost all applications. When the loaded vehicle was stationary for long periods, however, we found it necessary to provide additional independent power packs on the vehicle, typical examples being the liquid chocolate tankers for Cadbury and Fry where the heating elements were required to be continuously operative until the vehicle was fully discharged.

Almost all of the low density products could be aerated sufficiently for unloading purposes by the introduction of controlled volumes of low pressure air from varying types of power take off driven compressors. One of the exceptions, requiring high pressure containers and heavy duty Ingersol Rand compressors, was the locally produced salt. The eight-wheel vehicle illustrated was supplied to British Soda and was fitted with three cylindrical high pressure containers, each with a conical base and inter-connected discharge manifolds specially designed by Yorkshire Engineering

Above left: The British Soda Co, based in Sandbach, did not have to look far for the chassis of this vehicle delivering salt in bulk.

Left: The ICI logo of Imperial Chemical Industries Ltd had yet to be applied to this eight-wheeler liquid chemical tanker operated from its Wilton works.

A different solution to bulk transport was the fleet of eight special short-wheelbase tractors built for Tate & Lyle and used to haul 45 special trailers, each carrying 6 tons of raw sugar over a 1¼-mile route in Liverpool from the dock where the ships carrying it arrived to the refinery, where this one is seen. Adequate adhesion over stone setts liable to be slippery in wet weather was apt to be a problem, as was the need for a tight turning circle. Smart dark blue Tate & Lyle Foden vehicles have long been a familiar sight in both Liverpool and London.

and Welding Company.

Fodens' long standing working relationship with the salt and chemical manufacturers in the Cheshire area was a favourable factor when the inevitable problems relating to the bulk transportation of chemical products came to be discussed and with the three individual headquarters of ICI Alkali, General Chemical and Salt Divisions located at Northwich, Runcorn and Winsford respectively, it was to be expected that we would be favoured with at least a proportion of their road vehicle requirements. From the mid-'fifties through the following decade, there were very few monthly production schedules issued at Fodens without a vehicle for one or the other of our three major bulk haulage customers; ICI, Tate & Lyle, and Associated Portland Cement Manufacturers.

Most of the bulk material haulage problems submitted to Fodens at this time were solved by minor modifications to a standard model, but occasionally, a special vehicle was necessary. This proved to be the only solution when Tate & Lyle submitted a requirement for a highly manoeuvrable short wheelbase vehicle to haul a fleet of 45 specially built independent raw sugar trailers from Liverpool's Huskisson Dock to the Tate & Lyle Refinery, a distance

of 1¼ miles, mostly on dockside roads paved with granite 'sets'.

The fleet of eight specially built, short wheelbase Gardner engined tractors were fitted with a ballast body and special water ballasted Goodyear tyre equipment to ensure maximum road adhesion and by modifying the steering linkage, the minimum turning circle was reduced to 31ft, thereby ensuring a high degree of manoeuvrability.

During this same period, at Arnhem in Holland, Foden vehicles of a completely different type were demonstrating their manoeuvrability and other attributes to the Dutch Ministry of Transport and associated Road Transport officials at a specially arranged competition and demonstration, terminating in the main market square of Arnhem.

The giant eight-wheeler Foden vehicles with Gardner 8LW engines and twelve-speed epicyclic gearboxes were hauling six-wheeler independent trailers which, when fully laden, resulted in a total vehicle payload capacity of 35 tons. Their successful demonstration in Arnhem helped to stimulate Foden sales in Holland, fast becoming the company's principal continental customer base.

On 1st January 1955 the revised 'Construction and Use

In Holland, regulations permitted the use of eight-wheelers towing six-wheel trailers and special vehicles with the eight-cylinder Gardner 8LW engine were used by H. Hawkes & Zonen to carry a total payload of 35 tons. Three are seen at a special demonstration in Arnhem, a town which, a decade earlier, had witnessed the valiant but vain attempt by British parachute troops to secure a key bridgehead in the advance towards Germany. The broad traditional-style radiator of these vehicles was specified to meet Gardner's cooling specification for the 8LW.

Regulations', which had been under discussion for some time within the governing bodies of the Transport Industry in the UK, came into force, and had an immediate effect on the specification and earning capacity of almost the whole of our standard home market vehicle range.

Fortunately, as Fodens normally had representation on one or the other of the relevant Technical Committees at the Society of Motor Manufacturers and Traders, we had prior notice of impending changes and could prepare accordingly. The changes related to increased gross vehicle weights, individual axle weights and maximum overall vehicle width. Fodens decided to take this opportunity to revise the whole range of FG vehicle type designations to denote the gross vehicle weight rather than the payload capacity. Thus the four-wheeler FG 4/7½ became the FG 4/14, the 6 wheeler FG 6/12 became the FG 6/20 and the eight-wheeler FG 6/15 became the FG 6/24.

The change in the allowable gross vehicle weight of the four-wheeler made the FE 4/8 range of 12-ton four-wheelers virtually obsolete and unsaleable, but the 14-ton four-wheeler which now replaced it had a very practical specification. Maximum overall width had now been increased to 8ft 0in and the maximum single axle weight limit increased from 8 to 9 tons, so that the new four-wheeler specification would include a 5 ton front axle, 9 ton 8ft 0in wide rear axle with 10.00 x 20 tyres all round. Some of the six and eight-wheeler vehicles in service at this time could operate at the new gross vehicle weights with recommended changes confined to road springs and tyre equipment, so that, for Fodens and its customers the ability to carry increased payloads and achieve higher profit margins was gained without excessive modification costs.

One other significant development during this period was the initial application of the Foden engine in a range of locomotives manufactured by H. C. Hibberd of Park Royal.

These were fitted with the Foden six-cylinder two stroke engine direct coupled to a Vulcan Sinclair 'Fluidrive' fluid coupling. Other industrial applications of the Foden engine now included air compressors, power mules, cranes, pumping units and self-contained generator sets.

One of the most notable new product features of 1955 from my own viewpoint however, was the design and subsequent development of our first airfield refuellers, built for British Petroleum for worldwide application. The prototype vehicles were heavy duty rigid six-wheelers with Gardner 6LW engines, five-speed gearbox

The first Foden aircraft refueller appeared in 1955, being developed for use by British Petroleum, which designated it the Cornwall type. It was based on an FG6/20 18ft-wheelbase chassis with tanker bodywork by Thompson Bros of Bilston, Staffs.

with superlow forward and reverse gears, 12-in channel section frames, uprated axles, Michelin D20 metallic tyres and an 80hp gearbox mounted power take off driving a 500gpm Pegson pump.

The solo vehicle payload was 3,400 gallons of aviation spirit which could be increased to 5,900 gallons when operating with a trailer tank.

The new unit was designated the Cornwall type refueller by BP and marked the introduction of a complete new range of vehicles by Fodens to meet the specific requirements of the Petroleum Industry for aircraft refuelling.

As aircraft increased in size and operational radius over the following years, we were destined to design a similarly increasing range of refuellers to meet their requirements, culminating in the refuelling of the first supersonic aircraft, the Concorde.

Our crane carrier development programme had, at this time, developed to a stage where we could now offer a special 'split' cab to more readily accommodate the lower section of the crane jib in the travelling condition, and one of the first customers to benefit from this improved feature were our original crane carrier customers, Smiths of Rodley.

Throughout the years of our crane carrier development, Smiths could normally be relied upon to co-operate with Fodens on any new design feature and this close association eventually resulted in a complete change in crane carrier design.

The year 1955 had proved to be a most interesting and progressive period of my time at Fodens and my good fortune that year extended to the cricket field where, more by good fortune than any particular ability, I was awarded the first 'Sportsman of the Year' trophy.

The following year, 1956, was celebrated as Fodens' Centenary Year. The celebrations were, to be strictly accurate, somewhat premature, because 1956 merely marked the 100th anniversary of Edwin Foden starting work as an apprentice at Plant and Hancock's foundry in Elworth in the year 1856. It was ten years later, in 1866 that the Foden name was added to the company title to become Foden and Hancock and 46 years later in 1902 before the company Fodens Limited was established.

An echo of the Foden shunting engines of the 1920s came with the application of Foden engines in a range of industrial locomotives made by H. C. Hibberd. This was an 18-ton model for the standard 4ft 8½in gauge but examples were also built for narrow-gauge lines.

The 'split' cab enabled the jib of a mobile crane to be carried at a lower level than hitherto, opening up fresh avenues of design development. This was the prototype developed jointly with Smiths of Rodley in 1955. It had a Gardner 5LW engine, a joist-type frame and could lift 15 tons at a 10ft radius.

However, the idea of a celebration was popular with all concerned. Fodens' net profit after tax for the previous year, 1955, had totalled a record £188,000, so it was accordingly decided to arrange a Centenary Celebration in July of that year.

My particular responsibility on the Centenary Committee, which was formed at that time, was to organise a 'Cavalcade of Transport' which eventually included over 100 vehicles covering the total period of the Company's existence. It included horse-drawn vehicles, steam traction engines, tractors and steam road vehicles, veteran cars and motor cycles, customers' decorated vehicles, departmental tableaus and even penny farthing bicycles. I still have a copy of the Centenary Programme which lists all the vehicles taking part and provides details of all the other events of the day, which included a comprehensive sports programme and continuous outdoor entertainment during the afternoon on the sports field, dancing and cabaret provided by Syd Phillips and his Band in the evening and a firework display to end the day. The date was Saturday, 7th July 1956 and the illustrations that follow show

a few examples of the 100 vehicles and almost 300 personnel who participated in the Cavalcade of Transport.

Twenty individual Departments entered lorry mounted tableaux in the Centenary Cavalcade. Drawing Office were eventually declared to be the winners, but sadly, our prediction of a Foden Drawing Office in the year 1984, as displayed on the vehicle, was not be attained. Centenary Year 1956 also marked the introduction of several important new vehicle features, the most easily identified being a new cab for the FG and FE range of standard road vehicles to replace the now somewhat dated S18 cab.

The new cab, which retained the basic construction materials of ash framework and aluminium panels used on previous cabs, was designed with a similar double curvature outer shape as the FE 4/8 cab, but was subjected to a 1,000 mile road test on the Motor Industry Research Association pavé test track before design finalisation and production.

The new cab, pictured opposite on a Derbyshire Stone eight-wheel bulk tanker, was undoubtedly one of the best ever produced

The parade held on 7th July 1956 was headed by members of the 'beard club', all with beards specially grown for the day, and carrying the Foden centenary banner. They were followed by the Fodens Motor Works Band.

Representing the Company's original self-propelled product, this Foden steam traction engine, number 1174, dated from 1903 although its design was much as built from the 1880s. In 1956, it is possible that the driver, clearly elderly, would have had experience of such engines when in normal commercial use.

The Foden steam wagon was represented at the 1956 Centenary celebrations by a 1916 5-ton model, originally a tipper supplied to the Portsmouth gas undertaking.

This imaginative float, based on a dumper chassis but with features evidently inspired by Foden's steam era, was designed and built by the Company's student apprentices.

by Fodens and was destined to be the last of the wood frame/aluminium panel designs. On the lighter range of Gardner 4LK engined vehicles, now redesignated the OG 4/9 type, a new all alloy cab, designed and built by the local bodybuilder Bowyer Brothers of Congleton was introduced at the same time.

In addition to the introduction of the new cabs, two other basic elements of the vehicle specification were the subject of radical changes at this time. The Foden hydraulic brake system, introduced on the bus chassis and subsequently incorporated on the complete range of FG and FE vehicles, had been the subject of service complaints, particularly on vehicles operating under adverse road conditions, and overseas. It was accordingly decided to introduce the more robust and easily serviced air pressure brake system, incorporating an engine driven compressor, high pressure storage tanks, a progressively operated pedal valve and diaphragm type brake actuators. The basic components for this system were available from Clayton Dewandre in the UK and from Bendix Westinghouse on a worldwide basis. We had, for some time, been fitting air

pressure trailer brake equipment to our range of vehicles from the same suppliers and the change in specification was implemented with very few problems in production or service.

One other feature introduced at this time, again mainly to meet dump truck and overseas operators' requirements, was power assisted steering. Our initial arrangement involved the fitment of a frame mounted hydraulic powered ram operating on the steering linkage, a system fitted successfully by many of our competitors, but it was destined to be superseded by a much improved integral system of our own design in due course.

At the Earls Court Commercial Vehicle Exhibition held later in the year, the new S20 cab and the other new mechanical features were incorporated in the various Show vehicles which significantly included a four-wheel and six-wheel dump truck. Fodens' dump truck business had expanded rapidly from the original quarry requirement, to steel works, mines, road construction and so many other civil engineering applications that we now had a total of 29 alternative bodies available for varying payloads on the four-and

The lightweight model with Gardner 4LK engine remained in production, now designated OG4/9, and an all-aluminium alloy cab made by Bowyer was introduced. The vehicle shown, dating from 1955, was an early example.

A new styling era for Foden's main range of FG and FE models began in 1956 when the S20 cab replaced the S18 type. It was to remain characteristic of the firm's products for some time and indeed this eight-wheeler for Derbyshire Stone Sales Ltd dated from the early 1960s. A change in the chassis specification introduced at about the same time was the standardisation on air-pressure brake systems in place of the previous hydraulic operation.

six-wheel vehicles.

The six-wheeler 15 ton dumper, with alternative Foden or Gardner six-cylinder engines and an eight-speed epicyclic gearbox with double drive four-spring rear bogie, was now based on a 14in x 6in joist section main frame.

1957 was the year of the Suez crisis and, as a result of the anticipated fuel supply problems we were expecting a serious fall in demand for home market vehicles. Fortunately, Fodens' diversification into the manufacture of engines for a wide variety of non-automotive applications, together with our continued involvement in the contractors' plant, bulk material handling, airfield refuelling and other industries, often observed and quoted by some of our competitors as a possible dilution of our abilities; at times like this, were a priceless asset. We received repeat orders from British Petroleum for updated versions of the original Cornwall type six-wheel refueller at this time. These later models could be identified on airfields around the world by the S20 type cab and were destined to have a service life of over twenty years.

During this same period, after several meetings with Esso Aviation Products representatives we received our first order for a number of special four-wheel tractor units with heavy duty gearbox, mounted power take off and special extended cabs for operation with 6,000 gallon capacity aviation fuel semi-trailers manufactured by Steel Barrel Tank Trailers of Uxbridge. This order for the new refuellers, code-named Pluto by Esso, marked the commencement of a long and profitable relationship with the company, during which time we built a series of airfield refuellers of increasing capacity, culminating in the 12,000 gallon Python in 1959, at that time, the largest articulated refueller in the world.

The continuous requirement for increased refuelling capacity during this particular period was generated by the introduction of larger jet engined aircraft in place of piston-engined and turbo prop machines and also an increasing cost-effective need to reduce the turn round time at the air terminal.

Comprehensive sales literature had always been available for each individual type of vehicle made at Fodens, from the steam era onwards, outlining the basic performance and maximum load capacity, but in 1957 our first 24-page data book on home market goods and dump truck models was introduced.

In April of 1957, as a result of increasing vehicle sales in Holland, Fodens decided to exhibit a range of dump trucks and left hand drive road vehicles at the RAI Commercial Vehicle Exhibition

Aircraft refuellers were an increasingly important market. In addition to further six-wheel models for BP, an articulated design was produced for Esso in conjunction with Steel Barrel who built the 6,000-gallon tank semi-trailers. The cab was extended upwards, partly to match neatly with the trailers but also allowing the driver extended upward vision to enable him to negotiate the vehicle safely into position without risk of damage to the wings of parked airliners.

The special heavy-duty Gardner 8LW-engined eight-wheeler had become a standard type for the Dutch market, some operators running fleets of twenty or more, building up very large mileages hauling six-wheel trailers at gross train weights of up to 50 tons. This one was operated by Kluitkalk of Den Haag.

in Amsterdam. This bi-annual Show was to prove one of the most effective means of publicising our range of products in Europe and also presented the opportunity to gather technical information relating to our European competitors and operational data from our European customers.

The most popular and most profitable Foden vehicle operating in Holland continued to be the special heavy duty eight-wheeler, fitted with the Gardner 8LW engine, twelve-speed Foden epicyclic gearbox, double drive rear bogie and dumper type axles. Operating with a three axle independent trailer, this vehicle combination was now capable of hauling gross train weights of 40 to 50 tons with a resultant high earning capacity. A number of our customers in Holland now had fleets of twenty or more of this vehicle type, many with astronomical mileages recorded.

Meanwhile, on the home market, Fodens' dump truck sales received a further boost with the introduction of special six-wheeler side dump models for a number of large quarry owners in Derbyshire and North Wales.

The particular application of this vehicle which I can recall most vividly was the Penmaenmawr and Welsh Granite Company's

requirement for a fleet of high capacity side dump trucks to operate at the quarry at the top of Penmaenmawr mountain where their huge primary crusher was located.

The method of travel to the top was by narrow gauge, cable operated rail truck and this was the way the dumper components were transported for final assembly at the top by a team of our Service Department fitters. The lower section of the narrow gauge rail system was destined later to be replaced by a fleet of four-wheel Foden dump trucks, raising the total Foden fleet of vehicles on this one site to a level which ensured a profitable after-sales service and spares level. It later became the practice, on home and overseas work sites where the concentration of Foden vehicles was of a sufficiently high level, to allocate Foden Service personnel on a secondment basis, together with stocks of fast moving spares on a consignment basis. It was a procedure which worked well in the UK, but as I was to discover later, when I became Service Manager, it could result in significant financial losses in certain undeveloped overseas areas.

In the European sales market at this time, the Foden dump truck range was being exhibited at Trade Fairs in Oslo and Milan, the

Italy has always been a particularly difficult country into which to export commercial vehicles, even of special types, in view of its own large heavy-vehicle industry, so the receipt of an order for four six-wheel dumpers for the Cornigliano Steel Works obtained after this vehicle was sent to a trade fair at Milan was a remarkable achievement.

Italian venture resulting in a demonstration and order for four 6 wheeler dumpers for the Cornigliano Steel Works.

One other significant event of the 1957 period which was destined to have a marked effect on our future methods of cab construction, involved a visit arranged for Frank Nicholls, my first foreman in the Assembly Shop in 1937, together with Bill Burrows, one of our former Crusader tank conversion team, both now promoted to senior Works Management status, and myself, to an ICI plant near Wolverhampton, where a range of components was being manufactured in fibreglass. The aim was to evaluate the material for possible use in making such components as mudguards and cab panels.

We saw various parts from bonnets for the Singer Hunter car to Beardmore taxi headlamp nacelles being made by the 'cold lay-up' process using multiple layers of fibreglass sheet and resin. We were all impressed, though having reservations on the time-consuming methods, reporting accordingly on our return. Even so, this visit was to lead to a fibreglass application programme and eventually our first fibreglass cab.

The year 1957 ended with a successful Scottish Motor Traders Show at the Kelvin Hall, Glasgow in December, which generated several substantial vehicle orders North of the Border and about this time our Engine Sales Department received their first order from the "Japanese Maritime Defence Force" for a number of Foden Generating Sets. Another milestone around this period was the completion of a new office block to accommodate most of the Company's administrative and sales staff.

1958 was destined to mark yet another interesting and progressive year in the Drawing Office and also a profitable year for the Company. One of my first assignments involved a visit to the American Harnischfeger Corporation's crane factories in Dortmund and Dusseldorf with our South African Company Director, Harold Hymans.

Apparently, one of our South African customers had requested the specific combination of a 20 ton capacity P & H 255 ATC crane on a Foden eight-wheel crane carrier and my job was to ensure their complete compatibility when the crane was fitted to the carrier in South Africa.

Our meetings in Germany and subsequent co-operation with the Harnischfeger engineers went extremely well, and the successful

The compatibility of an American crane and a Foden FC20 crane carrier to operate in South Africa was confirmed by meetings at the crane maker's German factories in 1958. Here the resulting vehicle is seen in use. By that date, a wider range of proprietary engines was becoming necessary and the model was offered with a choice of Foden, Gardner, Rolls-Royce or Cummins engines. The success of this operation led to contact with other German crane makers and substantial orders for similar crane carriers.

conclusion to our joint effort, we learned later, had been noted with considerable interest by other German crane manufacturers who were destined later to provide Fodens with substantial orders for similar crane carriers to operate in Europe.

On the earthmoving side of the business, we had received information to the effect that the National Coal Board would welcome the advent of a high capacity British dump truck to replace the American vehicles operating at that time in the more extensive NCB open cast coal extraction sites. The various divisions of the National Coal Board already had fleets of Foden four and six-wheel dump trucks employed on their sites mainly for pit waste disposal and it was accordingly decided to proceed with the design of this highly specialised vehicle for a very good customer, without the assurance of a confirmed order.

The new dump truck specification included a Rolls Royce 300hp turbocharged engine, a specially designed new Foden three-speed gearbox with ratios from .75 to 1 down to 2.03 to 1 with automatic three-stage torque convertor ratios from 1 to 1 down to 5.3 to 1, Kirkstall 15 ton rated front axle and 30 ton rated rear axle with overall spiral bevel and hub reduction ratio of 18.4 to 1. Maximum payload was 28 tons and the maximum body capacity 18 cubic yards. Tyres were 18.00 x 25.00, 28-ply rock lug in single formation on the front axle and twin formation on the single rear axle. The main chassis frame was constructed from 18in x 6in steel joist section and the rear axle casing was bolted directly to the main frame using Belleville washers to allow only limited movement between frame and axle. The front suspension incorporated two semi-elliptic springs mounted transversely by trunnion brackets on each side of the front axle beam in a similar manner to the Model T Ford front suspension. The vehicle was fitted with a special single ram high speed tip gear and attained a body tipping angle of 85 degrees. On test, the vehicle performed well with its maximum designed payload under varying site conditions, but unfortunately the anticipated orders from the National Coal Board did not materialise.

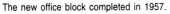

The new office block completed in 1957.

Large-scale design investment was put into the Foden FR6/45 dump truck, of which the prototype seen here was built in response to a National Coal Board need, though no specific order had been placed and in the event, despite successful operation, was not forthcoming. Although some other dump truck users did place orders for the type, the outlay was not capable of being recovered from the sales achieved.

Fortunately for Fodens, Earls Cement, Richard Thomas and Baldwin and other traditional customers which had utilised our range of high capacity dump trucks for some years, were impressed with the capabilities of the new Foden product and eventually purchased a number of vehicles, but in this particular case, the considerable design and development costs could not possibly be justified by the resultant limited sales.

Usually, when a new Foden vehicle type was introduced, there would be a number of existing components, or even complete units, from current models which could be successfully incorporated or adapted for the new product, but in the case of the FR 6/45 dump truck, this, unfortunately, was not the case. From radiator to rear end it was completely new and none of the units and components embodied in its manufacture could be used on other vehicles.

Fortunately, the production of Fodens' standard range of goods vehicles maintained an acceptable level and the demand for customer

Fortunately, sales of standard models were buoyant, particularly for the bulk transport of specialised products, in which several Foden design staff were engaged on a permanent basis. This FG6/24 for the ICI Alkali Division, Northwich, was an end tipper to carry granulated polythene.

engineering to suit the transportation of manufacturer's special products increased to a degree which resulted in a number of our staff in the Drawing Office being permanently allocated to this type of work. The examples illustrated were all designed and built during the relatively short production life span of the S20 type cab in the late 1950s and early 1960s.

There were many other products carried in these specially designed container vehicles at this time, each presenting varying problems of loading, storing and discharge which had to be discussed in detail with the respective manufacturers and customers before the eventual equipment design was finalised. We developed a close working relationship with the various tank and container manufacturers such as Carmichael, Butterfield, Metalair and Whessoe, and our task was made easier by the availability of a wide range of power take off points on the Foden gearbox.

It was perhaps appropriate, in view of our intense involvement with this type of vehicle at this particular time, that one of the largest exhibits on Fodens' stand at the 1958 Earls Court Commercial Vehicle Show was an 8-wheeler bulk cement tanker for Blue Circle Products.

The most interesting eight-wheeler on the stand, however, was a new lightweight 'K' type model with a dry chassis and cab weight of only 5ton 12 cwt, but which, with an aluminium body, would accommodate a payload of at least 17¾ tons without exceeding the legal allowable gross vehicle weight of 24 tons.

The 'K' type 8-wheeler specification included a new Mark III version of the Foden six-cylinder two-stroke engine developing 150 gross bhp at 2,400rpm, a four-speed Foden gearbox with ratios from direct 1 to 1 down to 6.18 to 1 and a single drive four-spring rear bogie axle assembly with a final worm drive ratio of 7.5 to 1.

Other weight saving measures included 4 ton front axles, a 'Neate' type handbrake in lieu of the transmission handbrake and Michelin 'X' type 9in x 20in tyres all round. The standard cab included in the 'K' type specification was the S.20 standard ash frame, aluminium panel type, but the unladen weight could be

This view of the Foden stand at the 1958 Earls Court Show conveys how important a part bulk transport was playing in Foden's business. In addition, the sheer height of the two different types of tipping body supplied to two cement concerns helped to draw attention to the stand – under the arrangements for the Show made by the SMMT the name banners for each exhibitor had to be of uniform size and style, so tall exhibits were useful in this way. The placing of three eight-wheelers with S.20 cabs, all facing the same way, emphasised the level of Foden's output of this type, whilst the rugged appearance of the two tractors on the corners was used to good effect. The Show was always an opportunity to examine competitors' products – here our neighbours included Atkinson and Scammell; the stands of trailer makers Taskers and Dyson are also visible in the background.

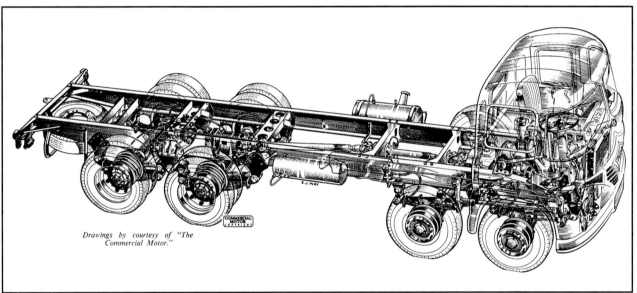

Drawings by courtesy of "The Commercial Motor."

The lightweight K-type eight-wheel model introduced at the 1958 Show (visible in the background of the view at the top of the page) was the subject of this drawing. The weight-saving features shown included the Foden two-stoke engine in its latest FD6 Mark III form, a four-speed gearbox, single-drive rear bogie and the new S.21 fibreglass cab, though the Show vehicle had the S.20 type. On the other hand, eight-wheel brakes were standard – it had been common practice to omit brakes from the second axle of eight-wheelers. With a lightweight body, up to 17.75 tons could be carried within the 24-ton gross limit.

reduced by a further 1½ cwt by the fitment of a completely new fibreglass cab designated the S.21 type.

The back, roof and front panels of the new cab were produced as a single moulding, reinforced with a timber frame encapsulated in the layers of fibreglass and resin. The cab floor, engine cover and internal bulkheads were incorporated in a second large reinforced moulding and the detachable front panel, door assemblies, bumper bar etc were produced independently in the same manner. The resultant assembly was light, strong, non corrosive, not difficult to repair and it looked good. The reinforced fibreglass cab as far as Fodens were concerned, was here to stay. There were four other vehicle types from the Foden standard range exhibited on our own stand at the Show with eight additional exhibits on body and container manufacturers' stands and a joint Foden/Dyson tractor

unit and articulated trailer exhibit in the Demonstration Park. The Foden tractor unit was fitted with the new Mark III two stroke engine and fibreglass cab and was also equipped with air suspension and disc brakes to match up with the similarly equipped Dyson 15/16 ton semi trailer. The technical press was favourably impressed and offered the following comment:-

'With the continuing trend towards the use of articulated vehicles for trunk haulage, the Foden tractor and Dyson semi trailer probably represent, by virtue of their advanced specifications, the long distance vehicle of five years hence. The Foden/Dyson outfit is the most advanced goods vehicle on show'.

As was his usual practice, Mr William Foden, the Company's Governing Director, attended the Show each day and took an active

The fibreglass S.21 cab had a more rounded appearance than the S.20, the windscreen glass sweeping back as far as the door pillars, eliminating the corner pillar, admittedly slim, of the previous type. This example on a K-type eight-wheeler with platform body was supplied to Concrete (Midlands) Ltd, of Lichfield, makers of Bison floor beams.

role in welcoming customers and discussing their problems and requirements. His personal comments in the pre-Show edition of the *Foden News*, are well worth noting:-

'Once again I take this opportunity to welcome old friends and new customers to the Foden Stand at the Commercial Motor Show. This year, we are presenting a range of exhibits which will, I feel sure, meet the anticipations of those who are motivated to look at Fodens by the expectation of new developments. I shall be ninety three days before the Show opens and, as I look reflectively back over the years, I don't think that Fodens have often failed to come up with something new annually. We have contributed our share to Commercial Vehicle development. I say that not boastfully, but as a man who, on looking back, may be permitted the assumption that

his life has been lived usefully if the premise be permitted that all successful engineering increases economic welfare. Progress in engineering is a three phase advance. You demonstrate feasibility, develop reliability, and then do you best to meet customers on price. That, at any rate, is how we work at Elworth. When Sales are established you back them with Service, not solely for profit, but as engineers who never lose interest in their machines, nor in the men who operate them. That is why we hope to see old and new customers at our Stand. We are glad to hear the former expressing their seasoned views on past developments and to have the opinion of all potential customers on what we are offering in relation to present requirements'.

The first significant event of 1959 was the National Boat Show, held at Olympia in January. Fodens exhibited the Marine version of the Mark III engine in four, six and twelve-cylinder configuration with alternative Self Changing Gear Company and Thornycroft gearboxes and immediately created a great deal of interest.

Mr William Foden, Governing Director, who attended the 1958 Show each day, just after his 90th birthday.

The Mark III version of the Foden FD6 two-stroke six-cylinder engine developed up to 150bhp, a remarkable figure for a 4.1litre diesel engine. Its appearance had altered only slightly, though there were now individual covers over the rockers operating the exhaust valves for each cylinder. This example also had various auxiliaries not seen on early units, these varying according to the application.

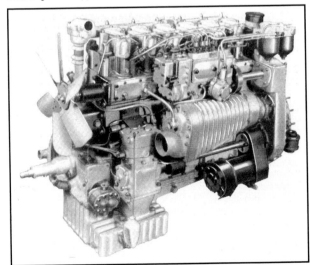

Dump truck design continued to advance and higher-rated axles led to the appearance of this FED6/30 version capable of operating at 30 tons gross and having a 40,000-lb payload – in terms of capacity, the body was rated at 11 cubic yards. It had the Foden Mark III engine, twelve-speed double-underdrive gearbox.

In response to requests from our dump truck and contractors plant customers for increased payload for off-road applications, we had, at this time, introduced heavier front and rear axle assemblies rated at 6 tons and 12 tons respectively, the 12 ton rear axle incorporating double reduction hubs, so that it was now possible, with a three axle vehicle, to operate at gross vehicle weights of 30 tons, and with a two axle vehicle at 18 tons. Almost at the same time we had a new Foden twelve-speed double underdrive, epicyclic gearbox available.

The introduction of the higher rated axles and the availability of a wider choice of more powerful engines also expanded the choice of specification for Fodens' range of heavy duty four and six-wheel tractors and tractor units for independent and articulated trailers. The six-wheelers with independent multi axle trailers could handle gross loads of 100 tons, when the need arose. The Gardner 8LW engine was often favoured for such duty until the introduction of the long-awaited Gardner 6LX, with the same external dimensions as the 6LW, but with bore size increased to 4.75in, giving a 10.45-litre capacity and output of up to 150bhp at 1700rpm. It was announced in 1958 but such was the demand that no appreciable quantities were received by Fodens until 1959.

There were alternative engines available in this power category, however, and from 1959 onwards, Fodens offered the Rolls Royce 210bhp and the Cummins 180 and 212bhp six-cylinder engines in addition to the Foden and Gardner units in the tractor unit sales

literature. In many overseas sales areas, the Cummins range of engines, with well established service facilities, was the favoured power unit and, as a high proportion of Fodens heavy duty tractor and dump truck sales were destined for these areas, Cummins engines became prominent in our overseas vehicle specifications.

Many of the tractor orders received included a requirement for winch gear to facilitate loading and to meet these requirements, we provided a range of Darlington winches driven by a gearbox mounted multi speed power take off, controlled from the cab.

Fodens' range of independent ballasted tractors in the late 1950s and early 1960s was not confined solely to multi-axled monsters. There were many requirements for four-wheel tractors to haul relatively modest loads in confined areas, this British Railways tractor being a typical example.

This KGHT5/15 tractor with Gardner 5LW engine, five-speed gearbox and S.21 fibreglass cab was supplied to British Railways Western Region, a regular user of Foden four-wheel tractors, though usually with longer wheelbase to allow incorporation of a Foden worm-drive winch as used on the timber tractor.

British Railways Western Region frequently placed orders for Foden four-wheel tractors, usually with a longer wheelbase to accommodate the fitment of the Foden worm drive winch gear, as used on the Foden timber tractor.

Undoubtedly, the most impressive tractor unit produced by Fodens in 1959 was the specially designed six-wheeler unit, forming the motive section of the Esso 'Python' aircraft refueller, claimed at that time to be the largest in the world. Some 55ft long, 13ft high, 8ft wide, with an unladen weight of 25 tons and a laden weight with 12,000 imperial gallons of jet fuel, totalling 70 tons, it was most certainly an impressive vehicle with an equally impressive fuel

The heavier-duty axles allowed the development of heavier-duty tractor units. Such vehicles could handle gross loads of up to 100 tons, and considerably more when used in pairs. This one dating from 1958 operated by A. E. Farr Ltd was doubtless making light work of the multi-wheel articulated trailer with dolly and its load. It had the wide radiator used with the Gardner 8LW engine, and an extended crew cab, though with the 8LW the centre part of the rear section would have been occupied by the rear cylinders of that unusually long engine, about to be superseded by the much more compact 6LX with similar 150bhp output.

Claimed to be the largest aircraft refueller in the world at the time, the Python had been developed for Esso from the earlier Pluto design. Two of them could refuel a Boeing 707, at the time the most widely used large jet airliner, in under 10 minutes. The Foden tractor unit had a Rolls-Royce engine and the 12,000-gallon capacity tanker semi-trailer was by Steel Barrel, carried on Carrimore running gear attached directly to the tank. In service, they performed well in excess of their specified requirements and through continuing contact with Esso engineers benefits for subsequent more standard Foden models ensued.

dispensing capability of 1,000 gallons per minute. Two Python refuellers could refuel a Boeing 707 with a fuel tank capacity of 19,000 Imperial gallons in less than ten minutes.

The six-wheel Foden tractor unit specification included a Rolls Royce 210 HP six-cylinder engine, twelve-speed Foden double underdrive gearbox with full torque power take off and heavy duty dumper type axles with double reduction rear hubs. The power take off was directly coupled to a hydraulic generator which, in turn powered two Pegson fuel pumps, all mounted on the tractor unit so that in addition to the primary capability of aircraft refuelling, the tractor could operate as a mobile fuel pipeline boosting unit in the event of the future installation of a fuel pipeline and hydrant installation around the airfield.

The 12,000 gallon capacity tank semi-trailer was designed and built by the Steel Barrel Company of Uxbridge and incorporated Carrimore Trailer running gear, but had no trailer subframe, the tank structure in itself having sufficient strength to meet the low speed transit requirements involved in the refuelling operation.

By the year 1959, another of our specialist vehicle designs, the crane carrier chassis, which had originated as an off-standard single order, had developed to an extent whereby we had a continual demand for carriers in three distinct weight categories for various types of cranes and, on occasion, excavators and draglines. The three crane chassis types were classified in relation to their respective main frame hoist sections, FC 14, FC 16 and FC 20.

All types incorporated the standard Foden crane chassis features of a solid beam, spheralastik rubber bushed rear bogie suspension system, lockable front axle suspension, cross braced frame and 'trough' type cab, but there was a choice of four alternative power units, the Foden four-cylinder 100bhp and six-cylinder 150bhp engines and the Gardner five-cylinder 95bhp and six-cylinder 112bhp engines. Gearbox alternatives at this time were confined to

The crane carrier chassis, originally a one-off special product, had become a production range of models from 1959, offered in three versions, FC14, FC16 and FC20, according to the loading required and with a choice of Foden FD4 or FD6 or Gardner 5LW or 6LW engines. Here a chassis is shown in the form supplied to the crane or excavator makers, together with a complete crane on an FC14 chassis in use.

The drilling of foundation shafts for tall buildings created a demand for earth-boring drill rigs of the type already in use in the United States, and Foden was asked by the contractors John Laing and Son if it could provide a suitable chassis for a drill rig supplied by Hugh B. Williams of Dallas. The completed unit with 78ft jib was delivered to the site shown, at the junction of Gower Street and Euston Road, where it was used to produce the foundation shafts for a 16-storey office block, then one of the tallest in London.

the five-speed unit with ratios from direct top to 13.4 to 1 bottom, or the eight-speed epicyclic gearbox with ratios down to 20.8 to 1 in underdrive bottom gear. Maximum road speeds were 27mph with the Gardner engines and 38mph with the Foden engines. For dragline and excavator applications and also for crane work where laden mobility was required, selective double reduction rear hubs were considered to be an essential fitment.

In the Drawing Office we now had draughtsmen permanently allocated to the design and adaptation of our crane chassis range to suit the requirements of an increasing number of crane and excavator manufacturers and, in line with Foden tradition, we began to consider the basic design criteria for a completely new crane carrier which would more readily meet the needs of the operator in both transit and working conditions. In the meantime, we built a variety of FC 20, FC 16 and FC 14 carriers in ever-increasing numbers.

When we were asked by John Laing and Son if we could provide a chassis suitable for the mounting and transportation of an American earth boring drill rig which had already been successfully truck mounted in the United States, we immediately accepted the job on the basis of "Anything they can do we can do better".

With the aid of one or two drawings and photographs of the drill rig, together with the assistance of an engineer from the manufacturers, Hugh B. Williams of Dallas, Texas, a project engineer from the customer, John Laing, and two top class fitters from our own Repair Shop, we completed the fitment of the rig to a specially built eight-wheeler Foden chassis in our Service Department without too many serious problems, in approximately fifteen working days.

The drill rig was capable of drilling shafts up to 8ft in diameter to a depth of 110ft, but the procedure normally adopted when drilling foundation shafts which, when filled with concrete, acted as support columns for multi storey buildings; was to drill the shafts to the required depth at diameters around 3ft to 4ft and then open out the base of the shaft with an expanding reamer to the maximum

diameter of 8ft. Each of the resultant concrete columns had a load bearing potential of some 2,000 tons.

The specially built vehicle operated efficiently in service, but there was no great demand for vehicles built for the specific purpose and repeat orders were not forthcoming. On the other hand, Fodens' ability to design and build special vehicles of this nature did not pass unnoticed and this growing confidence was to serve the company well, not only in the maintenance of Fodens' traditional overseas sales areas in Australia, South Africa and Rhodesia, but also in the fast developing areas around the oilfields of the Middle East.

A prime example of Fodens' expansion in traditional trading areas could be seen in Australia where the main agents, Diesel Motors, now had well equipped sales and service establishments in all the state capitals and offered the complete range of Foden products from rear engined passenger vehicles to dump trucks. It was representative of the well-established organisations in traditional Foden overseas sales areas.

In the rapidly expanding new trading areas of the Middle Eastern oilfields however, the operational and servicing problems, at least for some time, were more difficult and, due to adverse climatic and operational conditions, unskilled drivers and initially, a lack of adequate spares and field service coverage by some of the new customers, there were occasional service problems to be identified and solved. Most of the new customers fortunately, were large experienced operators which maintained their extensive fleets to an acceptable operational standard, a prime example being the Bahrain Petroleum Company.

During the 1960s and through into the 1970s, Fodens extended its Middle Eastern market area into the United Arab Emirates and eventually into the Kingdom of Saudi Arabia, at which time I became more closely involved with the continuity of Foden vehicle operations in this and many other overseas market areas. However, back in 1959 that was all part of the distant future.

Foden

Model FG 8/40 Stock Transporter, 8-cylinder, 150 h.p. Capacity up to 500 sheep. Operated by Mr. J. Allison beyond Darling River.

HAUL THE BIG WAY THE "FODEN" WAY

PROFITABLE

If you're in the "big" end of hauling, where big loads mean big earnings, you'll be interested in these examples of Foden heavy-haulage vehicles. Whether it's "droving" 500 sheep per trip, or moving tons of rock in the Snowy River project, hauling coal or chemicals, milk or machinery, there's a big rugged Foden to multiply your tonnage and profits.

Right: One of the fleet of Foden dumpers operated by Selmer Engineering Pty. Ltd. at their Snowy Mountains Works project.

Australian styles of publicity were a little more brash than Foden favoured at home, but this was a substantial market. This advertisement was issued by the main agents, Diesel Motors, and showed an FG8/40, with Gardner 8LW engine, basically much as favoured in Holland, but with right-hand steering and hauling two two-axle drawbar trailers, the complete outfit equipped to carry 500 sheep. The lower picture shows a six-wheel dump truck used on the Snowy Mountain hydro-electric project.

The Australian market had its own needs, with big distances, and specialised vehicle types – this eight-wheel tractive unit and refrigerated semi-trailer was operated by Gascoyne Trading Pty Ltd on the Perth to Carnarvon coast road.

Operating conditions in the Middle East revealed their own problems. This scene shows some of the Bahrain Petroleum Co Ltd's Foden six-wheelers with Gardner 6LW engines, Foden five-speed gearboxes and S.19 cabs. The fully-open windscreens and cab doors left wide open while parked give some indication of the climate.

The market for the rear-engined passenger chassis had proved disappointing and deliveries had virtually ceased by the mid-1950s, but early in 1959 a PVRF6 chassis with Foden two-stroke engine was fitted with an early example of the Plaxton Panorama body for Toppings of Aintree, Liverpool. It is seen at Wembley on 2nd May 1959 on the occasion of the FA Cup Final. In all, a total of 79 Foden rear-engined single-deckers, comprising 48 PVRF6 and 31 of the Gardner-engined PVRG6 version, had been built. Most were coaches for British operators, though 25 (13 PVRF6 and 12 PVRG6) were exported, including ten for Australia and New Zealand. It could be said that the model was ahead of its time, for rear-engined coaches gained a significant share of the top end of the British coach market about 20 years later.

7   THE 'SIXTIES

Self-loading vehicles began to figure in Foden's output in 1960, these views showing an eight-wheeler so equipped that was used for extensive trials by British Railways. Palletised bricks were being unloaded on to a railway Conflat wagon after being conveyed to the railway depot on the Foden. No order ensued on this occasion but many others did specify Foden vehicles of this type from then on.

From my records of the period, the year 1960 marks the start of Fodens comprehensive involvement in the refuse collection and self-loading container business. In the Drawing Office it presented no great problem to select a wheelbase to suit the specific container length, and a power take off from the gearbox to drive the high pressure hydraulic pump, which, in turn, provided the power to load and unload a fully laden container and also to operate the stabiliser jacks at the rear of the vehicle.

Although there was some loss of payload when compared with a conventional tipping vehicle due to the weight of the subframe, hydraulic equipment and lifting arms, the vehicle self loading capability provided the feature required by many operators and resultant sales of both six and eight-wheel versions of the vehicle were rewarding. Initial orders for the six-wheeler model came from the Steel Company of Wales and they were quickly followed by orders from a large number of municipal and private waste disposal operators. The hydraulic lifting gear was available from two alternative European suppliers, Bennes Marrel of France and Meiller of West Germany and it was with a special Meiller equipped eight-wheeler that we hoped to secure a substantial order from British Rail for the loading and unloading of palletised materials, notably bricks, and brewers' malt, onto and off British Rail 'Conflat' goods wagons.

Despite extensive trials with various products, the most difficult being palletised bricks, we did not receive the expected order from British Rail, or, to my knowledge did any other manufacturer. From my records it would appear that both Meiller and Marrel loading equipment was fitted to Foden vehicles at some time during the extensive trials, but on this occasion, with no positive result.

Fortunately, there were many other large operators who found the Meiller and Marrel equipment ideal for their needs and we had no shortage of orders, particularly from the waste disposal industry where Fodens already had large customer fleets of six and eight-wheeler vehicles equipped with 'Dempster Dumpmaster' and other special bodies and loading equipment.

Most of the large Foden waste disposal vehicle fleets such as A. & J. Bull, Drinkwaters and Pannels operated in the London area.

However, early in 1960 our Manchester based dealer salesman, Len Bebbington, negotiated the sale of a sizeable fleet of eight-wheeler Gardner engined refuse disposal vehicles to the City of Salford and this redressed the North/South balance to some extent. I recall that the negotiations involved Jack Mills and myself in a memorable lunchtime function with the Lord Mayor and a sizeable proportion of the Salford City Council prior to the delivery of the first vehicle. Events of this nature were normally attended by senior representatives of the Sales Department. The Drawing Office staff were the 'Back Room Boys' at that time and rarely attended functions of this nature.

Fodens crane carrier business continued to expand in 1960 and our first new application of the year was an FC16 six wheel double-drive chassis with Foden Mark III six-cylinder engine, five-speed gearbox, double drive solid beam rear bogie and dumper type half cab to suit the fitment of an all-hydraulic powered crane manufactured by the King Aircraft Company of Glasgow. The hydraulic power was derived from the vehicle power take off and the rated capacity of the crane was 10 tons at 10ft 0in radius on outriggers and 6 tons at 10ft radius free on tyres.

Although of somewhat unorthodox design, the crane operated well enough and was promoted efficiently by an enthusiastic Scottish salesman named David Kilgannon.

The City of Salford placed a fleet of Foden eight-wheeler refuse disposal vehicles with Dempster Dumpmaster 30 cubic yard bodywork in service in 1960, the author and his chief, Jack Mills, being invited to the official lunch to mark the delivery of the first vehicle. They had Gardner engines, made at Patricroft and thus in the Salford locality, as well as the fibreglass cab.

The King Aircraft Co 10-ton hydraulic crane on FC16 chassis was of unusual design but resulted in few repeat orders.

Orders were more plentiful for another Foden crane carrier designed and produced later in the year for Ruston Bucyrus of Lincoln. We had been supplying Rustons with an eight-wheel carrier for their 22RB crane on a regular basis for some time and had established an excellent working relationship with their senior design engineers at that time, Robert Chevassut and Neville Parker. The carrier in current supply was an FC 20 type eight-wheeler with Gardner engine, Foden transmission, solid crane suspension, trough type divided cab and extending outriggers and with a lifting capacity of 44,000 lbs.

Crane chassis of the FC20 type were being supplied to Ruston Bucyrus for the 22RB crane on a regular basis, this one dating from November 1960.

The Ruston engineers then required a carrier for their 30 RB crane which had a lifting capability of 70,000 lbs. at a maximum radius of 15ft, a considerable increase in intermediate capacities and a proportional increase in total weight. To meet the increased transit weight and operational requirements it was necessary to design a completely new 8 x 4 carrier with a 22in x 7in steel joist main frame and 16in x 6in box section outriggers, powered by a 210bhp six-cylinder Rolls Royce engine with a twelve-speed Foden gearbox and a new double drive solid beam rear bogie axle assembly, rated at 24 tons, as shown overleaf.

This vehicle for Rustons was by far the largest carrier we had produced and again demonstrated Fodens' capability to meet the increasing demands of our civil engineering customers quickly and effectively.

The carrier designed for the Ruston Bucyrus 30RB crane was by far the largest Foden had produced, with 22in by 7in steel joist main frame and Rolls-Royce 210bhp engine.

Another interesting vehicle combination built during this period was a four-wheel tractor unit and container trailer combination for Westburn Sugar Refineries of Glasgow.

Unlike the single compartment tipping container design adopted by Tate and Lyle and British Sugar for the transportation and discharge of bulk granulated sugar, Westburn fluidised and displaced the sugar from each of the three separate alloy containers by means of a power take off driven Godfrey blower on the tractor unit which had a maximum output of 600 cubic feet of free air per minute at a maximum pressure of 10 psi.

The final important event of 1960 was the biennial Earls Court Commercial Vehicle Exhibition and it is interesting to note that the general range of vehicles on the stand was very similar to that exhibited at the same show two years previously, in 1958. It included a six-wheel dumper, two eight-wheel bulk material vehicles, one a tipper, the other a tanker, a short wheelbase four-wheel tractor unit and trailer and a high powered six-wheel overseas tractor unit. The range of standard vehicles exhibited, together with the four-wheel dump truck and the specialist crane, excavator and contractors' plant chassis, plus a significant contribution from engine sales, had contributed to an increase in Fodens' annual turnover from £1,544,000 in 1946 to £4,260,000 in 1959 and a simultaneous increase in annual net profits from £50,000 to £150,000 during the same period.

The sugar transporter for Westburn Sugar Refineries of Greenock had an unusual three-compartment layout, allowing various grades to be carried. It had a KETU6/24 tractor unit and the Bonallack tanks were mounted on a Crane semi-trailer chassis.

The one completely new Foden exhibit at the 1960 Commercial Vehicle Show was, in fact, a turbo-charged version of the six-cylinder Mark III two-stroke engine, designated the Mark IV and claiming a significant increase in developed power from 150 to 210bhp together with a 50% increase in peak torque from 365 to 550 lbs ft.

With the introduction of the new engine Fodens now had an available Elworth-built alternative to the Cummins and Rolls Royce 200bhp engines included in the heavy duty range of six-wheel tractor unit and dump truck specifications, and although a Marine version of the engine had not been built at the time, the future availability of the Mark IV Marine engine was well publicised at the 1961 International Boat Show held at Earls Court in January.

Although there had been no completely new vehicle types introduced at the 1960 Earls Court Show, many new and often unusual applications of our existing range of vehicles continued to be submitted for our attention in the Drawing Office and one particular inquiry which I recall at that time was submitted by ICI Salt Division, which operated a rock salt mine at the nearby town of Winsford. A high proportion of the salt mined was subsequently sold in granular form to various municipalities and county councils for clearing the roads of ice and snow in the winter months, and ICI was now able to supply a specific type of ground rock salt which did not coagulate when stored in the open, even in wet weather. Consequently, orders for this modified product increased dramatically, to an extent whereby production from the mine needed to be increased threefold. Higher capacity crushing and screening plant was to be installed, together with new drilling equipment and a modified mine ventilation system.

Our task was to increase the transportation capacity from the working faces to the primary crusher at the bottom of the mineshaft by a factor of three, and our subsequent proposals involved the replacement of the existing narrow gauge rail system which needed continual time consuming modification as the working face progressed, with a fleet of four-wheel, 8-ton capacity, dump trucks.

The vehicles supplied to ICI were virtually standard four-wheel dump trucks with four-cylinder Foden engine, five-speed gearbox and 8-ton capacity body, the only special features being a Venturi fitment on the exhaust system to dilute the exhaust emission to acceptable mine regulation standards and a special roofless cab.

Assembled at the foot of a mineshaft, these dump trucks ran for five to six years conveying rock salt from the working face to the primary crusher in the ICI rock salt mine at Meadow Bank, Winsford, Cheshire. They were basically standard 8-ton models with four-cylinder Foden engines, apart from the roofless cabs and a modified exhaust system – when replaced by larger vehicles, they were dismantled, brought to the surface, reassembled by the Foden service department and resold.

There was a problem, however, in delivering the vehicles to the bottom of the mine shaft which had a maximum cross sectional measurement of approximately 8ft 6in x 3ft 6in. This restriction resulted in each vehicle being stripped down after final road test into suitably sized units and then reassembled down the mine; the most difficult problem being the dumper body sections which had to be finally welded together in a well ventilated area at the foot of the mineshaft. To assist the ICI personnel in the operation and maintenance of the new vehicles, we had Foden Service Department staff allocated to ICI for an initial period, but the vehicles operated quite efficiently in this unusual environment for five to six years and were then replaced by higher capacity six-wheel Foden dumpers when the mine production rate was again substantially increased. The original four-wheelers were then stripped down, extracted from the mine, reassembled in our Service Department and resold.

One other special vehicle application undertaken at this time involved the supply of a massive double tractor and low load trailer combination for a French company entitled 'Le Materiel Electrique' of Paris. At a meeting with the customer's representatives in London we found that the vehicle was required to carry transformers and other heavy electrical equipment for a new hydro-electric scheme to be established in the Cameron Highlands area of the Malay Peninsula.

Total payloads would be in the order of 65 to 70 tons and road and grade conditions would include difficult sections with 'hairpin' bends and grades up to 1 in 7.

The eventual combination designed to meet the customer's specific operational requirements was made up of two independent ballasted six-wheel tractors powered by six-cylinder 212bhp Cummins engines with Foden epicyclic gearbox and double drive, double reduction rear bogie axles together with an independent twelve-wheel double 'gooseneck' trailer built by Cranes of Dereham and rated at 75 tons. Each trailer bogie was independently steerable and a 'Tannoy' communication system was fitted to maintain contact between the two tractor drivers and the trailer bogie steersman. Even so, we had an exciting few moments on test when, on a grade of about 1 in 8, an emergency stop-start test left the lead tractor with the front axle two feet off the ground.

This combination, comprising two six-wheel tractors with Cummins 212bhp engines coupled fore and aft to a 75-ton 'gooseneck' trailer by Cranes of Dereham was built for use by a French concern, Le Materiel Electrique, in connection with a hydro-electric scheme in the mountains of Malaya. The broad traditional-style radiator originally associated with the Gardner 8LW engine was also suited to the cooling needs of other large engines of the period, such as the Cummins 12-litre six-cylinder engine used here, and so continued to be found on some Foden products.

The 'own-account' market was another important part of the eight-wheeler output, these vehicles more often having specialised bodywork, like this short-wheelbase example for Tate & Lyle, with pneumatic discharge tipping tank body. The curvaceous fibreglass cab was well suited to this operator's high-gloss dark blue paintwork, set off by gold lettering.

It was subsequently arranged for a senior Foden test driver to accompany the vehicles to Malaya in order to train the customer's drivers and to supervise the initial delivery of electrical equipment to the power station site.

This initial delivery, although not without incident, was completed successfully, as were subsequent journeys, so that another special Foden vehicle combination had achieved the customer's specific requirements.

These special vehicle applications, no matter how successful, could never generate sufficient profitable business to fill our production schedules and it was generally the standard Foden eight-wheeler, in either tipper, flat platform or container application which fulfilled this critical requirement. The Society of Motor Manufacturers and Traders periodic goods vehicle registration figures regularly indicated Leyland and Foden at the top of the eight-wheeler registration table and occasionally, the order changed to Foden and Leyland.

The vehicles illustrated were typical of the eight-wheeler range produced by Fodens in the early 1960s and the major increase in demand was noted in the short wheelbase tipper model, mainly for bulk material container transport and generally for the reason indicated in the Tate and Lyle vehicle illustration, ie a considerable saving in delivery and handling costs. With a 15 ton payload bulk

sugar tanker, this reduction would amount to £60 per delivery, a significant cost factor in 1961, a year when Fodens' turnover totalled a record £5,700,000 with net profits after tax amounting to £197,000.

These record figures, however, were destined to stand for only one year until 1962, which turned out to be another profitable and progressive period.

The first notable event of the year was the Boat Show at Earls Court in January when the Foden exhibits included three Marine propulsion engines in four, six and twelve-cylinder categories, the twelve-cylinder version rated at 270bhp, with Self Changing Gears. A significant number of Foden marine engines was now operating in privately owned craft and reports from their respective owners were most favourable.

Further extensions to both engine and vehicle assembly lines were in progress to meet the increased demand, which, on the vehicle side was particularly evident in relation to the requirements of the construction industries. As an example, we were now building special short wheelbase eight-wheelers suitable for mounting and driving 9 cubic yard capacity concrete mixers.

Some of the principal ready-mix concrete suppliers in the UK now operated fleets of four, six and eight-wheel mixers totalling almost 100 vehicles and a high proportion of these vehicle fleets

Ready Mixed Concrete Ltd was one of Foden's biggest customers, operating a mixed fleet of four-, six- and eight-wheeled models with the engine-driven hydraulic pumpsupplying power for the mixer drive.

were Fodens; another illustration of a special vehicle application which developed into a major production element. In the UK, the largest operator and Fodens' prime customer, was Ready Mixed Concrete Ltd., with a total fleet of over 400 vehicles and up to 70 mixing plants located strategically around the country. The company operated a mixed fleet of four, six and eight-wheeler vehicles to suit the varied requirements of their customers and the Foden vehicle element was generally concentrated in the heavier six and eight-wheeler section of the fleet.

Another vehicle type commonly utilised by the construction industries was the low-loader machinery transporter and over the years, Fodens, in conjunction with various trailer manufacturers, had produced a range of four and six-wheeler tractor units to suit the specifications of their contractor customers. During this time, we had developed a close working relationship with Dysons of Liverpool who, not unlike Fodens, manufactured a standard range of products, but were willing and able to design and build special purpose units to meet individual market requirements. The customer for the outfit shown was the National Coal Board and the requirement was a matched four-wheeler tractor unit and 20ft 0in low-loader trailer to carry a payload of 30 tons.

The year 1962 was particularly notable for a significant increase in Fodens' crane chassis sales, both in the United Kingdom and in Western Europe. Ransome and Rapier and NCK placed orders for

six and eight-wheel carriers respectively for the UK market, and DEMAG of Dusseldorf and Fiorontini of Rome ordered eight-wheel carriers for their respective home markets.

The Fiorontini order was confirmed on the understanding that an Italian OM engine and associated components would be utilised in a prototype chassis which we built in the Service Department, and that subsequent vehicles would be delivered in kit form for assembly in Rome.

DEMAG initially agreed to accept an all British specification for its prototype carrier and initial production orders, but eventually in return for a substantial multiple order, we agreed to offer a Deutz F8L air cooled engine as an alternative to the standard Gardner unit. The subsequent engine installation did present one or two problems, mainly in relation to engine driven auxiliary units, but they were quickly solved and we were able to deliver the prototype vehicle to Dusseldorf in accordance with the agreed schedule.

The order from DEMAG was followed by inquiries and subsequent orders from other West German crane manufacturers and we finally decided that the amount of business now generated in this specific vehicle type justified a completely new design project and the result of this decision was destined to constitute one

A substantial order from DEMAG of Dusseldorf for a carrier for its K406 crane called for a Deutz F8L air-cooled engine but retained the Foden 12-speed double underdrive gearbox.

Dyson trailers were often used with Foden tractor units, and a close working relationship with them was built up. This lowloading 30-ton machinery transporter outfit was for the National Coal Board, the tractor being powered by the Gardner 6LX engine developing 150bhp, driving through the 12-speed gearbox.

An exhibit causing some surprise on the Foden stand at the 1962 Show was the 'Superpayload' semi-trailer, designed for minimum unladen weight so as to carry up to 17 tons if coupled to a Foden-engined tractive unit. It incorporated standard Foden hub and brake components in the four-in-line rear end.

of the prime engineering features of the following year, 1963.

However, it was now September 1962, and the Commercial Vehicle Show was due to open at Earls Court on the 21st. There were five vehicles exhibited on Fodens' stand, all incorporating new features to maximise performance, increase payloads, improve driver comfort and reduce service costs.

The four-wheel tractor unit with four-in-line articulated trailer exhibited provided a good example of weight saving and resultant increased payload capacity. There was also a welcome degree of component interchangeability introduced by utilising the Foden tractor unit front hub and brake assembly on the '4 in line' trailer axles. The unladen weight of the complete vehicle with Foden Mark VI 175bhp "Dynamic" engine and five-speed gearbox was less than 7 tons, thereby resulting in a payload allowance of 17 tons. With the heavier Gardner 6LX engine and twelve-speed gearbox, the payload allowance was reduced by 7 cwt. to 16 tons 13 cwt.

The other four-wheel tractor unit on the stand was specifically designed for the European market, with a Foden Mark VII 225bhp 'Dynamic' engine, twelve-speed double underdrive epicyclic gearbox, left hand drive, and a wheelbase extended to 12ft to accommodate a special fibreglass sleeper cab with a detachable 2ft-

A new two-spring bogie introduced in 1962 for the eight-wheeler was designed to eliminate all metal-to-metal wearing surfaces, using rubber mountings, and was also of interest in using springs having only two leaves, of specially tapered shape.

wide bunk extension, double skin roof and additional heating and ventilation equipment. Completing the range of four-wheel vehicles on show was a short wheelbase end tipper with a Foden four-cylinder Mark VI 120bhp engine, five-speed gearbox and a 12ft alloy body. The unladen weight of this vehicle was 4 tons 16 cwt, allowing a maximum payload of 9 tons 4 cwt.

There was also a lightweight six-wheeler fitted with the same four-cylinder Foden engine, but with a twelve-speed overdrive gearbox and a single drive four-spring bogie, resulting in a total chassis and cab weight of 5 tons 3 cwt. and a total body and payload allowance of 14 tons 17 cwt. Super single tyres contributed to the weight saving and improved flotation for off-highway applications.

The fifth and final vehicle on show was Fodens' latest version of their top selling model, the 24 ton eight-wheeler, and the new design features embodied in this exhibit virtually 'stole the show'. The vehicle was exhibited in chassis and cab form with a wheelbase to suit the fitment of a 24ft body; the engine fitted was a Foden six-cylinder Mark VI developing 175bhp at 2200rpm., the front axles were the standard 5 ton Foden units, but almost all the other major vehicle assemblies were newly developed. First, a completely new seven-speed, twin layshaft, gearbox designed to transmit the higher torque developed by the latest range of engines in current use, and with gear ratios available from 7.5 : 1 low to .78 : 1 overdrive top.

Another completely new feature of the eight-wheeler specification was a two spring rear bogie axle suspension system which eliminated all metal-to-metal wearing points and required no lubrication. It gave 7in of axle-to-axle articulation and was designed to keep wheel loadings constant under all conditions.

However, the outstanding new feature on the eight-wheeler, which every visitor to the show had to see, was the impressive fibreglass tilt cab.

The basic concept of tilting the cab, or at least the upper section of the cab, to facilitate engine maintenance, had been discussed in the Drawing Office for some time, but with the successful production of the fibreglass cab the concept became a distinct possibility and possibility quickly became reality. There were problems, of course, in establishing the method of activation, the ideal pivot point, the specific sealing line between the upper tilting section and the lower fixed section of the cab, and a safe and positive locking device between cab and chassis, but with these and other production problems solved, the advantages to be gained by the new concept became increasingly apparent and were quickly confirmed by the reaction of the technical press and our customers at the show.

The tilt cab introduced at the 1962 Show was said to be the first application of such an idea on this side of the Atlantic, and was to prove a trend-setter for the whole industry. It also established another generation of Foden cab styling set to become familiar over subsequent years.

Fodens had a highly successful 1962 Show. The stand was crowded with customers and potential customers each day and in addition to the five vehicles exhibited on the Foden stand there were twelve additional Foden vehicles on ancillary equipment manufacturers' stands at the Exhibition. The *Commercial Motor's* post-show comments underlined Fodens' success as follows:- 'The Foden tilt cab has no equivalent on this side of the Atlantic and forms part of one of the most subtly advanced heavy vehicles to have been developed in this country for many years'.

The new models and new specification features introduced at the Show resulted in a substantial increase in an already heavily loaded production programme, but fortunately, new planned extensions to the Machine Shops, Erecting Shop, Engine Department and Garage were now being commissioned with the result that the year 1963 marked the start point of another significant period of expansion in the Company's history.

The expansion programme was not confined solely to production workshops. A completely new Spares and Repairs building was under construction at this time for the Service Department and the Foden Recreation Club premises were extended to provide two additional canteen areas for staff and workshop personnel, together with a new and better equipped kitchen.

In the Drawing Office, our continuing co-operation with Dysons of Liverpool had resulted in an order for a 43 ton capacity special tractor and semi trailer outfit for operation in Ghana. The Foden six-wheel tractor unit was fitted with a Darlington winch driven from a gearbox mounted power take off and was a fairly standard design from our aspect, but the low loader Dyson trailer incorporated a new folding goose-neck design to facilitate speedy loading and unloading of heavy equipment and this operation had to be carried out with the assistance of the tractor mounted winch.

In service, the Foden/Dyson outfit obviously operated satisfactorily and encouraged further joint ventures which included an arrangement whereby Dysons fabricated crane chassis frames for Fodens during periods when our own welding departments were overloaded. It was about this period in 1963 that we finalised

Ghana was the destination for this 43-ton outfit, the swan neck of the Dyson semi-trailer being readily folded down, allowing the Ruston 33RB to be loaded under its own power before driving away.

The primary assembly section of the erecting shop as seen in 1963, soon after extensions had been brought into use. Chassis were assembled on trolleys which could be rolled along the tracks at the centre and left of the foreground. Eight- and six-wheeled chassis predominate, Of the chassis visible in the foreground, three have Gardner engines and one a Foden two-stroke. A crane chassis is visible in the right foreground, this having a Gardner 6LX. Beyond the painting booths, chassis progressed through the finishing stages, cabs then being fitted.

our proposals on a revised design for our crane chassis and decided to build a prototype. Prior to this decision, we had long discussions with our original crane carrier customers, Smiths of Rodley, from which we identified the main operational problem areas with current designs and eventually agreed on an alternative layout.

The final agreement committed Fodens to design and build a prototype, which, after approval by Smiths, would be followed by

a further four chassis for the same customer before offering the new carrier design to the open market.

The principal design feature of the new crane chassis was the relocation of the driver's cab forward of the engine and radiator, and low down on the main chassis frame so that the jib sections in the transit condition did not encroach on the cab space.

With this layout it was possible to house the driver and up to

The prototype Low Line eight-wheel crane carrier, seen before delivery to Smiths of Rodley, opened up a new concept for this type of vehicle. Moving the cab forward and as low as possible meant that the jib section of the crane when lowered for transport did not encroach on cab space and the driver gained better vision and reduced noise.

three additional crew in the cab, and the crane designer had virtually no restriction on the width of the main jib section. In addition, the driver's visibility was improved and the cab interior noise level was considerably reduced.

Two examples of the new carrier design were exhibited at the International Construction Exhibition held at the Crystal Palace site in June 1963, one on the Smiths stand complete with a 30 ton lifting capacity crane fitted, and the other on Fodens stand in chassis and cab form. The new crane carrier attracted considerable attention and highly favourable comment, and it soon became obvious, even before the end of the Show, that our output forecasts would need to be increased.

Fodens was the only British manufacturer exhibiting road vehicles at the show, and our exhibits included three six and eight-wheel truck mounted concrete mixers for Stothert and Pitt and Ransome and Rapier on our own stand, together with two dump trucks and three further mixers on the stands of Ritemixer, Concrete Engineering Services and NCK-Rapier Ltd.

This International Exhibition, together with the Public Works Exhibition held at Olympia later in the year, which Fodens now regularly attended, illustrated the Company's growing involvement in the design and manufacture of an ever increasing range of contractors' plant. It was a development which was destined to

serve the company well in the future, particularly at times when vehicle production for the UK market was affected by significant changes in Construction and Use Regulations.

Fodens' increasing participation in the construction industry also provided the opportunity to increase the Company's export business, particularly on projects where major British contractors were involved. It was at the International Construction Exhibition that we had our first informal meeting with representatives of Costain, which eventually resulted in the provision of an extensive fleet of special Foden eight-wheel vehicles for the Dubai harbour construction project, which, in turn, marked the start point of Fodens' comprehensive involvement in the industrial development of the Gulf area in general and the Trucial States of Abu Dhabi, Dubai and Sharjah in particular. The immediate benefit gained from the 1963 Exhibition however, was a significant increase in demand for the new Foden 'Low Line' crane carrier, and, in order to meet this demand by increasing our production rate, additional workshop space was allocated specifically for the fabrication of the new chassis.

With most of the main workshops now extended and reorganised to reduce material handling and assembly times, Fodens were in a position to significantly increase production rates and reduce delivery times for their complete range of vehicles. There were, however,

The demand for crane carriers justified the construction of an assembly shop designed to suit this work, the spacious working conditions being conveyed by this view. Here too, assembly was carried out on wheeled trolleys, though the positioning of parts containers indicates that the welded frame assemblies were expected to remain in position for some time. In the centre of the picture, a Leyland engine, already having received a Foden twelve-speed gearbox, is being made ready for installation, whilst in the left background a supply of front axles is evident.

The 'Light Heavyweight' six-wheeler was designed to allow up to 13 tons payload within the 20-ton gross figure, using the Foden FD4 four-cylinder engine in its latest Mark VI form – John F. Moon of The Commercial Motor, testing one, commented that the FD4 was developing almost as much power as the six-cylinder model used to do, but few of the type were sold. The vehicle shown was for Hargreaves Motors Ltd of Rothwell, Leeds.

always new vehicle specification variations required either to meet a customer's specific operational needs or to generally increase payloads and resultant profitability. One vehicle type in this latter category introduced in the final quarter of 1963 was a lightweight six wheel tipper designed to achieve an unladen weight of 7 tons and a resultant available payload of 13 tons.

The main weight saving features were the four-cylinder Foden engine which now developed 120bhp at 2,200 rpm and 293 lbs ft torque at 1,400 rpm, and the aluminium alloy body made by Andrassy of Wakefield. The commercial vehicle technical press commented favourably on the performance of the new model, but subsequent sales were not impressive. Conversely, another vehicle type, introduced during the same period, but with completely different design parameters, had an extended production and operational life span, initially in the home market, but later, and more extensively, in the Middle East.

The vehicle was designed for off-road, site operation only; with a joint section main frame, Gardner engine, twelve-speed gearbox, dumper axles and suspension with double reduction rear hubs and a dumper half cab, to operate at a gross vehicle weight of 30 tons. There were at least two versions built for the original UK customer, Eccles Slag, who eventually had quite a sizeable fleet, and then four

years later in 1967 an overseas version of the original design formed part of a considerable fleet of 90 Foden vehicles utilized by Costain and its associate companies in the construction of Port Rashid in Dubai.

The first new vehicle design released from the Drawing Office in 1964 was a six-wheel 22 ton payload dump truck incorporating many improved design features including a new front axle design rated at 7 tons, a 28 ton double drive rear bogie axle assembly with double reduction hubs, a range of abrasion resistant steel bodies with capacities from 13 to 15 cubic yards to suit varying payloads, an improved tipping angle of 70° and power return tipping rams.

The new vehicle design embodied the benefits of Fodens' many years of practical experience in the earthmoving and mineral extraction industries and proved to be highly successful in service both in the UK and in many operational areas overseas.

Another Foden product now leaving the factory in ever increasing numbers, for both home and overseas customers, was the new low line crane carrier, now offered in six or eight-wheel format to suit the customer's specific requirements.

The first prototype version of the new carrier had been delivered to Smiths of Rodley in accordance with our joint agreement but, with the completion of this initial order, Fodens was now dealing

Another new design of 1963, the eight-wheel dump truck, was to prove more successful. Eccles Slag was the initial customer, as shown here, following up with further orders but in 1967 an overseas version was adopted by Costain for a fleet engaged in the construction of a harbour in Dubai.

The Low Line crane carrier was now in regular production, the initial range including six- and eight-wheel models. This rear view of the CC8-10/30 model shows the engine location, much as in a conventional eight-wheeler in relation to the front axle, but with the cab moved forward and at a lower level to allow the jib to project forward over its roof.

The 22-ton dump truck was the first new vehicle design to appear in 1964 – it was rated at 35 tons gross and alternative engines giving an output of between 150 and 225bhp were available. Among its new features was a 70° tipping angle, as seen here.

with enquiries from almost the whole of the European Mobile Crane Industry and the newly commissioned crane carrier assembly shop was soon operating to maximum capacity. Up to this point, the year 1964 appeared to be progressing according to plan, but this was not to be. On 2nd June our Governing Director, William Foden, died.

He was 95 years old and therefore, the sad event was not unpredictable, but his vital involvement in saving the company from complete collapse in the mid 1930's and his continued record of sound and progressive management during the following 30 years as Manager Director, and later as Governing Director, was a fine achievement and would be difficult to match by his successors. As a 'back room boy' in the Drawing Office and even as Chief Draughtsman, I rarely came in contact with William Foden until we were preparing for the Centenary Celebrations in 1956, at which time I was consulting him on a regular basis regarding the veteran steam vehicles we were including in the Centenary 'Cavalcade of Transport'. His memory was remarkable, not only in relation to the vehicle specification details, but more particularly in relation to the individual customers, many of whom he referred to almost as personal friends.

He was 87 at the time of the Centenary Celebrations in 1956, but his enthusiastic appreciation of the vehicles on display, both old and new, remained undiminished. Often referred to in the

When Mr William Foden died in June 1964 at the age of 95, it seemed fitting that the coffin should be carried on a Foden steam wagon. He was buried in the family vault at St Peter's Parish Church, Elworth. He had reached normal retiring age when he returned from Australia to save the company from collapse in 1935 and his sound judgement was to guide the Company to a level of success that could hardly have been foreseen in that period of uncertainty.

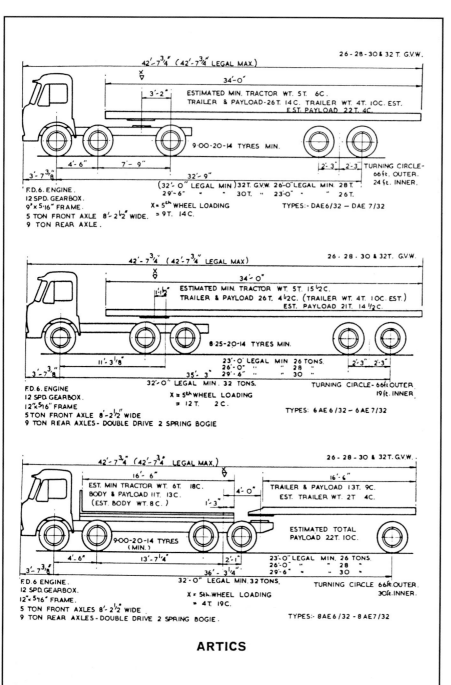

The double-front-axle tractor for use with a two-axle semitrailer was a new type of vehicle, specifically created as a result of the 1964 regulations. Steering adhesion would be improved by the double front axle configuration.

The conventional six-wheel tractor with double-drive rear bogie gave better traction, but was heavier, more complex and more expensive. This model was normally used for indivisible loads in the UK and for the export market.

Foden proposed this adaptation, christened 'Twinload' of what was effectively a standard eight-wheeler, with a shortened rear overhang on which was mounted the fifth wheel to support the front end of a single-axle semi-trailer, as a machine retaining the stability and manoeuvrability of the standard eight-wheeler while meeting the requirements to run at 32 tons gross. It actually offered a better payload, up to 22 tons 10 cwt, than either of the more conventional artics, but sales response was poor.

ARTICS

The new Construction and Use Regulations introduced in 1964 opened up load ratings of up to 32 tons for five-axle articulated vehicles while continuing to restrict the standard types of eight-wheeler, as made in large quantities by Foden, to no more than their existing 24 tons gross. This latter figure could be increased to 26 or 28 tons but only by using a wheelbase much longer than previously, raising problems of manoeuvrability. The objective was to spread the weight imposed on bridges or road surfaces; corresponding requirements applied to the new heavier-rated articulated vehicles but the relatively short tractive unit ensured that adequate manoeuvrability was retained in such cases. The drawings are taken from the data sheets produced for guidance by the Sales Department and reproduced in Foden News. They show what could be offered, though some of the options were not very practical. Note that the type identifications included letters for the alternative engines following the A for Artic: E signifying the Foden engines, F signifying the Foden supercharged engines, G the Gardner LW types and X the Gardner 6LX.

Commercial Vehicle Press as 'The Father of the British Commercial Vehicle Industry', his was a name to remember.

Apart from losing our Governing Director, there were other problems to be faced in 1964 following a series of significant changes in the commercial vehicle 'Construction and Use Regulations' issued by the Ministry of Transport and due to become effective from 21st August. The specific feature in the new regulations which affected Fodens was the change which now allowed articulated vehicles to operate at a maximum gross vehicle weight of 32 tons, whilst confining the eight-wheeler, Foden's top selling model, to a maximum gross vehicle weight of 24 tons. The resultant payloads of the two vehicle configurations would be approximately 22 tons and 16 tons, thereby providing the articulated unit with a significant operational advantage. It was legally possible to build an eight-wheeler to operate at a gross vehicle weight of 26 tons and even 28 tons, but the qualifying wheelbase, particularly for the 28 ton model was impractical. Included in the regulations were similar qualifying wheelbases for four-wheel and six-wheel

This was the standard long-wheelbase eight-wheeler as in large-scale production in 1964. Such vehicles could still be sold but where maximum weight-carrying capacity was wanted the artic now had an advantage, thus tending to reduce the market for what had been Foden's main product in terms of sales volume and profitability.

By increasing the wheelbase length to meet the new regulations' requirement for a 23ft outer axle spread, as it was called, the gross weight could be increased to 26 tons. This was possible by moving the rear bogie nearer the rear of the frame, retaining the same overall length and body space. Some redesign to improve steering lock resulted in a turning circle marginally better than the previous standard model.

To run at up to 28 tons gross, the outer axle spread had to be increased to 26ft and this meant that a far longer wheelbase was required, to the point where its lack of manoeuvrability tended to be unacceptable to most users – although the overall length of 36ft 1in (equivalent to 11 metres) was the same as the by then legal and commonly used dimension for single-deck buses and coaches. These latter vehicles had a considerably shorter wheelbase of around 18ft 6in, and could thus cope with most road conditions.

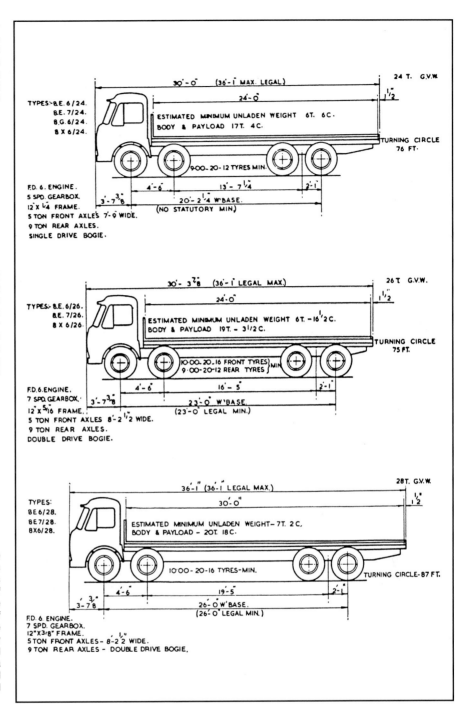

rigid vehicles to operate at maximum gross vehicle weights of 16 tons and 22 tons respectively, but we anticipated no problems in meeting these requirements and remaining competitive. To illustrate the effect of the revised Construction and Use Regulations on our standard range of four, six and eight-wheeler vehicle types, we prepared and issued a series of data sheets for the Sales Department, indicating the operations legally acceptable for the UK market.

One other qualification requirement included in the new regulations was a footbrake efficiency of 50% and a handbrake efficiency of 25%, both to be measured with a decelometer. The standard Foden air pressure brake system fitted at that time would satisfy the footbrake efficiency requirement but to meet the handbrake specification and performance criteria, it was necessary to incorporate assistance from the air brake system by fitting triple diaphragm brake chambers on the front axle to achieve the required

Air assistance for the handbrake was provided by use of triple diaphragm brake chambers on the front wheels which came into operation as the lever was applied.

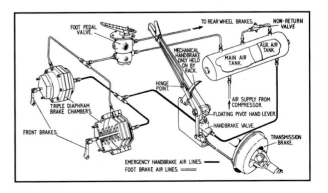

Foden's 'Twinload' 32-ton gross combination of eight-wheeler and semi-trailer had much to commend it, with a slightly higher payload capacity than conventional articulated outfits and the better natural stability of the eight-wheeler. Both tractor and trailer bodies had a load-carrying length of 16ft 6in, adding up to a total of 33ft. It was praised by the technical press yet did not sell well. Ironically, in recent years a not dissimilar concept, with a single-axle or close-coupled two-axle trailer behind a load-carrying vehicle has become quite a common sight on British and European roads. This is the 1964 Show example, type 8AE7/32, with 225bhp Foden Mark VII engine.

The articulated outfit became much more common in the aftermath of the 1964 legislation. This 4AE6/30 was also a Show exhibit, with 30-ton gross weight rating and 21-ton payload on a total of four axles. Here there could be a load length of 34ft, and for some forms of transport this was a valuable merit.

retardation level, and the fitment of a transmission brake to ensure that the vehicle could be parked safely in the event of an air pressure system failure.

All the vehicle types illustrated on the revised data sheets were to carry a manufacturer's plate indicating the rating for which the vehicle was designed and also the legally allowable loading limits for each axle. Modifications to existing vehicles to qualify for the increased gross vehicle weight ratings would, of necessity, be confined to tractor units only, at the discretion of the manufacturer.

Vehicles built to the revised regulations were identified by the new designations indicated on the new data sheets, the first number denoted the number of wheels, the first letter – the type of vehicle, the second letter and number – the type of engine and, finally, the last two numbers indicated the gross vehicle weight. At the 1964 Commercial Vehicle Exhibition held at Earls Court in late September, the four principal exhibits on the Foden stand were all, of course, designed to conform with the revised Construction and Use Regulations and we had made an attempt, with one specific vehicle configuration to retain the inherent stability of the rigid eight-wheel design in a 32 ton articulated vehicle.

This particular model was equipped with Foden Mark VII engine developing 225bhp, seven-speed gearbox, lightweight two spring bogie, 9in x 20in Michelin 'X' tyres all round and braking equipment conforming to the new regulations. The eight-wheel tractor unit and single axle articulated trailer were each fitted with 16ft 6in bodies resulting in a significant total body space of 33ft. Payload capacity totalled 22½ tons, and the vehicle was more manoeuvrable and had significantly less 'cut in' on corners than a conventional short tractor unit and long trailer configuration.

The technical press reports on the new Foden 'Twinload' articulated vehicle, both during and after the Show, were highly favourable but subsequent sales were not encouraging and, not for the first time, we were disappointed with a poor customer response to a new and well implemented design feature.

Also exhibited was a 4AE6/30 tractor unit and tandem axle semi trailer with a payload capacity of 21 tons. With a total gross vehicle weight limit of 30 tons under the new regulations, the tractor specification included a Foden Mark VI engine developing 175 BHP, five-speed gearbox, 5 ton front axle and 9 ton worm drive rear axle. The trailer body length was 34ft and both tractor units were fitted with the standard fibreglass tilt cab. The two remaining vehicles on the Foden stand were an 8 X 6/24 short wheelbase eight-wheeler with Gardner 6LX engine, seven-speed gearbox, double-drive rear bogie with super single tyres and engine-mounted hydraulic drive for concrete mixer application, and a left hand drive 6TE6/40 export tractor unit with Foden Mark VI engine, seven-speed gearbox, double drive, double-reduction rear bogie, power-assisted steering and overseas fibreglass cab with double roof insulation.

Foden vehicles were also exhibited on nine other body or container manufacturers' stands, mainly with eight-wheel chassis, indicating that this vehicle type would still be required despite the considerable payload advantage now gained by the tractor unit and trailer combinations under the terms of the new Construction and Use Regulations.

It was these same Regulations which resulted in so many changes to Fodens' production schedules in the following year, 1965, while customers decided which new vehicle configuration

Green Island Cement, of Hong Kong, placed these six-wheel tractor units with bulk cement semi-trailers in service to feed the huge demand of the building industry in that city. In 1964-65, the proportion of export business increased, partly due to the uncertainty created by the new regulations in Britain,

would best suit their specific needs. Fortunately, Fodens now had their updated production lines fully operative and a new ICT equipped Computer Department to handle outside material supply and internal manufacturing requirements more efficiently. In the twelve months following the introduction of the Regulation changes, it was estimated that over 70% of the heavy commercial vehicles sold in the UK were 32 ton tractor units. During this same period, Fodens derived over 20% of their total turnover of £7,500,000 from overseas sales, with contractors' plant in the form of dumpers, tractor units, and other specialised vehicles contributing the major proportion of this massive total.

Foden vehicles were now exported to South Africa in kit form and assembled at the Johannesburg Depot facility, a procedure which saved time, reduced shipping costs, and allowed vehicles to be modified during assembly to suit individual customer's specific requirements. The volume of Foden exports to South Africa was expanding rapidly and it was accordingly decided in 1965 to increase the area of the facility by 50%.

Foden exports to South Africa, Australia, New Zealand and other traditional overseas sales areas were generally increasing, but the sales situation in the UK was more difficult, due, in no small measure, to the effect of the revised C&U Regulations. Customers, which previously had replaced or increased their vehicle fleets with the same type of vehicles as in the past, if not the same manufacturer, were now uncertain as to which of the new vehicle configurations now being offered, would best suit their particular operational needs. Vehicle specification selection was now becoming a much

more complicated technical exercise and in the Drawing Office we were now being called upon to provide this advice to large fleet operators on a direct basis.

Esso Petroleum was only one of many operators, some with large fleet replacements to implement, others with one or two vehicles, but both with the same question to answer: 'Which will be the most profitable vehicle configuration for my specific operation under the conditions established by the revised regulations?'. In relation to the revised legal braking requirements and the recommended power to weight ratio of 6bhp per gross tonne, Foden had no difficulty complying with these factors on any vehicle in the UK range, but to offer a specification which would provide a higher payload and earning capacity with no loss of overall manoeuvrability or stability could occasionally present a problem.

The subsequent applications of the rigid eight-wheeler vehicle, Fodens former top selling model, illustrates the varied solutions offered.

In cement mixer applications, in view of the limited length of the mixer and water tank assembly and the important manoeuvrability requirement for restricted site operation, there would be no point in offering the longer wheelbase models to qualify for higher payloads.

A long distance vehicle application with the intermediate 23ft wheelbase requirement presented no operational problems. The 26 ton eight-wheeler with a 23ft qualifying wheelbase proved to be the most suitable for the traditional eight-wheeler long and medium distance operator. There was only limited interest in the 28 ton

In the event, some operators found that the traditional 24ton short-wheelbase eight-wheeler was still the best proposition for their needs, notably where manoeuvrability was important, as often the case on building sites.

To qualify for the 26-ton gross weight limit, eight-wheelers had to have a minimum qualifying wheelbase length, measured from the leading axle to the rearmost one, of 23ft, and although this was longer than had been standard for the previous generation of long-wheelbase models of this type, it proved acceptable for normal long-distance operation. Such vehicles were often of much the same overall length, approximately 30ft, as previously, as was so here. The reduced rear overhang was actually helpful in the design of a vehicle such as this, with end-tipping bulk sugar container body.

model with a 26ft minimum wheelbase requirement, but some of the models of this type that we did build were worthy of note. By far the most interesting was the special eight-wheeler produced for T. A. Bulmer of Middlesbrough for the transportation of steel channels and joist sections up to 50ft long.

Based on the Low Line crane carrier design with a four-man crew cab, the vehicle was 35ft long and had a payload capacity of 18 tons. The specification included a Gardner 6LX engine, Foden twelve-speed gearbox and double-drive four-spring rear bogie and complied with all requirements of the revised Construction and Use Regulations.

The other eight-wheeler type built during this period formed the motive section of the 'Twin Load' articulated vehicle introduced at the 1964 Earls Court Show. Despite the acclaim generated by the

newly designed unit at that time, very few customers had followed up their interest with an order, one of the exceptions being Harveys of Bristol. The total capacity of the two containers was 6,000 gallons and with a Foden 225bhp engine and epicyclic gearbox, the articulated outfit had a cruising speed exceeding 60 mph on the regular journeys from the wine producing regions of France and Germany to the bottling plants at Bristol.

Previously, the six-wheeler category, other than applications for concrete mixer mounting, had provided Fodens with only moderate sales outlet. At an increased allowable gross vehicle weight of 22 tons we anticipated an increased share of the total market.

In actual fact the most notable increase in six-wheeler sales was subsequently noted in the tractor unit models where customers

This ingenious combination of the Low Line crane chassis layout with a load-carrying frame to meet the requirements allowing an eight-wheeler to operate at up to 32 tons gross was built in 1965 for T. A. Bulmer & Co Ltd of Middlesbrough. The low-level cab allowed the carriage of up to 18 tons of steel joists in lengths of up to 50ft. They were carried on a bolster, allowing them to extend over the cab, this also allowing them to clear the engine cover protruding above the platform level of the body. At the rear, the chassis and body was cut short, allowing the vehicle itself to comply with the 11-metre overall length limit;.

operating with 32 tons gross vehicle weight articulated vehicles rightly considered that a three axle tractor unit provided increased overall vehicle stability.

In relation to four-wheeler vehicles, Fodens output was concentrated almost exclusively on high powered tractor units with multi-speed transmissions to suit the 32 tons gross vehicle weight articulated vehicles which, under the terms of the revised regulations, had a profitable payload advantage over any other vehicle type.

The final notable event in the year 1965, a significant year of change in the industry, was the Scottish Commercial Vehicle Exhibition at Kelvin Hall, Glasgow, where some examples of the new vehicle types were on display.

Appropriately at this time, James Hemphill of Glasgow took delivery of the first vehicle in a newly ordered fleet of nine similar 32 ton articulated tankers incorporating Foden six-wheel double front axle tractor units and 5,000 gallon capacity Butterfield tank trailers.

Incoming home market vehicle orders in the early months of 1966 indicated a varied pattern similar to the previous year, as operators came to terms with the extended range of vehicle load capacities now available. George Armitage of Wakefield, an old established brick manufacturer, decided to operate his eight-wheelers with independent trailers, whilst Coalmoor Refractories of

Shropshire, with similar payloads, decided that the new 'Twin Load' eight-wheeler and articulated trailer would best suit their particular needs.

With so many variations in the standard vehicle range now available, together with the dumper, crane carrier, and overseas vehicle types in production, the value of the extended manufacturing and assembly facilities introduced in the early 1960s was now appreciated more clearly. One specific example of the dumper

The double-front-axle, or twin-steering, tractive unit was a creation of the 1964 regulations, being one of the possible configurations permitting operation at 32 tons gross when coupled to a two-axle semi-trailer. James Hemphill Ltd, of Glasgow, was taking delivery of this vehicle, one of a batch of nine hauling 5,000-gallon tank semi-trailers by Butterfield, at the time of the 1965 Scottish Show.

Replacing the four-wheel dump trucks operated at the ICI rock salt mine at Winsford illustrated on page 103 was a new fleet of special 35-ton six-wheel models which, again, had to be taken down the mine shaft and assembled at its foot by the team of fitters and welders from the Service Department seen here with one of the completed vehicles. This time, a covered cab with windscreen was provided, together with a tubular framework covering the front and top of the cab.

requirements at this time was an order for a fleet of special 35 ton six-wheel dump trucks for the ICI rock salt mine at Winsford to replace the four-wheelers supplied some years previously.

Annual production had increased in five years from 30,000 to 1 million tons and during this period, the Foden dumpers had performed well. Following the completion of the new vehicle fleet, the task of dismantling each vehicle for lowering down the mine shaft and then the reassembly operation at the foot of the mine, was again entrusted to a selected team of fitters and welders from our Service Department. Their final task in the mine was the dismantling of the four-wheel dumper fleet, which was later re-assembled in the Service Department and subsequently resold.

Fodens overseas sales, already providing the company with an appreciable proportion of total turnover, was now expanding in the Far East and, in addition to the substantial fleets operating in Hong Kong, Foden six-wheel concrete mixers, tippers and tractor units were now working in the Philippines.

This specific vehicle fleet of tippers and mixers all had Foden Mark VI engines, six-speed gearboxes in the tippers, twelve-speed double underdrive gearboxes in the mixers, overseas type fibreglass cabs and heavy duty 12in x 4in channel section main frames. The tipper bodies were the Neville alloy panel type with an alloy subframe.

The Philippines was another export market in which Foden had made an appearance. Among the vehicles in operation there was this FE6/20 end tipper for Concrete Aggregates of Manila.

Fodens' continued involvement and dependence on export sales was exemplified at the Earls Court Commercial Vehicle Show in September by the inclusion of a six-wheel 40 ton gross vehicle weight tractor, specially built for the overseas market with a Cummins six-cylinder 210bhp engine, twelve-speed underdrive gearbox, 8 ton rated front axle, 24 ton double drive bogie with selective double reduction hubs and a special S21 type non tilting fibreglass cab with double skin roof for heat insulation.

The six-wheel overseas tractor unit is seen at the top left corner of the stand in the picture on the opposite page. Also on show for the first time was a six-wheel double front axle tractor unit fitted with a Leyland engine and an RV 47 Self Changing Gears gearbox. This vehicle was designed to operate with a semi-trailer at 32 tons gross vehicle weight and was fitted with Michelin tubeless tyres on the front axles and super single tyres on the rear axle. There was also a four-wheel 30 ton tractor unit fitted with a Foden Mark VI 180bhp engine and twelve-speed overdrive gearbox and this vehicle was fitted with the tilt cab. Fodens' stand was never complete without an eight-wheeler on show and this year's exhibit was an 8 X 6/24 short wheelbase concrete mixer chassis with Gardner 180bhp engine, Foden twelve-speed overdrive gearbox, tilt cab, and four-spring rear bogie with 10.00 x 22.5 Michelin tubeless tyres all round.

Our exhibits at the Earls Court Show in September were, at this time, normally confined to road haulage vehicles, leaving off road, contractors' plant vehicles to be exhibited at either the International Construction Exhibition at the Crystal Place site in June, or alternatively at the Public Works Exhibition at Olympia in December. However, on this occasion, our new four wheel 15 ton payload dump truck was shown for the first time at the Commercial Vehicle Show and created considerable interest.

The new vehicle was ideally suited for the smaller quarry or restricted working site and, with low pressure super single tyres was able to operate in poor ground conditions. The prototype vehicle was exhibited again at the Public Works Exhibition in December and resultant sales both home and overseas were highly satisfactory. Another interesting new design feature introduced during this period, which was to prove a valuable asset to Foden drivers, was the air-operated range change arrangement on the twelve-speed epicyclic gearbox.

The Foden stand at the 1966 Commercial Vehicle Show, like others before and since, gave an indication of the Company's main markets and aspirations to serve them. At the top left in this view is the six-wheel overseas tractor unit with Cummins 210bhp engine. Nearest the camera, the double-front axle tractor was intended for the home market and was of interest in having a Leyland engine and Self Changing Gears RV47 semi-automatic epicyclic gearbox – both of these vehicles had the non-tilting S.21 fibrelass cab. Between them was an eight-wheeler, with Gardner 6LXB 180bhp engine, Foden twelve-speed gearbox and the tilt cab.   Foden-engined models were represented by the four-wheel tractor in the background, set at right angles to its semi-trailer, used to entertain visitors to the stand. Home market models had tubeless tyres, then becoming available on heavy commercial vehicles. On the right-hand rear of the picture is seen the 15-ton payload dump truck which was also exhibited at the Public Works Exhibition at the end of that year. It was offered with options of Gardner 6LX or 6LXB engine and had super-single rear tyres.

There were also a number of additional engineering changes to be introduced in the near future, which were dictated by the requirements of the Ministry of Transport rather than Fodens' Design Department. It was agreed that from 1st January, 1968 all unplated vehicles would have to comply with the intermediate braking standards, and from 1st January, 1972 they would be required to comply with the full braking standards of 25% emergency or parking brake retardation and 50% footbrake or service brake retardation.

Although a high proportion of Foden vehicles in service would meet the 1968 requirements, it was necessary to design and prepare conversion kits to enable all Foden vehicles in service to comply by the designated dates. The kit parts lists and explanatory drawings were our responsibility in the Drawing Office. Our Service Department prepared, issued and often fitted the kits as required and the conversion exercise was eventually completed with rather less trouble than we had originally anticipated.

The primary event in January on the Foden calendar was usually the International Boat Show and 1967 was destined to be a special year. The previous year, 1966, the *News of the World* had entered the *Daily Express* offshore power boat race with an Anthony Needell designed power boat, built by W. A. Souter of

Cowes and fitted with four Foden six-cylinder Mark VII turbocharged engines.

Of the 40 boats which stated the race, only eighteen finished due to poor weather conditions, but the Foden powered boat had performed well and the decision was subsequently taken to enter the 1967 race. At the International Boat Show in January, the power boat was exhibited on Souter's stand, together with one of the Foden engines, and in the subsequent race held in April over a

With four turbocharged Foden six-cylinder engines, the News of the World powerboat entered in the 1967 offshore race was not short of power, and duly won the event.

One of the special eight-wheel dump trucks used by the Steel Company of Wales makes a dramatic sight as it discharges its payload in the huge plant at Port Talbot.

total distance of 48 nautical miles, the Foden powered craft subsequently won the race in 64 minutes 10 seconds. The win again underlined the capabilities of the Foden two stroke engine design in a marine application and marked a satisfactory start to yet another eventful and progressive year in Fodens' history.

It was a year of expansion for one of our principal contractors' plant customers, the Steel Company of Wales, already operating a fleet of some 50 Foden six and eight-wheel dump trucks, crane carriers and site vehicles at its huge steel plant and dock facility, now extending 4½ miles along the coast at Port Talbot, in South Wales.

The special eight-wheel high-speed end-tip site vehicles were designed to handle payloads up to 30 tons and were operated on the site on a shift basis, thereby resulting in high total tonnage and low total mileage data which could be somewhat confusing when related to occasional warranty claims. The vehicle design was based on the original eight-wheeler site vehicles supplied to Eccles Slag some years previously and consisted mainly of dump truck engine, transmission and suspension units mounted on an exceptionally strong chassis frame.

The Steel Company expansion programme resulted in further

orders for similarly equipped Foden vehicles for operation on the extended site.

Another significant delivery implemented at this time followed an order from the Ministry of Defence for several six-wheeler general service vehicles. The vehicles were required for the Royal Corps of Transport and were based on the standard 20 ton double drive six wheeler design with an overseas type of fibreglass cab and an all steel hinged side body with detachable canvas tilt cover on tubular steel frame.

1967 was also a good year for overseas dump truck sales with repeat orders received from Whytes of Malaya and Selection Trust of West Africa. The Whytes dumpers had a gross vehicle weight rating of 24 tons and the specification included 8 ton front and 16 ton rear axles, a Gardner 6LX engine and aluminium alloy section dumper bodies.

Those supplied to West Africa were rated at 35 tons gross vehicle weight and with a specification also including a Gardner 6LX engine, Foden axles, 10 speed epicyclic gearbox and an aluminium alloy body. Both vehicle types also shared a common feature in the all steel half cab which had proved to be highly suitable from an operational service access viewpoint, but could

In February 1967, the Royal Corps of Transport was the recipient of a fleet of long-wheelbase six-wheelers with canvas tilt body, ordered by the Ministry of Defence. This was the beginning of a regular association with the supply of Foden vehicles for Army use, still a common sight today.

These six-wheel dump trucks were supplied to the Sierra Leone Selection Trust, West Africa.

The all-steel cab produced by Coventry Motor Panels was adopted mainly for use on overseas applications calling for a heavy duty cab where weight was not a critical factor, being given the Foden designation S.40. It was available in optional forms including a sleeper cab and could have an insulated roof where needed but it was also favoured for heavy haulage applications in Britain, including this independent haulage tractor for Strathclyde Transport.

become fairly hot in tropical operating conditions, despite the partial shade provided by the cab protection canopy extension on the dumper body.

On standard overseas road vehicles fitted with the fibreglass cab, the double skin roof proved an effective insulation feature, but there was a growing number of overseas applications and some home market operations where, apart from additional insulation requirements, there was a need for a generally more heavy duty cab.

After a good deal of discussion and a number of adaptations to suit Fodens' specific requirements, it was decided to utilise an all steel cab designed and produced by Coventry Motor Panels. The cab was designated the S.40 type and was made available in right or left hand drive format, with additional versions featuring modified front panels to suit higher capacity radiators and others incorporating additional crew seating or sleeping accommodation. For tropical overseas conditions, a double skin roof and large roof ventilator were available.

Other commendable features included a four point mounting system incorporating conical rubber units with rebound restrictors at the front, and coil spring mountings and telescopic hydraulic dampers at the rear. Service access to the electrical equipment mounted on the front bulkhead was provided by detachable panels located on either side of the main radiator grille panel. There were many other minor but worthwhile features embodied in the Coventry Motor Panels cab which had been in production for some time for other applications before the Foden version was introduced.

At that time the S.40 cab was undoubtedly the best of its type available in the UK and it was destined to serve the company well in a varied range of applications over the next decade. Fitment was by no means confined to vehicles destined for the overseas sales areas.

Many UK operators, particularly in the heavy haulage sector of the industry where a second crew member was essential, found the S.40 steel cab more suitable for their requirements than the lighter fibreglass cab, and the resultant increase in unladen weight in their specific sector of the transport industry was of no importance.

In December of 1967, responding to the continuing requirement for higher payloads from both home and overseas operators, we introduced a new six-wheel dump truck with a payload capacity of 56,000 lbs.

The vehicle specification, which offered a range of alternative Gardner, Foden and Cummins engines from 180 to 240bhp, also

The 40-tons gross dump truck offered a capacity of over 20 cubic yards and incorporated a new heavy-duty twelve-speed gearbox.

listed a number of completely new features including the following: 17in diameter air cooled clutch units, 32 ton rated four spring rear bogie assembly, 16in joist section main chassis frame, 'Ducol' high tensile, abrasion resistant, steel body, and a new twelve-speed Foden gearbox.

The new six-wheel dump truck and a whole range of vehicles fitted with the new S.40 steel cab were also selling well in the UK, but the year was most notable for Fodens' first significant penetration of the Middle East sales area via a major British public works contractor.

The sales area was the Trucial State of Dubai, the contractor was Costain, and the project was the provision of a deep water harbour for the Port of Dubai. We had discussed the transport requirements of the project with representatives of Costain at the International Construction Exhibition the previous year and it was obvious at that time that reliable transport would be a critical element. The initial £9.4 million contract with Costain Civil Engineering Ltd, was signed by Sheik Raschid, the Ruler of Dubai, in October 1967 for the construction of a deep water harbour which would eventually provide 15 berths of 390 feet minimum draught. The scheme also involved the construction of two protecting breakwaters, one of which was 1.5 miles in length. A secondary contract was later signed which resulted in a total commitment of £24 million with Costain for additional transhipment berths, warehouses and other major port facilities. The initial transport problem involved the construction of a road from the harbour site to the only rock quarry in the area which was 20 miles inland over open desert and the first Foden vehicles required were 4 and six-wheel dump trucks initially to assist with the road construction and subsequently to operate in the quarry.

These vehicles were shipped to Dubai during the months of February and March 1968 together with a number of six-wheel end tippers for transporting sand and aggregates for the road construction. Each of the six-wheel end tippers was supplied with a single axle gantry type trailer.

During the following months of April, May and June the special eight-wheeler tippers designed to transport the rock from the quarry to the two breakwater sites were delivered and the major part of the massive order was complete.

As agreed during our meetings with the contractor, the eight-wheel rock carrier design was based on the special eight-wheel site tipper design introduced for, and operated successfully by, Eccles Slag and the Steel Company of Wales, and we were confident that

A contract awarded to Costain to build a deep water harbour for the Trucial State of Dubai resulted in the supply of 90 Foden vehicles of varied types, including dump trucks of both four- and six-wheel types, with Rolls-Royce and Cummins engines respectively, shipped in the early months of 1968.

the Costain vehicles, properly maintained, would satisfy the customer's rather more arduous requirements. For this specific project Fodens supplied a total of 90 vehicles of various types during 1968.

In addition to the heavy duty tippers, dump trucks and rock carriers, there were a number of crane carriers and concrete mixers included in the total, all of which were shipped as deck cargo and landed by means of shallow draught barges and lighters in Dubai.

The advent of a deep water harbour facility in Dubai acted as a general stimulant to all business activity in the area and our appointed dealers in Dubai, General Navigation and Commerce, or 'GENAVCO' as they were more generally known, were now receiving orders for a wide variety of Foden vehicles for the many new subsidiary industries becoming established in the area.

The two examples illustrated are typical of the multiple orders for many vehicle types received by Fodens during this period. Engine specifications included Rolls Royce, Cummins, Leyland and Gardner. Cab types varied between S.40 steel and S.39 overseas fibreglass, driving axle tyre equipment was usually low pressure sand tread type; steel or aluminium alloy body designs varied in

Six-wheel tippers of road-going type were also supplied to Costain for the Dubai contract. These were 26-ton gross vehicles and had Cummins engines. Unusually for tippers, they were supplied with trailers to allow them to be used for other duties.

The eight-wheel 40-ton-gross rock transporters supplied to Costain for use in Dubai played a crucial role in the whole project, for their reliability was essential to its completion within an acceptable time. They were fitted with Rolls-Royce 220bhp engines.

The Costain order led to further demand for Foden vehicles for other operators in the Trucial States, an example being this 50-ton articulated outfit, with sand tyres and double-reduction hubs on the driving axles. The cab in this case was the S.39 overseas version of the fibreglass type.

The effect on business extended to neighbouring countries. Ths six-wheel tipper with sand tyres and S.40 steel cab was supplied via General Navigation for operation in Saudi Arabia.

By 1968, assembly of chassis exported in kit form was being carried out at the Foden depot in Main Reef Road, Johannesburg. In this scene, two four-wheel dump truck chassis with Gardner 6LW engines are almost complete, and a bodied example is visible in the background. In the foreground, chassis frames for road-going six-wheelers are being prepared for assembly.

relation to the load to be carried, the tip gear was either Pilot or Edbro and the remainder of the specification was completely Foden.

Fodens' increasing overseas sales expansion in 1968 was by no means confined to the newly developing areas of the Middle East. In South Africa, where Foden vehicles were now received in kit form and customised during assembly to suit individual operators' requirements, there was a considerable increase in activity, which had now included the design and fitment of their own cabs. Kits were assembly by a crew of two in eight working days, despatched to the body builder for the fitment of the cab and body and then returned to the depot for final inspection, road test and delivery.

In Hong Kong, one of Fodens' major customers, Green Island Cement, was building up an extensive fleet of mobile contractors plant, mounted almost exclusively on Foden chassis, a successfully proven, cost effective method of reducing spares and service costs due to the high degree of parts interchangeability between the various Foden chassis utilised.

For the construction of the second Mersey road tunnel, special vehicles based on the short dumper chassis but fitted with special bodywork were used to carry the roof section formers. Two are seen at work in June 1968.

For the very local home market of Liverpool we were engaged by the main contractor for the second Mersey Tunnel, Nuttall Atkinson, to provide a number of short wheelbase four-wheel vehicles for transporting and supporting the roof section formers during the construction of the tunnel. The vehicle was basically a four-wheeler short-wheelbase dumper chassis with driver's half cab and special body.

At the 1968 Commercial Vehicle Show held at Earls Court in September, we exhibited the Foden S.50 half cab for the first time on two of the show vehicles. We had considered for some time that there were certain categories of short-haul road vehicles, normally manned only by the driver where a heavy-duty, safer, and more easily repaired cab than the standard fibreglass saloon pattern cab would be more suitable.

Apart from the safety aspects of the new cab, service access on the nearside was considerably improved and, when compared with the full width S.40 Motor Panels steel cab, there was a considerable weight saving. Other new features introduced at the show included the fitment of spring brakes in place of the transmission brake for secondary and parking brake applications, and the introduction of sintered iron friction pads in lieu of the conventional fabric wearing face on the clutch plate, a measure destined to increase clutch facing life by a factor of four.

On a heavy duty six-wheel haulage tractor exhibited at the show, a new load transfer device was incorporated which, in effect, energised a pair of Dunlop Air Bags located between the frame and the rearmost axle and thereby reduced the tendency to lose steering adhesion under adverse grade conditions.

Early in 1969, two major airfield refueller projects engaged our attention in the Drawing Office. The first enquiry and subsequent order came from Gloster-Saro for a double front axle tractor and independent trailer combination with a total payload capacity of 30,000 gallons of aviation spirit for Mobil Oil Company.

The vehicle and trailer were designed with the tank and chassis as integral units and, to meet the required laden wheel loads and performance, we incorporated the heavy duty axle suspension and

The S.50 half-cab was introduced at the 1968 Commercial Motor Show as part of the following year's range of options, intended for use on duties such as public works contracts where a more rugged cab for the driver only was considered more appropriate. The reverse-rake windscreen was becoming more common on stationary or slow-speed applications of other kinds, such as airport control towers or ferries, having the practical merit of tending to remain cleaner in adverse weather.

The 30,000-gallon Gloster-Saro refueller outfit designed for Mobil was not based on existing chassis, except that the axles, suspension and transmission were as used on the 40-ton dumper. The main unit was of double front axle layout, this being because it used the concept of mounting the cab and power unit ahead of the front axles. No attempt was made to 'glamorise' the appearance, and this was another instance of use of a reverse-rake windscreen.

transmission utilised in our 40 ton dumper specification. The vehicles were destined for service on airfields in North Africa and to our knowledge, attained their designed payload and operational requirements.

This specific design was hardly off the drawing board when we received an order from Thompson of Bilston for three special six-wheel tractor units to form the motive section of a prototype 12,000

gallon capacity articulated tanker fleet for refuelling Concorde. Following a meeting with Thompson's engineers, it was also arranged for Foden to supply the trailer tank bogie axle assemblies in order to improve component interchangeability between tractor and trailer.

The Foden tractor unit specification included a six-cylinder Leyland engine developing 200bhp at 2,200rpm, a twelve-speed

For refuelling Concorde, an outfit using a more conventional sixwheel tractor unit was decided upon by Thompson, which supplied the tank semi-trailer and equipment. Here the capacity requirement was not so great, at 12,000 gallons, but even so the combination weighed up to 70 tons fully laden. The three vehicles supplied were on display at the first public viewing of the prototype aircraft and, no doubt partly due to the immense interest the aircraft aroused, they attracted even more interest than the previous refuellers we had built, which eventually resulted in several further orders.

Foden gearbox with 140bhp power take off driving the main pumps at a total fuel delivery rate of 900 gallons per minute, and a four spring double drive rear bogie axle assembly with double reduction hubs. Pumping and metering equipment were fully enclosed in a separate compartment located behind the cab. Each articulated unit was 54ft long and weighed up to 70 tons in the fully laden condition. When servicing the aircraft the standard refuelling procedure involved two tankers operating simultaneously from each side to fill the main tanks, which were located symmetrically.

A fresh development in this period was the publication of *Service News* as a separate exercise from *Foden News*, so as to ensure that information of value to customers' service personnel would reach its target.

Liaison between the Design and Service Departments at Fodens was generally well organised and effective. Regular service meetings attended by all Depot Managers and Senior Field Service Engineers, were organised by the Service Manager and were always attended by the Chief Designer or the Chief Draughtsman, who were called upon at the following meeting to report on any necessary rectification or preventative measures taken to overcome or prevent the service problems reported.

A significant addition to the Foden dump truck range in September 1969 was a six-wheel 39 ton model with Cummins engine and Allison automatic gearbox, a combination which was destined to become widely used, both for UK and overseas markets. At that period, sales in Britain were strongly boosted by motorway construction. Sales of low loader outfits also increased and, at one point, we built examples for both JCB and Poclain to convey demonstration machines.

There were significant changes taking place in the field of material handling which would result in a wider field of application for vehicles designed to carry standardised containers and pallets.

To illustrate the suitability of our standard four wheel tractor unit and articulated trailer for this type of work, Fodens participated in a three day demonstration of a new Rubery Owen self-propelled straddle crane, designed specifically to handle standard containers. The "Karricon" straddle crane could load, unload, traverse and stack containers quickly and safely and became a standard item of equipment at many container terminals.

The final notable event in my records for 1969 was the Scottish Motor Exhibition held in November at the Kelvin Hall, Glasgow.

In accordance with Fodens' usual practice, we had a representative range of Scottish customers' vehicles on the stand and during the show our distributors finalised orders for many more. The Kelvin Hall Show, organised by the Scottish Motor Traders Assocation was a much less formal affair than the Earls Court Exhibition and there was a higher proportion of actual operators in the total numbers of stand visitors. Consequently, time spent on stand duty was more interesting and more rewarding to the company. Scottish operators in general appeared to remain loyal customers to a greater degree than their English counterparts. On reflection, I am inclined to believe this may well have been due to the high standards of our Scottish sales and service staff.

Movement of stadardised containers grew rapidly in the late 1960s and here a Foden tractor unit is seen taking part in a three-day demonstration of the Rubery Owen Karricon self-propelled straddle crane.

A 39-ton dump truck introduced in 1969 incorporated a Cummins 310bhp engine, Allison automatic gearbox and the S.40 cab.

A regular Service News bulletin began to be issued in the late 1960s.

8 EXPANSION AND CHANGE

As we moved into the 1970s another round of Construction and Use Regulation changes were under discussion, which, if and when implemented, would extensively modify our basic vehicle parameters yet again. It is opportune to review briefly the basic changes to Fodens' range of vehicles during the 1960s.

Allowable gross vehicle weights, and consequently payloads, had increased substantially, particularly in relation to articulated vehicles, and, with a required power to weight ratio of 6 bhp per ton, higher powered engines, with correspondingly uprated transmissions, had become a subsequent necessity. Later refinements had reduced the fuel consumption of these engines, and automatic and semi-automatic transmissions had become more popular, particularly for off-highway applications where the frequent combination of bad site conditions and poor gear changing ability could prove disastrous.

Braking efficiency had been improved, initially by legislative requirement and subsequently by the introduction of additional braking systems; for example, the spring brake and the transmission brake. Power assisted steering and clutch operation had further reduced the driver's work load and his working environment had been changed dramatically by insulated cabs, hydraulic suspension seating and air conditioning.

A comprehensive range of good-quality vehicle electrical equipment was now available from both UK and continental suppliers, and a similar situation prevailed in the case of hydraulic equipment. A wider range of tyres with higher load ratings and reduced rolling resistance tread patterns were now produced by Michelin, Goodyear, Dunlop and other leading manufacturers.

Serviceability, or more specifically, access for service, had been improved dramatically with the advent of the fibreglass tilt cab and some time later, the steel half cab, and the preparation and distribution of service information generally had been improved by reorganisation of the Service Department.

A new test track and more comprehensive test equipment was now available to provide more precise data for our experimental and research engineers, and in general terms it could be claimed that the 1960s had proved to be a progressive and rewarding period for Fodens.

During the 1970s we were destined for a period of expansion and change, and the new decade commenced on a favourable personal note with promotion from Chief Draughtsman to Design Department Manager. The new title made very little difference to my responsibilities in the Drawing Office, but the appointment gave me more scope when dealing with inter-departmental affairs, particularly at times when my immediate chief, Jack Mills, now an executive director, was not available.

Fodens' trading performance for the 1969/70 financial year indicated a record total turnover of £12,946,000, an increase of 31.5% on the previous year, and a total profit before tax of £1,086,414, an increase of 51.2% on the last year and the first time this important statistic had reached the one million pound mark. Total vehicle orders had increased by 36% and the value of export turnover had reached a record level of £2,650,000, an increase of over £1,000,000 on the previous year.

The list of main depots and agents had become extensive, with Foden depots in Johannesburg, South Africa; Moorebank, New South Wales, Australia, Auckland, New Zealand; and Venlo, Holland. In addition there were agents in six other African countries, five in the Middle East, seven in Asia, eight in Europe, two in South America and one in the West Indies.

Orders continued to come from Dubai, as addtional industries grew as the harbour project progressed. This 40-ton dumper truck was for the Dubai Rock Co.

Bamburi Portland Cement, a Kenya concern using Foden vehicles since 1947, expanded its fleet considerably when it became a supplier to the Dubai harbour, this 32-ton bulk cement outfit being among those added to the fleet.

The most rapidly expanding area in terms of vehicles delivered continued to be the Middle East, where, with the Dubai harbour construction project well advanced, vehicle orders for newly established subsidiary industries in the area were being placed. In addition to the local vehicle requirements relating to the development of Dubai, there were many additional orders for Foden vehicles received at this time from associated industries located far away from the Trucial States.

One clear example was a substantial vehicle order from the Bamburi Portland Cement Company in Kenya, a major supplier of cement for the new harbour and an old established Foden customer. This firm had operated Foden dump trucks at their Mombasa plant since 1947 and now required additional dump trucks and bulk cement carriers.

If, as it appeared, all was going well with Fodens' overseas vehicle applications, this was most certainly not the case with the

With uncertainty about proposed new regulations which held the prospect of increased gross weight limits, Fodens decided to take a bold line and exhibit models which could take advantage of the proposed new limits at the 1970 Commercial Show. This 8LXB6/30 eight-wheeler was limited to 26 tons under existing regulations but was designed to run at up to 30 tons. It had a Gardner 6LXB engine and heavy-duty transmission and axles as well as the S.50 steel half cab.

Designed to run at up to 38 tons gross, this DAXB6/38 double-front-axle tractor unit had the new eight-cylinder Gardner 8LXB engine developing 240bhp and used some of the same units as the new eight-wheeler but had a newly-designed 10-ton rear axle with double-reduction hubs. This had a new S.70 fibreglass cab, having a similar profile to the S.50, but of full width.

Anticipating the legalising of operation at 44 tons, the 6AC6/44 double-drive six-wheel tractor had a Cummins NT270B engine with 270bhp output and the same 19-ton bogie as the eight-wheeler. In this case the cab was the S.60, of all-metal construction, but of similar appearance to the S.70. Cummins engines were gaining increasing acceptance in Britain, partly because of the power outputs needed for heavier vehicles. As it turned out, the weight limits for articulated vehicles remained a matter of controversy in Britain, delaying changes in the regulations, although the ability to offer such models opened up export possibilities.

home market, where proposed changes to the UK Construction and Use Regulations, which would have a considerable effect on individual axle weights, gross vehicle weights and consequent payloads, had still not been finalised. Progress at the many technical committee meetings we had attended at the Society of Motor Manufacturers and Traders and discussions with the Ministry of Transport had been held up repeatedly, not by any disagreement between the manufacturers, but by restrictions imposed by the civil engineers and objections from various organisations claiming to represent the general public. Proposals had been discussed which would, if implemented, allow six-wheel rigid vehicles to operate at a gross weight of 24 tons, eight-wheel rigid vehicles at 30 tons and six-wheel double drive tractor unit and bogie axle trailer combinations up to a staggering 44 tons. Other qualifications would include a minimum engine brake horsepower requirement of 6 bhp per ton, and most important of all, limitations on maximum axle loadings and minimum axle spacing. It was these last two factors which were causing serious problems with the civil engineering section of the Ministry of Transport which, quite naturally, was concerned about the detrimental effect of increased loadings on roads and bridges.

With the opening date of the 1970 Commercial Vehicle Exhibition rapidly approaching, Fodens decided to exhibit three prototype vehicles built to conform with the latest Construction and Use proposals, but with no certainty that these proposals would be approved and the vehicles legalised. It was a bold and potentially costly decision to make at this time, but at least it indicated to customers that Foden would be ready to build vehicles to take advantage of the higher payloads and earning capacity. Three vehicles were exhibited, an eight-wheeler – a vehicle type favoured by many of Fodens' traditional customers – and two articulated units.

The specification of the eight-wheeler included the 180 bhp Gardner 6LXB engine, an air assisted clutch with sintered iron clutch plate, a twelve-speed overdrive 5 DP gearbox, new 6½-ton rated front axles, and 19-ton capacity double drive rear bogie, a 12 in x 4 in channel section high tensile frame, an S.50 type hydraulically mounted all steel half cab, and a 23 ft 0 in wheelbase, which, under the existing regulations, would permit a gross vehicle weight of 26 tons.

The 38-ton tractor unit specification included the new 240 bhp Gardner 8LXB engine with the same clutch, gearbox and front axles as the new eight-wheeler, but with a new 10 ton capacity rear axle incorporating high speed double reduction hubs. The cab fitted to this model was the full width S.70 type hydraulically mounted, fibreglass unit.

The other tractor was fitted with a Cummins 270 bhp NT270B engine and the same clutch and twelve-speed overdrive gearbox as the other two show models. This vehicle specification included the same double drive 19-ton capacity bogie axle assembly as the eight-wheeler and a 6½ ton rated front axle. The cab fitted on the show model was the S.60 all metal full width type. This tractor unit, when operating with a suitable trailer equipped with a similar 19 ton capacity bogie axle, had a total gross vehicle weight capacity of 44½ tons.

Despite the keen interest shown in the new Foden models at the Earls Court Show and the obvious advantage to be gained in higher payloads and earning capacity, there was no immediate decision on the proposed regulation amendments and we were destined to wait

This 45-ton machinery transporter was introduced for the contractor industry, with Cummins six-cylinder engine and Dyson trailer, incorporating some of the units from the new heavy-duty range. It is seen carrying a Foden 40-ton dump truck.

until June 1972 after a series of meetings with other manufacturers and Ministry of Transport representatives before a compromise solution could be agreed upon and a modified series of Construction and Use Regulations issued.

Fortunately, during the interim period, Fodens had sufficient home market customers willing to take a chance on the higher payload capacity vehicles we were building becoming legally viable in the not too distant future, and also a continuing off-highway, contractors plant, and overseas vehicle market, to maintain the required production and sales levels. A new model introduced at this time for the contractors' plant customers was the 45 ton machinery transporter. It had a Cummins engine, Foden eight-speed gearbox, the 6½-ton front axle and a 16-ton double-reduction rear axle.

A completely new, dual purpose vehicle model coming off the drawing board in 1971 was the aptly named "Twin Load" six wheeler site vehicle. Designed to operate on the road at a gross vehicle weight of 24 tons with a payload of 13 tons, the vehicle specification was also suitable for off-road, site operation at a gross vehicle weight of 28 tons and a resultant maximum allowable payload of 17 tons.

To achieve an unladen weight which would allow a viable payload under normal road regulations and at the same time meet the operational needs of site conditions, the site vehicle specification needed careful consideration and was eventually finalised to include

The 6C6/28 six-wheel dual purpose site vehicle was intended to work either at 28 tons when on a site but could also operate on the road at 24 tons. The half cab is not visible in this view of a demonstrator.

129

The Bucyrus Erie crane, mounted on a specially adapted Foden low line carrier, made an impressive sight. The crane incorporated hydraulic jib extension and elevation and the carrier had hydraulically-operated outriggers, all designed to reduce the time needed to operate the crane.

a Cummins NHK 230 six-cylinder 204bhp engine, twelve-speed Foden gearbox and sintered iron clutch with air assisted gear change and clutch operation, power assisted steering, double drive rear bogie axles with double reduction hubs, a high tensile steel 12in x 4in x $^3/_8$in channel section main frame, a hydraulically mounted all steel half cab, an abrasion resistant steel body with cab protection canopy and automotic tail door operation and high speed, power return, tip gear. *Construction News* gave a highly favourable report on its performance and it soon became clear that the Sales Department had identified a new and profitable market.

A further addition to our comprehensive range of contractors' mobile equipment was finalised in 1971 when a prototype lowline carrier for a new range of Bucyrus Erie mobile cranes was completed and satisfactorily tested. The crane had been designed by Bucyrus Erie, the American parent company of Ruston Bucyrus, and in a series of meetings at Lincoln, we had to meet the engineering requirements of each company to obtain the order.

The principal new feature in the crane design was the hydraulic powered extending and elevating jib mechanism which, although reducing the time needed to set up and operate the crane, had the adverse effect of increasing the total transit weight. The retracted telescopic jib assembly was a massive structure which could only have been transported effectively on a low line carrier. This adaptation, which included hydraulically operated outriggers, was destined to be my last involvement with crane carrier design and was certainly the most impressive.

It was around the same period in 1971 that our Sales Department received an enquiry from the American Ryder Truck Rental organisation for a number of tractor units to operate in the United Kingdom. The required specification and the final decision on the make of vehicle purchased would be decided following a visit by one of the company's senior engineers, Mr. Tom Mannix, who, when he eventually came to Fodens, appeared to be a highly experienced senior automotive engineer interested in a quality specification with sound evidence of reliability and availability of

after sales service. He obviously had little time for the average sales presentation, but got along extremely well with my immediate chief, Jack Mills, and it came as no surprise when we received an initial order for the four-wheel tractor units required.

The tractor unit specification included a Cummins NK 250bhp engine, 17in diameter mechanically operated, sintered iron clutch, twelve-speed gearbox, high speed double reduction rear hubs, 11.00in x 22.5in tubeless tyres, an S.40 hydraulically mounted, all metal cab and full petroleum regulation equipment. The additional items fitted to meet the customer's specific requirements included a Kysor radiator shutter, a CAV high output alternator and higher capacity batteries, a 45 litre sump on the Cummins engine in lieu of the standard 31 litre type and higher capacity oil and air filters to extend servicing intervals. Pat Kennett of *Motor Transport* tested the Ryder tractor unit at the full operational gross vehicle weight of 32 tons on the road in Derbyshire and on the MIRA test track at Nuneaton and his subsequent report was highly favourable.

Later in the year at the Scottish Motor Show in Glasgow, one of the Ryder tractors was exhibited on the Foden Stand at Kelvin Hall, together with two other tractor units with widely varying specifications.

The Kaye Goodfellow tractor shown in the right foreground of the picture was a six-wheel 75 ton model with a Gardner 8LXB 245bhp engine, twelve-speed gearbox, a double drive rear bogie with selective double reduction hubs and an S.41 type all metal cab with extended front panel to house the high capacity radiator. The four-wheel tractor unit in the immediate foreground was a standard 32 tons gross vehicle weight model with the Gardner 6LXB 180bhp engine and fibreglass S.39 type cab. The special feature incorporated in this model was a new nine-speed gearbox with an input torque capacity of 1,000 lbs.ft. and a more simplified 'Range Change' gear selection arrangement than the standard twelve-speed gearbox "Splitter" change.

In the Demonstration Park at Kelvin Hall, Fodens exhibited yet another version of the four-wheel 32 tons gvw tractor unit, this

A significant event was the development of a special tractor unit specification to meet the requirements of Ryder Truck Rental, then establishing a hire operation of such vehicles in Britain. The choice was for 250bhp Cummins engines and features designed to ensure reliable operation under all conditions and extended service intervals. The vehicle is seen during a road test by *Motor Transport*.

The Foden stand at the Scottish Show of 1971 displayed three tractor units. Nearest the camera was a standard 32-ton gross weight model with Gardner 6LXB engine and the new nine-speed gearbox. On the right, the vehicle for Kaye Goodfellow was designed for operation at 75 tons gross on special heavy-duty work, with Gardner 8LXB engine. On the left, one of the Ryder Cummins-engined vehicles can be seen.

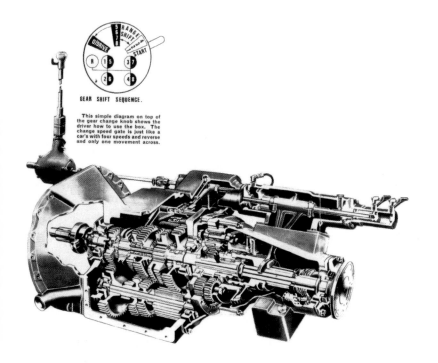

GEAR SHIFT SEQUENCE.

This simple diagram on top of the gear change knob shows the driver how to use the box. The change speed gate is just like a car's with four speeds and reverse and only one movement across.

The nine-speed gearbox was designed to give much easier operation than the twelve-speed unit, which required an expert driver to make effective use of its capabilities. Although similar to previous Foden multi-speed designs in using an epicyclic unit behind the main four-speed box, the method of use was much simpler. There was a small three-positon switch on the gear lever, gears 1, 2, 3 and 4 being obtained quite conventionally with the switch set to the right, then 5, 6, 7 and 8 with switch straight ahead, and finally 9, the overdrive, was obtained by switching to the left, this operating only from 8th gear. It allowed a typical 32-ton vehicle to cruise at 60mph and yet be capable of climbing 1 in 6 gradients; it could cope with 1,000 lb.ft input torque, enough for engines in the 300-350hp class. Particular attention was paid to easy gear-change action and, to quote the publicity material, "the lowest gears, up as far as third, can be flicked through without even double-declutching".

model with a Cummins NHK 205 engine, the new nine-speed gearbox, S.39 fibreglass cab, and a fully loaded flat bed trailer.

Despite the absence of an eight-wheeler on the stand at the Scottish Show, we were convinced from the regular meetings with the Ministry of Transport representatives at the SMMT that eventually the industry's proposals for increased six and eight-wheeler gross vehicle weights would be accepted and that such vehicles would regain their popularity with our customers. We continued to sell these types, now built to the proposed standards, but restricted to the existing limits until the new ones became legal.

There were also other significant managerial changes taking place at Fodens in the Spring of 1972, which were destined to have a marked effect on my own future responsibilities at the company. In March, 1972, Mr Edwin Twemlow and Mr Ted Foden, at that time joint Managing Directors of the company, decided to retire and were succeeded by Mr Bill Foden, Mr David Foden and Mr Patrick Twemlow. The newly appointed joint Managing Directors were assuming control at a significant point in the development of the UK commercial vehicle industry and were obviously determined to see that the company gained full advantage of the opportunities presented by the proposed changes to the Commercial Vehicle Construction and Use Regulations in the UK and a rapidly expanding road vehicle and contractors' plant market overseas.

An expansion and redevelopment programme was accordingly planned and, as part of this development, it was decided to form a new department entitled 'Technical and Administrative Sales', to be responsible for the interdepartment liaison between Design and Sales, together with the responsibility for Sales Literature, Publicity, Estimating and the sale of Original Equipment.

I was offered the position of Technical and Administrative Sales Manager to head this new Department and after very little hesitation I accepted the offer, selected the four or five key technical personnel I needed from the Drawing Office to add to the existing Sales staff and moved out of my old department to take on the new job in April, 1972.

Up to that point, I had spent a total period of 32 years in the Drawing Office, as Draughtsman, Section Leader, Chief Draughtsman and finally Design Department Manager, all of that time under the leadership and guidance of Jack Mills, now elevated to Engineering Executive Director.

My time in the Drawing Office, from 1940 to 1972, had covered a most interesting period of continuous development, as can be judged from the preceding chapters. As well as the successive goods and passenger models, there had been a major expansion into purposes far removed from road haulage. There had been a policy of continual scrutiny and improvement, maintaining the Foden tradition that "Nothing but the best is good enough" for its customers. On many occasions the use of new materials had been pioneered. It was now part of my new job to see that our prospective customers were made fully aware of these, and the many other advantages to be gained by operating a Foden vehicle.

In April 1972, at the time of my new appointment, the proposed changes to the Construction and Use Regulations were still awaiting final approval, but the eventual outcome appeared to be inevitable and, after a lean spell, orders, particularly for the 28 and 30 ton eight-wheelers were pouring into the Sales Department. At the same time, our field salesmen and dealers were selling their normal quota of various vehicle types from the wide range offered and it soon became evident that, with our existing maximum production

rate, delivery dates would be extended to unacceptable points if we allowed the situation to continue. Fodens' newly appointed Joint Managing Directors already had plans approved for a completely new vehicle unit storage and assembly plant capable of producing up to 80 vehicles per week on a single shift basis, but this facility would not be available for another eighteen months at least.

We, therefore, suggested the introduction of a rationalisation programme to cut out the low volume, low profit margin models from our sales and production schedules at least until the new high output assembly plant was commissioned, and, after some slight opposition, our new Department's initial proposals were approved and implemented.

Not all of Fodens' reorganisation and expansion programme at this time was confined to the Elworth Works. On 20th April 1972 Fodens opened their subsidiary company's new premises in Alberton, Johannesburg. The new facility, comprising offices and workshops employing a total of 80 personnel, gave clear indication of Fodens' intention to expand its already significant representation in South Africa.

Back in Elworth, with the Engineering Director in South Africa, I was deputising for him at an SMMT Sub Committee Meeting, at which it was hoped we could finalise the Commercial Vehicle Industry's submission to the Ministry of Transport on the proposed increase in allowable vehicle weight. It turned out that several representatives felt it necessary to refer back to their companies, and a further meeting was arranged for the following week. During the intervening week-end, with the help of Steve Oxley, the Seddon Atkinson representative at the meetings, I did a little 'lobbying' to check the level of agreement, finding it to be favourable. The subsequent meeting then approved the proposals for submission to the Ministry and we expected them to be incorporated in the regulation changes without further delay. In the event, there was a disappointing delay, until the end of June, but no retrospective changes to the vehicles already delivered were needed.

The effect of the number of axles and the axle spacing on the resultant allowable gross vehicle weight was illustrated in the Ministry of Transport explanatory publications, some of which are reproduced on the opposite page.

At Fodens, we issued more detailed information relating to our specific range of vehicles which took into consideration the specification and relative unladen weight of our individual models.

At this specific point in time in mid 1972, the future growth of the company looked to be assured. There had been a reduction in overall profitability in the 1971/72 financial year, but this could be attributed to the uncertainty relating to the effect of the proposed gross vehicle weight changes, particularly in relation to Fodens' traditional market leader, the eight-wheeler.

With a determined sales campaign and a well designed, reliable range of models, Fodens had improved its relative position in the tractor unit section of the market and, as evidence of this favourable trend, three other major truck rental fleet operators had joined Ryder Truck Rental by adding Foden units to their respective fleets.

Now, with an assured competitive future for our complete range of vehicles and a number of new design features to offer, we approached the 1972 Commercial Vehicle Show at Earls Court with justifiable confidence.

The 30 ton gross vehicle weight eight-wheeler quite naturally attracted a good deal of favourable attention on the stand, but the most notable exhibit, and the 'Star of the Show' in the opinion of

The diagrams issued by the Ministry of Transport to explain the effect of the revised regulations adopted in June 1972 included a range of weights permissible on each type of vehicle, dependent on the distances between axles and, in some cases, the ratings of the axles, arrived at in conjunction with highway engineers as well as the representatives of manufacturers, of which the author was one. Some of the axle spacings for low weight ratings were very rarely used, but the requirements for six- and eight-wheel rigid vehicles did now permit the construction of practical vehicles of up to 24-ton and 30-ton gross vehicle weights respectively, which was of particular importance to Foden as a major builder of vehicles of these types.

On the other hand, the maximum gross combination weight for any type of articulated vehicle remained at 32 tons at that stage, the key dimension becoming that between the rearmost tractor unit axle and the leading semi-trailer axle. Additional axles had the effect of slightly reducing this distance but did not take the maximum GVW beyond 32 tons. Overall, this time the changes tended to aid the eight- or six-wheel rigid vehicle rather than the articulated types.

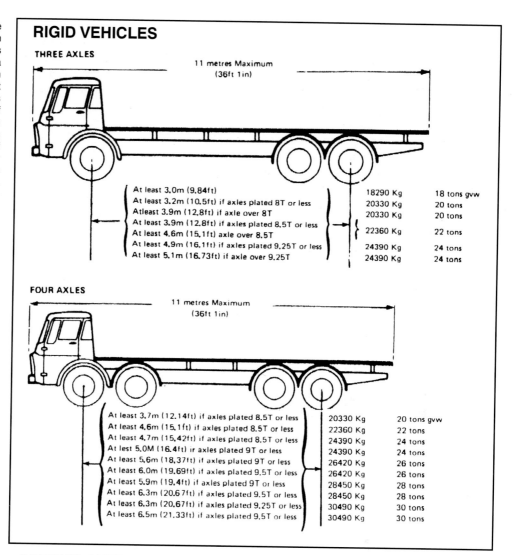

RIGID VEHICLES

THREE AXLES

11 metres Maximum (36ft 1in)

At least 3.0m (9.84ft)	18290 Kg — 18 tons gvw
At least 3.2m (10.5ft) if axles plated 8T or less	20330 Kg — 20 tons
Atleast 3.9m (12.8ft) if axle over 8T	20330 Kg — 20 tons
At least 3.9m (12.8ft) if axles plated 8.5T or less	22360 Kg — 22 tons
At least 4.6m (15.1ft) axle over 8.5T	
At least 4.9m (16.1ft) if axles plated 9.25T or less	24390 Kg — 24 tons
At least 5.1m (16.73ft) if axle over 9.25T	24390 Kg — 24 tons

FOUR AXLES

11 metres Maximum (36ft 1in)

At least 3.7m (12.14ft) if axles plated 8.5T or less	20330 Kg — 20 tons gvw
At least 4.6m (15.1ft) if axles plated 8.5T or less	22360 Kg — 22 tons
At least 4.7m (15.42ft) if axles plated 8.5T or less	24390 Kg — 24 tons
At lest 5.0M (16.4ft) ir axles plated 9T or less	24390 Kg — 24 tons
At least 5.6m (18.37ft) if axles plated 9T or less	26420 Kg — 26 tons
At least 6.0m (19.69ft) if axles plated 9.5T or less	26420 Kg — 26 tons
At least 5.9m (19.4ft) if axles plated 9T or less	28450 Kg — 28 tons
At least 6.3m (20.67ft) if axles plated 9.5T or less	28450 Kg — 28 tons
At least 6.3m (20.67ft) if axles plated 9.25T or less	30490 Kg — 30 tons
At least 6.5m (21.33ft) if axles plated 9.5T or less	30490 Kg — 30 tons

ARTICULATED VEHICLES

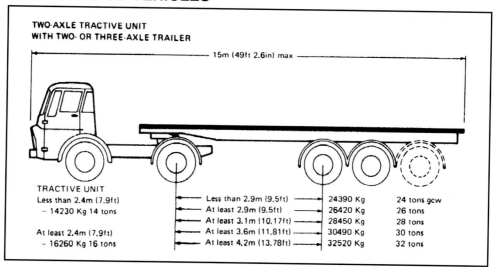

TWO-AXLE TRACTIVE UNIT WITH TWO- OR THREE-AXLE TRAILER

15m (49ft 2.6in) max

TRACTIVE UNIT
Less than 2.4m (7.9ft)
— 14230 Kg 14 tons

At least 2.4m (7.9ft)
— 16260 Kg 16 tons

Less than 2.9m (9.5ft)	24390 Kg	24 tons gcw
At least 2.9m (9.5ft)	26420 Kg	26 tons
At least 3.1m (10.17ft)	28450 Kg	28 tons
At least 3.6m (11.81ft)	30490 Kg	30 tons
At least 4.2m (13.78ft)	32520 Kg	32 tons

The data below relates to a three-axle tractive unit with two or three-axle trailer

TRACTIVE UNIT
Less than 3.0m (9.84ft)
— 18290 Kg 18 tons
At least 3.0m (9.84ft)
— 20330 Kg 20 tons
At least 3.8m (12.47ft)
— 22360 Kg 22 tons

At least 4.3m (14.1ft)
— 24390 Kg 24 tons

Less than 2.0m (6.56ft)	24390 Kg	24 tons gcw
At least 2.0m (6.56ft)	26420 Kg	26 tons
At least 2.3m (7.55ft)	28450 Kg	28 tons
At least 3.2m (10.5ft)	30490 Kg	30 tons
At least 4.0m (13.12ft)	32520 Kg	32 tons

Powerful backing for the Foden tractor unit came when Avis, Godfrey Davis and Hertz followed the example of Ryder by adding such vehicles to their fleets. By 1972, the use of hired vehicles in this size range had grown immensely. They were rated at 34 tons gross, even though this weight was beyond the limit in force in Britain.

the press and TV commentators was the newly designed S.80 type reinforced fibreglass tilt cab, fitted to the four-wheel, 32 ton gross vehicle weight tractor unit shown in the foreground of the Stand and easily identified by the 11 in diameter headlights.

The cab had been designed to meet the multiple demands of driver comfort, ease of control, and maximum access for service on our complete range of home and overseas road vehicles, although it was recognized that for some heavy duty and overseas applications the S.40 all steel cab option would have to be retained. The main cab shell was a one piece fibreglass moulding incorporating a reinforced steel bulkhead and floor, the underfloor reinforcing box sections extending rearward from the front suspension units. Four separate removable covers with special seals and clamps provided service access to the engine, air filter and batteries, and ensured that

the cab interior was completely insulated from engine heat and noise. Access for servicing with the S.80 cab was provided in three stages, lifting the front panel, tilting the radiator or tilting the whole cab.

All main driver's controls were power assisted, seating and steering wheel angle were adjustable and instrumentation was arranged with primary instruments and switchgear adjacent to the steering wheel. Sound and heat insulation had been provided by 2in thick ABS trimmed foam insulation material and in general, the driver's environment had been improved to a significant degree.

On Press Day at the Earls Court Show, the S.80 cab on the Foden stand was selected as the featured item for the BBC 2 'Wheelbase' programme by presenter Barrie Gill and thereby provided Fodens with a good deal of free publicity.

In addition to the new cab there were two other important new

The new S.80 fibreglass tilt cab introduced at the 1972 Show attracted much attention, including from TV, as seen opposite. It was beginning to become standard practice in advertising and elsewhere to identify model ranges by cab type. Great care was taken in its design to provide a much improved driving environment for the driver, with particular attention to noise and heat insulation, as well as ease of servicing. In addition to four removable internal panels with special seals, the T-shaped portion of the front panel hinged up to give access to such items as the windscreen washer reservoir. If required, removal of the radiator stay bolts allowed the radiator to tilt forward, giving access to the clutch linkage and other points, and for more extensive work the whole cab could be tilted to 45° by hydraulic linkage. The 11-in headlamps, adopted in place of the 7-in type, were a distinctive feature.

This overall view of the Foden stand at Earls Court in 1972 shows the three exhibits. In the centre can be seen the new S.80 cab on a four-wheel tractor unit with Rolls-Royce Eagle Mark II 220bhp engine and nine-speed gearbox. On the right, an eight-wheeler with S.40 steel cab, Gardner 6LXB 180bhp engine and the new eight-speed overdrive gearbox was displayed. On the left of the stand is a six-wheel tractor unit with Cummins NTK330 engine devloping 330bhp and driving through a nine-speed gearbox with torque converter, the latter another new feature. It had a sleeper version of the S.40 cab designated S.41. The chassis partly visible in the background was on the Ford stand, our neighbours at the Show that year.

transmission features introduced at the 1972 Earls Court Exhibition.

Firstly, there was a new eight-speed range shift gearbox with ratios from 0.77 to 1 overdrive down to 12.25 to 1 bottom, and an input torque limitation of 750 lbs ft (approximately 270hp). This was intended to replace the existing twelve-speed gearbox for suitable applications – the overall ratio spread was the same, and the range shift method of operation made it more suitable for a less skilled driver. The other new item was a Foden/Brockhouse torque convertor designed for use with the existing range of Foden gearboxes and engines in the 270 to 350bhp categories. This incorporated an electronically-controlled clutch to give a lock-up effect at speed, though the normal Foden clutch was retained. In normal use, the torque converter would allow smooth restart from rest without using the clutch, as well as having a useful torque ratio of 2 to 1, allowing use of the lower ratios in the gearbox to be much reduced.

The 1972 Show was the first major event in which our newly formed Technical and Administrative Sales Department had been involved, and I was pleased with the individual contributions made by members of the Department.

The final notable event of 1972 marked a complete change in the normal frequency of Fodens' shows and exhibitions. The Kelvin Hall Scottish Motor Traders Show alternated with SMMT Earls Court Show so that each event was biennial, but in 1972 it was considered that the Scottish operators should have an early opportunity to view the new Foden vehicles, and an additional show with explanatory presentations by senior Foden personnel was, therefore, arranged to take place at the Scottish MOTEC facility at Livingston, near Edinburgh in December.

The equipment and general layout of this new multi occupational

The FC20 dump truck of 20-ton capacity introduced in 1973 used newly-designed Foden axles as well as the combination of nine-speed gearbox with torque converter. The engine was a Cummins, this make being used on the whole range of four Foden dump trucks at that date, except that a Leyland unit was offered as an option on the 17-ton model.

training and education centre was well suited for our purpose and the Scottish and North of England customers were certainly much better informed on our latest products after our individual presentations than the average visitor to our stand at Earls Court.

The year 1972 had been dominated to some extent by the questionable competitive future of our six and eight-wheel range of home market road vehicles, a question now satisfactorily settled. During 1973, our attention was due to be concentrated more on our range of Contractors' Plant vehicles.

The new year saw the introduction of a completely new four-wheel dump truck with a payload capacity of 20 tons and a transmission specification selected to withstand the iniquities of unskilled or partially skilled drivers. Powered by a Cummins 250bhp engine, the nine-speed Foden gearbox was linked with the recently introduced Brockhouse torque convertor to provide a

A joint marketing arrangement with Faun of West Germany led to the sale of that concern's products in Britain as Foden-Faun. Under the agreement, Fodens Ltd became main service and spares agents.

semi-automatic transmission. The 10 ton rated front and 20 ton rated rear axles were both newly designed Foden units providing a total gross vehicle weight rating of 30 tons. The exhaust heated, high tensile, abrasion resistant steel body had a struck capacity of 14 cubic yards and, with high speed tip gear, could discharge its full load in less than 40 seconds.

During the same period the available range of dump trucks was extended further by reason of a joint marketing and service agreement arranged with FAUN of West Germany which, in practice, proved to be of more practical value to our Service Department than our Sales Organisation.

The final settlement of the Construction and Use Regulations which had such a favourable effect on the payload and operational profitability of the standard six and eight-wheeler range of road haulage vehicles had a similar effect on the payload capacity of another important sector of Fodens range of contractors' plant, the truck mounted concrete mixer.

The revised Construction and Use Regulations helped to boost demand for truck-mounted concrete mixers. This 6.5 cubic metre example was on a long-wheelbase six-wheel chassis but it had also beome possible to offer an 8 cubic metre design mounted on a 30-ton eight-wheel chassis.

The increased earning capacity of a significant proportion of Fodens' complete model range during 1972 had increased the backlog of orders to an unacceptable level, but fortunately this situation had been anticipated by Fodens' Directors who had sanctioned the commencement of the £3.8 million expansion programme, the major proportion of which was to be spent on a completely new vehicle assembly and feeder store facility on a site some distance away from the existing production and assembly shops.

The type of assembly plant selected was similar to a facility successfully operated by one of our competitors, Scania Vabis, which had a manufacturing philosophy very similar to our own, whereby a high proportion of the major vehicle units were manufactured in the factory rather than 'bought out' and therefore had a similar high labour force to total vehicle production ratio. Building commenced in December 1972 and nine months later, in August 1973, the first vehicles were assembled on the new line; a remarkable achievement by the builders, MHS International and our own Production Engineering staff.

Our sole contribution from the Technical Sales Department to this impressive enterprise was the formulation of a new vehicle ordering system which enabled a sales order for a specific vehicle type to automatically generate the necessary production orders for the parts needed to build that vehicle. In order to introduce this

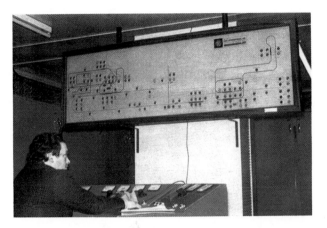

Said to be the most modern and sophisticated heavy vehicle assembly line in Europe, the new computer-controlled plant at Sandbach represented an investment of £3.8 million and came into operation in August 1973, doubling Foden's output capacity from 40 to 80 units per week, as well as being designed to build vehicles of any type in a range of gross weight capacity from 20 to 100 tons, and in any order. Above is seen the control panel, looking not unlike a modern railway signal system. It controlled a three-line overhead conveyer system of 279-metre length, part of which is seen on the right, feeding into a 69-metre moving floor system for the final stages of assembly. Subsidiary assembly lines linked to it fed in the various sub-assemblies. The system allowed for the varying frame length of each type, selecting appropriate components.

system, it was necessary to formulate a revised series of vehicle type identification codes which the computer would recognise and this did cause some initial familiarisation problems.

However, at a Sales Conference held in Jersey in March, 1973 we were able, with the aid of a cartoon type slide show presentation, to provide the assembled salesmen with the initial guidance needed, and there were no further problems when the new ordering system was activated. The new production facility was required primarily to substantially increase Fodens' vehicle production capacity and at the same time, reduce vehicle assembly costs and, quite apart from the need to actuate the new assembly line as soon as possible to meet the needs of Fodens' expanding home and overseas markets, there was an additional, as yet unconfirmed, requirement at this time, for a substantial number of military vehicles to be considered. In 1971 together with representatives from all the major British commercial vehicle manufacturers, we had attended a Ministry of Defence presentation at Chobham at which the Army's future transport needs were outlined in some detail. The following year, 1972, we duly received an enquiry for 37 six-wheeler tractor units for hauling tank transporter trailers and, after submitting our specification, drawings and quotation, we arranged a presentation at Chobham to outline Fodens' existing and planned manufacturing capabilities. The presentation was well received, the military personnel were obviously impressed with Fodens' extensive range of vehicles for various applications, but the eventual order was placed with Scammell. Early in 1973 we received a further enquiry for 927 General Service six and eight-wheel vehicles in the Low Mobility Category.

A high proportion of the vehicles required were virtually standard six and eight-wheel home market specification units, with the alternative requirement of the recently introduced Rolls Royce Eagle 200bhp Mark III engine, a new all steel cab design and the usual general service type steel body.

The remainder had a similar chassis specification, but required

fuel transportation tanks as an alternative to the general service bodies.

Apart from the new steel cab which was to be supplied by Coventry Motor Panels, it was not a difficult specification to meet and, following a comprehensive presentation to senior military transport personnel at the Army School of Transport at Bordon, we loaned an eight-wheeler demonstration vehicle to the military transport command in order to carry out their own road tests under service conditions in West Germany and the UK. During this evaluation period, many of our large road fleet customers were called upon to provide the Army Purchasing Authority with some comprehensive evidence of the reliability of their Foden vehicles.

The necessary positive evidence was successfully gathered from the operators selected by the Ministry during the summer of 1973 at a time when, had it been required, Fodens had ample evidence of their products' reliability in an environment much more taxing than any in Western Europe. The Dubai harbour project had been completed by Costain Civil Engineering some fifteen months ahead of schedule and the performance of the Rolls Royce powered Foden eight-wheel tipping vehicles in transporting the basic materials to build the harbour had been outstanding, as indicated by the operating data supplied by the customer.

Two additional factors normally detrimental to overall vehicle performance and service life not included in Costain's operating data were the facts that a high proportion of the total mileage covered was on the night shift and that almost all the drivers initially had no previous driving experience with a heavy commercial vehicle.

During the summer months of 1973 as the new vehicle assembly line neared completion and negotiations continued with the Ministry of Defence concerning our bid for the Low Mobility Military Vehicle Contracts, Fodens continued to design and build the usual multiple range of vehicle types which, at this time, included a bus chassis fleet, designed for short distance urban service in Nigeria.

The completion of Port Raschid, the Dubai harbour contract, in 1973, fifteen months ahead of schedule, was celebrated by all concerned. It was the largest man-made harbour in the Middle East, with fifteen deepwater berths having a minimum draught of 30ft. Many of the Foden vehicles used by Costain, the main contractor, had covered over 400,000 miles in shade temperatures of up to 125°F, among them the eight-wheel dump trucks with Rolls Royce Eagle engines – the records of one showed an average weekly mileage of 2,250, carrying an average payload of 22 tons over a 20-mile route at approximately 28mph and totalling 401,479 miles in a little over three years.

A rare instance of Foden chassis being used for passenger bodywork during the early 1970s arose when an order was received from Oshinowo Bus Company, Nigeria for models with Cummins NHK220 engines. The 50-seat two-doorway bodywork was by Strachans, of Hamble, near Southampton, and the chassis substantially to standard goods model specification of the period.

The chassis were designed for left hand drive and the specification included a Cummins NHK 220bhp engine, and Foden nine-speed gearbox. The bus bodies were designed and built by Strachans of Southampton, with seating capacity of 50.

With a full order book, a continuing demand for a wide range of home and overseas vehicles and the strong possibility of a substantial order from the Ministry of Defence in the near future, the future prospects looked very promising at this time, and when, in October, the Military vehicle order for almost 1,000 six and eight wheelers with a total value of ten million pounds was finally confirmed, the company's future prospects could hardly have been better.

In order to reassure our customers who had vehicles on order, that their promised delivery dates would not be seriously affected by the advent of the Military vehicle requirement, it was announced that MoD deliveries would not commence until 1974 and would be spaced out over period of 3½ years. It was also confirmed that no more than 15% of Fodens' total vehicle production capacity would be devoted to MOD vehicles at any one time

During the winter months, with the new assembly plant now fully operational, every possible effort was being made to increase the production rate and reduce the massive backlog of outstanding orders now substantially increased with the advent of the Military vehicle order.

Unfortunately, this was a period of unrest within British industry in general and with the basic elements of mining, power and dock workers in particular, the result of this industrial unrest was very soon made evident at Sandbach where material shortages increased and vehicles were cancelled during the early months of 1974. Fodens re-equipped manufacturing plant and new assembly facility, capable of producing over 100 vehicles per week, were restricted by shortages to less than half that total.

Prior to the advent of these multiple problems, Fodens had decided to introduce a new range of vehicles designed for the export market in general, and the European market in particular. This 'Universal' range as it was entitled, was due to be introduced at the Amsterdam Commercial Vehicle Exhibition in February 1974 and despite the growing supply problems at Sandbach, it was decided to go ahead as planned.

The first models in the new range were the 26 tonne rigid six-wheeler and a four-wheel tractor unit for operation at 38 tonnes gross vehicle weight. Both vehicles were fitted with a Cummins 14-litre 323bhp turbo-charged engine and the eight-speed range change Foden gearbox, although the Fuller RT 9509A 9 speed gearbox was later offered as an alternative in the 38 tonne tractor unit.

For me, the Amsterdam Exhibition provided a first opportunity to compare our Foden vehicle specifications with the whole of the European competition. At the London Show and even at the Belgian Exhibition in Brussels, only a proportion of the opposition was on view. From 1974 through to the earlier days of my retirement in the 1980s, I have rarely missed an opportunity to view the latest

Foden's new 'Universal' range intended for European export markets was planned for introduction at the Amsterdam Show of February 1974 and despite delays in production due to the enforced three-day week of the fuel crisis which had seriously affected British industry in general, it was decided to go ahead. One of the first two models was this 26-tonne left-hand-drive six-wheeler with Cummins 14-litre engine, seen here as a three-way tipper.

The Foden name appeared on a rally car in 1974, as a result of being a sponsor for the British Army team in the UDT World Cup Rally. The car was a special version of the Morris Marina coupe, with Rover V8 engine, driven by a team of two Majors. It is seen here in Spain, before an axle casing failure eventually brought the effort to an end.

products of the European commercial vehicle industry at the bienniel exhibition in Amsterdam. In 1974, Fodens' intention was to market the various vehicle types in the planned 'Universal' range with the aid of the West German specialist vehicle builder, FAUN, a combination, which under normal trading conditions would probably have been quite successful. Unfortunately at Fodens, material and component suppliers were becoming inconsistent, some vehicle orders had been cancelled and the production rate was accordingly reduced for what was hoped would be a temporary period.

Meanwhile, there were more modest activities back at home. The Foden Recreation Club, of which I was Chairman, had been in need of a new sports pavilion for some time, and having persuaded the local brewery, Greenall Whitley, to provide a loan for part of the cost, this had been achieved. It was named the Twemlow Sports Pavilion after our famous Managing Director and Chief Engineer, Edward Twemlow, who in time had turned out for the Drawing Office Cricket Team but was more widely known as a former Motor Cycle Tourist Trophy winner.

Another more significant involvement at this time was our sponsorship of the British Army team in the 1974 United Dominions Trust World Cup Car Rally scheduled to start at Wembley Stadium at noon on 5th May and then south through France, Spain, Morocco, Algeria and Nigeria down to Kano with the return journey through Tunisia, Italy, Greece, Turkey, Yugoslavia and Austria to reach the Football Stadium in Munich before 12 noon on 25th May. The Army team drivers were Major John Hemsley and

Major John Skinner, both highly experienced in the skills of rallying. The car was a Morris Marina Coupe fitted with a 3.5 litre V8 engine and a four speed gearbox with overdrive. The car was reasonably well placed on the return leg of the circuit in North Africa, when the rear axle casing failed and they were unfortunately unable to continue and therefore out of the rally. The major proportion of the sponsorship finance was raised from our suppliers during a busy afternoon on the telephone and in the light of the overall financial situation at the time, they were most generous.

Fodens' military vehicle involvement had extended during the year to the design and production of a 6 x 6 Medium Mobility category vehicle intended primarily to haul the FH70 gun, but also designed to house the gun crew and carry several pallets of ammunition which could be handled by a centrally mounted Atlas hydraulic crane.

The initial MoD vehicle requirement for the Low Mobility category of six and eight-wheel road vehicles had been similarly divided into specific operational categories whilst retaining the

The large military contracts were split into several sub-divisions, the Foden vehicles being classified by the Army into Low Mobility, which could be interpreted as intended for use on normal loads, or Medium Mobility, which were 6x6 types capable of negotiating cross-country terrain. The former were largely eight-wheelers, but included this 24-ton 6x4 tanker. Other vehicles in these groups are shown on succeeding pages.

The Foden 6x6 vehicles in the Army's Medium Mobility category were supplied in various versions, three of which are seen here. The specification included a Rolls Royce 305bhp engine, Kirkstall 8-ton front-drive axle, transfer gearbox, and 20-ton two-spring rear bogie assembly. A third differential was supplied on the forward axle and a differential lock on all axles.

The top illustration shows the tractor version as originally designed to tow the FH70 gun, house the gun crew and handle the ammunition pallets.

In the centre picture, the vehicle is shown as a 6x6 recovery vehicle, with crew compartment, winch, crane attachment and towing gear.

In the bottom picture, the vehicle is shown as a 6x6 gun limber, to transport and load ammunition pallets, etc.

The 'Low Mobility' version of the Foden 30-ton 8x4 military vehicles included the general cargo, tipper and tanker models seen in these illustrations.

The Foden stand at the 1974 Commercial Motor Show at Earls Court reflected considerable changes in emphasis in policy arising from changing circumstances and a different market emphasis. Nearest the camera is an example of the 'Universal' range of models aimed at the new market created by the formation of the European Economic Community, in this case a two-axle left-hand-drive tractor unit, model 24A 038 C33 09, designed to operate at up to 38 tons gross train weight – Foden's designations were becoming longer than ever. It had a Cummins NTC335 engine developing 335bhp at 2,100rpm, Lipe Rollway twin-plate clutch, Fuller nine-speed gearbox and Rubery Owen brakes.

In the centre was a rather more traditional 30-ton-gross eight-wheeler, model 08R 030 G18 08, with Gardner 6LXB engine, sintered iron clutch, eight-speed overdrive gearbox and S.80 cab. Three more Gardner-engined eight-wheelers were to be found on bodybuilders' stands.

On the right, representing the big Army contracts in hand, was a model 46R 026 R30 09 gun tractor of 6x6 formation with 305bhp Rolls-Royce Eagle engine, nine-speed gearbox and Kirkstall axles. Another military eight-wheeler was among the demonstration vehicles.

necessary high level of major unit interchangeability required for servicing purposes.

The vehicles involved include a 24 ton 6 x 4 tanker, and 30 ton 8 x 4 general cargo, end tipper and tanker models. At this time in 1974, the Low Mobility types of MoD vehicles were in production at Fodens but, owing to a delay in availability of the S90 type steel cab, which at one time resulted in a visit to the Saviem factory at Caen to consider the fitment of their steel cab, some of the initial deliveries of the 8 x 4 vehicles were fitted with fibreglass cabs.

At the 1974 Commercial Vehicle Show, which at the time was expected to be the last to be held at Earls Court before the scheduled move to the NEC and certainly the first to be held since our admission to the European Economic Community, the emphasis on the Foden Stand was concentrated on the 'Universal' range of vehicles introduced earlier in the year at the Amsterdam Exhibition and the Low and Medium Mobility vehicles currently in production for the Ministry of Defence, the one exception being a 30 ton gross vehicle weight eight-wheeler with a Gardner 6LXB 180bhp engine, eight-speed overdrive gearbox and S.80 fibreglass cab.

The relative specifications of the Foden vehicles exhibited at the 1974 Show gave a clear indication of Fodens' revised policy to utilise a much higher proportion of bought-out units and components in all of the vehicle range and to confine future additions to the model range to almost completely proprietary unit specifications. Market surveys had apparently indicated that the company's likely growth would be in this area, and in any event, the working capital requirements for this production method were undoubtedly more favourable, if not essential, at this point in time, when Fodens' financial resources appeared to be strictly limited. In fact, when

Fodens further financial requirements were made known to their Bankers some time later, the application was turned down, leaving the company with little alternative other than an application to the Department of Industry which at that time was empowered by the Labour Government in office to arrange financial assistance from a contingency fund to companies in temporary need. After an initial investigation by the Department's representatives, temporary financial assistance was arranged, and a more substantial long term arrangement was discussed which would depend on the results of an investigation into the company's affairs by Price Waterhouse.

For some weeks each department's financial viability was investigated in detail and the eventual overall report having proved satisfactory, it was expected that a long term Government Aid Package would follow in due course.

The Foden management, however, decided that the Price Waterhouse report was sufficiently encouraging to formulate a financial support package from private rather than Government investment and by the first quarter of 1974 had successfully raised over three million pounds of additional investment by means of a Rights Issue of cumulative preference shares.

In the company's Financial Report for the year ending March 29th, 1975 the worst appeared to be over and a recovery well under way, but it was obvious from our own observations and contacts that this would depend very much on our future profitable sales in areas other than the home market road haulage industry which remained depressed. A considerable proportion of Fodens' manufacturing capacity would, of course, be engaged in the completion of the Low Mobility Vehicle Contract which would extend over a period of three to four years and had now been

The military contracts played a major part in Foden's activities in the mid-1970s. The numbers involved had increased to 1,021 vehicles, including 148 eight-wheel tankers, this example having a 5,000-gallon fuel-carrying tank body.

extended to include 703 eight wheel cargo vehicles, 70 eight wheel tippers, 100 six-wheel tankers and 148 eight-wheel tankers.

Up to this time, only 23 of the multi-purpose 6 x 6 Medium Mobility vehicles had been ordered, but joint-user trials with the FH 70 gun were in progress at Hohne in West Germany with Britain, West Germany and Italy participating, each with their own tractor and limber, and it was hoped that other overseas military equipment buyers witnessing the trials might well choose the British vehicle to haul their guns.

Although the road haulage element of Fodens' UK market remained depressed, there was continued activity in the business of contractors' plant, both in the home and overseas sales areas and, not for the first time, Fodens' wide range of products, often condemned as a detrimental factor, again enabled a significant level of production to be maintained.

Among home-market examples, in the Kelmac limestone quarry at Carnforth the Foden/Faun sales team now had Faun K.30 loaders operating with a mixed fleet of Foden six-wheel and Faun four-wheel dump trucks. After Stothert and Pitt and Ransome and Rapier, Winget were probably the last of the traditional UK concrete mixer manufacturers to use a Foden chassis in their demonstration fleet. The short wheelbase eight-wheeler would be rated at 26 tons gross vehicle weight and the mixer capacity 8 cubic yards.

Overseas, and particularly in the Middle East, there was a good deal of construction work in progress with both UK and foreign public works contractors employing Foden vehicles.

Eight Foden dump trucks were operating on a continuous shift basis by Costain to prepare the site for an oil storage depot, an operation which involved raising the complete site area by as much as 6 metres.

Another customer, Joannou and Paraskevaides, had a fleet of FC 17 dump trucks engaged in a road building contract to connect the Eastern side of the United Arab Emirates with the Gulf of Oman, a road of considerable strategic importance due for completion in July 1975. The Foden dumpers were working 10 hour shifts for 6 days of the week.

By far the most valuable overseas order for this period involved the supply of 40 vehicles together with appropriate spares to Marples Ridgway of Bath for a 300km road building project in South Eastern Iran along the border with Pakistan. The total value of the order to Fodens totalled £800,000 and involved the secondment of Foden field service personnel for driver training and service instruction.

The vehicles in Fodens' overseas range were built to a high quality, heavy duty specification, designed to withstand the frequent problems of difficult operational conditions and indifferent driving standards, and we were therefore surprised to learn that a heavy duty six-wheel tipping vehicle, exported as a demonstration vehicle to a newly appointed associate dealership in Canada had experienced a gearbox failure at a very low mileage. It was accordingly decided that I should visit the company, not only to check the specific failure reported, but also to report on the actual long term feasibility of Foden vehicle sales in Canada. British Leyland had at one time set up an organisation to market an overseas version of the Leyland Comet in Montreal and this venture had not been successful. My contact in Montreal was a former Leyland (Canada) executive, now retired, who would provide assistance and advice.

Together with a former Drawing Office colleague, Richard Meadows, and the ex Leyland executive, we visited the company's fabrication factory at Alma, a small town on the Saquenay River, near Lake St. John, checked his gearbox problem, and ordered the replacement parts required and then proceeded, with the Canadian company's assistance, to check the heavy commercial vehicle market situation in the area.

Not surprisingly, the heavy commercial vehicle fleets we viewed in the area consisted almost exclusively of the products of the huge American automotive manufacturing plants located in the northern states, all with subsidiary assembly facilities in Canada. I had made prior arrangements with the British service manager of the Kenworth assembly plant in Montreal to visit the facility and gain some specific knowledge of the competition that any Foden dealer would need to compete with.

The conclusion we reached, after checking other aspects of the proposed activity in Canada, was that a full scale attempt to open up a complete new market, even in the Eastern Provinces of Canada, would be financially impractical, and that the only possible activity with any chance of success would be confined to the Foden dump truck range with the dealer utilising his comprehensive timber trailer fabrication workshops to build the chassis frames, bodies and cabs and with Fodens supplying the remainder of the specification in kit form in a similar manner to our practice with other overseas market areas. Our proposals, although approved in principle, were never fully implemented, owing to the intrusion of other, more significant financial factors.

As had happened on previous similar occasions, orders for contractors' plant helped to compensate for depressed demand from Fodens' traditional road haulage customers. The Middle East continued to be an important market, and the well-known British contractors, Marples Ridgway, with headquarters in Bath, ordered 40 vehicles for a road-building contract in Iran, along the border with Pakistan – one of the six-wheel end-tippers is seen here being loaded.

The final important event of 1975 was the Scottish Motor Traders Show at Kelvin Hall, Glasgow in November. The Show marked the introduction point for yet another new cab type, the S.83.

In addition to announcing the introduction of the new S.83 cab, which was fitted to the two tractor units on the Foden stand, a new marketing and service organisation entitled 'Foden Scotland', structured to provide better and more concentrated sales and service to Scottish operators, was also introduced at the Show.

The Scottish operators, to my mind, deserved a degree of special treatment if for no other reason than their loyalty to the specific manufacturer of their choice. Through good years and bad, the majority of our customers in Scotland appeared to retain their preference for the Foden product, and whether this was due to the attention received from the dealer or the parent company mattered little in the final analysis.

The S.83 cab, which in effect was marketed as the S.83 range of models, was introduced at the Scottish Show held at Kelvin Hall in November 1975. This was a fibreglass unit, derived from the S.80 but with improvements to allow more rapid tilting, now possible in under one-and-a-half minutes. An automatic locking device with warning light on the instrument panel was also included and other changes included a more robust air intake and modifications to the accelerator and power steering to reduce effort and unwanted reaction respectively. Two tractor units with this cab were on the stand and an eight-wheeler with another cab variation, S.80 Mark II, was also displayed.

9 SERVICE & THE FINAL YEARS

A short time after my return from Scotland, I was offered a completely new position at Fodens, with rather better long term prospects than my existing responsibility as Technical Sales Manager. Fodens' Service Manager, Ted Gibson, had decided to retire and, after the management had advertised the position and interviewed several unsuccessful applicants, I was informed that if I was interested in the change of responsibility, then the appointment would be confirmed immediately. The proposal involved working with the existing Service Manager in a joint capacity until his retirement and then taking on the responsibility for the Service and Spares organisation, initially as Service Manager and eventually as Executive Director – Service.

I was sure that I could work effectively with the current Service Manager, Ted Gibson, I was confident that I could handle the job, particularly after a period of direct guidance from him, and I knew that Technical Sales, the department I was leaving, would be in the competent hands of my former assistant, Brian Lomas.

The first major sales event of the new year was the Amsterdam Show in early February where the Foden 'Universal' Range exhibits were shown on the stand of our newly appointed dealer, 'Geveke'.

The Foden stand at the 1976 RAI Show in Amsterdam.

On the stand, we had an eight-wheel 8 cubic metre concrete mixer chassis powered by a Rolls Royce engine and a three-axle rigid six-wheeler fitted with Cummins engine. Both vehicles featured the new S.90 all steel cab. On the demonstration park we had a further eight-wheel 'Universal' model in chassis and cab form, again with the S.90 cab.

I visited the show in my new capacity as Joint General Service Manager, with David Roberts, our European Regional Service Manager and we seized the opportunity to visit the new dealer's service facility and several customers in the area around Amsterdam. I very soon realised that in my new job, I was back in the basic engineering sector of the business, dealing with the realities of today rather than the possibilities of tomorrow and I knew then that I was going to enjoy my new responsibilities.

The Service Department management structure at that time was divided into the two basic elements of Technical and Field Service, and Spares and Service administration, and it was in the Technical and Field Service sector that I considered I could be of most immediate assistance.

However, at this time in the spring of 1976, the company had far more serious problems to face than any I would encounter in the Service Department.

In April 1976, despite achieving a record turnover exceeding £28 million, the company reported a loss of £1 million. It was explained at the AGM that the loss was entirely due to loan interest and repayments, and that there had been a net trading profit of £358,000, but nevertheless, the financial future of the Company at the time appeared to be questionable. The UK heavy goods vehicle market continued to be generally depressed at this time, although Fodens continued to obtain a reasonable share of the few multiple vehicle orders placed.

Freightliners placed an order for 40 tractor units fitted with Rolls Royce 265 turbocharged engines and S80 Mark II cabs. The vehicles were scheduled to operate in London and Scotland.

There were other multiple home market orders from Wills, the tobacco concern, of Bristol, Bridgewater Transport of Manchester, Penllyne Haulage from South Wales and Geest Transportation of Spalding, but the more consistent high value vehicle business

Typical of home-market orders in 1976 was that for Freightliners.

Sometimes the area of operation for new Foden vehicles was far removed from the owners' headquarters, as with some eight-wheel end-tippers with Cummins engines for Laing of Borehamwood, Herts, which were for operation in Poland, creating a new area of responsibility for the Service Department.

continued to be generated from Fodens' overseas market areas, in particular, the Middle East. Marples Ridgway's road construction contract in south eastern Iran continued to develop and generate additional vehicle requirements and the latest vehicles to be delivered were six-wheelers, some with Hiab loading cranes and others with Hands-England hydraulic rotary drills.

In order to carry out driver instruction and supervise maintenance on this type of overseas project, Fodens' Service Department was required to provide personnel who were not only skilled in their job, but also had the ability to instruct others, very often with the additional complication of a language barrier.

We had three overseas regional service areas, each controlled by a regional service manager who, in turn, was responsible to the overseas field service manager at Sandbach. Service personnel on temporary overseas assignments were directly responsible to the relative regional managers for the duration of the specific job and then reverted to control by the Repair Shop Superintendent at Sandbach between assignments. It was not a perfect arrangement by any means, but it was practical and sufficiently flexible to allow

the Service personnel a reasonable opportunity to apply for the more lucrative overseas assignments.

Although Fodens' overseas market areas were generally clearly defined, there were occasional exceptions. Some left hand drive end tippers fitted with Cummins 335bhp engines, S.40 steel cabs and Edbro bodies were ordered by John Laing of Borehamwood for operation in Poland, presenting our European Field Service Department with another area of responsibility. During the same period, Gloster Saro were completing a number of the twin steer six wheel tractor unit and independent trailer airfield refuellers with Foden 12 and 24 ton axles and Foden/Brockhouse torque convertor transmission, and five of the same model had been sold to Sonotrack for operation in Algeria, creating another assignment for our Field Service staff.

In September of 1976 there were two notable events in my diary. The first was the appointment of my former chief in the Drawing Office, Jack Mills, as a full Director of the company, a measure well deserved and overdue, and the other was the 28th Commercial Vehicle Show, this time confirmed as the last to be held at Earls Court.

Fodens' exhibits on the Stand included the new six-wheel Universal model with S.90 steel cab and 290 bhp Cummins engine, previously shown at the RAI exhibition in Amsterdam, and rated at 36 tons gross vehicle weight as an independent vehicle, and from 65 to 100 tons gross train weight with a suitable articulated trailer. There was also a four-wheeler tractor unit with a Cummins 250bhp engine and S83 fibreglass cab. The eight-wheeler on the Stand was fitted with a Rolls Royce 265L engine and had a redesigned double front axle steering arrangement which attracted a good deal of attention.

The exhibit which created the most interest, however, was the new rear engine bus underframe which marked Fodens' return to the passenger vehicle business. Built with the co-operation of the design team at the Northern Counties Motor and Engineering Co Ltd of Wigan, the underframe assembly was suitable for most integral bus body designs and incorporated a Gardner 180bhp engine, and Allison MT 640 transmission.

At Earls Court, the complete passenger vehicle with double deck body was exhibited on Northern Counties' stand and generated a good deal of interest. Prior to the delivery of the prototype

The final Commercial Vehicle Show to be held at Earls Court took place in September 1976, and Foden exhibited, as had been the case on every occasion since the Show was first held there in 1937. Nearest the camera in this view is the Universal six-wheel model with Cummins 290bhp engine, with a four-wheel tractor unit to the left and another home-market goods model on the right. Partly visible in the background is the Foden NC bus underframe illustrated overleaf.

The Foden NC underframe was designed for incorporation into a double-deck bus in the manner which had become common practice by the mid-1970s, when even what were nominally double-deck chassis depended quite strongly on the metal-framed body to provide overall rigidity in the complete vehicle. The general concept, with Gardner 6LXB engine mounted transversely at the rear, conformed to standard up-to-date practice in this market at the time, but the use of Allison automatic transmission struck a more distinctive note. The prototype is seen here outside the experimental department – the rear panels, like the wheel arch framing, were designed to be built into the bodywork.

The prototype Foden NC double-decker is seen after completion with bodywork by Northern Counties, registered LNA 258P but before receiving its fleet number 1435 in the fleet of Greater Manchester Passenger Transport Executive (better known as GMT) after delivery in April 1976. Co-operation in its design had involved both the bodybuilder and GMT, the latter having begun in 1974, when its title had been changed from South East Lancashire and North East Cheshire PTE, generally shortened to SELNEC, and engineering design matters there largely guided by Harry Taylor, SELNEC's Group Development Engineer. The 1976 Show exhibit was the second vehicle to be delivered on an extended evaluation trial basis to GMT, No.1436 (PNE 358R).

underframe to the body builder, we carried out a thorough check of the complete unit in the Service Department to ensure service access to all major units for maintenance and replacement, a procedure which did highlight one or two critical areas which were rectified immediately. One of the first passenger vehicle operators to show a positive interest in the new vehicle was GMT, which agreed to take two vehicles for extensive evaluation trials.

On October 1st, 1976 Fodens' Service Department introduced a UK Service Directory for general distribution. The new publication indicated the specific location, normal services available, opening times, emergency services available and all relevant phone numbers for all of the 50 Service facilities operative at that time in the UK. At the same time, all Foden spares and service depots in the UK and overseas were to be more clearly identified by the new yellow and blue Foden logo.

In November, the Public Works Exhibition, hitherto held at Olympia, was relocated at the new National Exhibition Centre at Birmingham. Fodens utilised the Public Works Exhibition to exhibit their extensive range of heavy contractors' plant vehicles, but, at

the 1976 show the vehicle which attracted the most attention and subsequent sales was a lightweight six-wheel model with a Gardner 6LXB engine, Foden eight-speed gearbox, Eaton double drive rear bogie, taperleaf springs and the S.39 fibreglass cab.

The vehicle specification was selected to achieve an unladen weight of 6 tons and thereby provide an allowance of 18 tons for either a tipping body and payload or a hydraulic drive concrete mixer and payload, this latter category considered to be the more likely application. The vehicle was produced with two alternative wheelbases, but it was the short wheelbase mixer or tipper model which proved the more popular and fully achieved the sales objectives.

In the new year there were changes. In January 1977, after 48 years with the company, 24 years of this period as Service Manager and twelve years in the Experimental Department, my colleague Ted Gibson, retired. He was obviously a man of considerable ability and vast experience, but his principal assets to my mind were his ability to operate effectively under pressure and his ability to pass on the benefit of his own knowledge and experience to others.

Costain was the original main contractor for the initial Dubai Harbour Project which had been completed well within the stipulated period and had now been awarded an additional contract together with Taylor Woodrow, for an extension to the harbour facility and the provision of a dry dock.

By far the most comprehensive overseas requirement during the early months of 1977 was an order from the Fairclough-Al Medani consortium for a fleet of standardised Foden vehicles to operate on strategically located airfield construction sites around Ha-il in Northern Saudi Arabia.

The vehicles were required for various operations on and around the sites and also for transporting equipment and materials from the coast at Jeddah. All the vehicles were of a six-wheel double drive configuration with S90 steel cabs, and Cummins 290 bhp engines, but the applications were varied.

An earlier generation of Foden was recalled by the lightweight six-wheel model with Gardner 6LXB engine and S.39 fibreglass cab produced to meet a 6-ton chassis and cab unladen weight for concrete mixer applications. This was also Foden's first appearance at the National Exhibition Centre, Birmingham, when the Public Works Exhibition was held there in November 1976.

However, shortly after his retirement I was appointed to the position of Executive Director – Service and there were changes to be made in the structure of the Department which, when completed, would allow me the opportunity to spend some time with Field Service, particularly in the overseas area of our Service operations, where effective field service, whether provided by Fodens or the customer, was essential.

In the home market, it was reported that sales of tractor units and six wheelers, in particular, the lightweight 'Sixer', were maintaining satisfactory levels, but the eight wheeler market was not so consistent. Overseas, and more specifically, in the Middle East, the sales perspective was vastly different. An order worth £800,000 was received from Foster Yeoman for six-wheel 35 tonne tippers for operation in a Saudi Arabian limestone quarry.

There was also a requirement from a joint British consortium of Costain and Taylor Woodrow for twenty AC 29/60 Cummins powered six-wheel tractor units and twin axle tipping trailers for use on the Dubai port extension project.

A fleet of Foden vehicles using a standardised double-drive six-wheel chassis with Cummins 290bhp engine and S.90 steel cab was supplied in 1977 to the Fairclough-Al Medani consortium for use in connection with airfield sites in Saudi Arabia. This example had an Edbro tipper body but others were used with fuel tanker, cement mixer, breakdown crane and personnel carrier bodywork as well as with semi-trailers for bulk cement, low-loading and conventional semi-trailers for various purposes as well as on long-haul journeys to Jeddah.

In addition, there were two tractor unit applications for alternative end tipping and low loader trailers. It was an effective way of reducing the quantity and value of the spares stock and simplified the service problems. It was an effective way of reducing the quantity and value of the spares stock and simplified the service problems. On the other hand a common unit or part failure quickly

Orders from the Middle East were healthier than from the home market in 1977. An order for 20 AC29/60 six-wheel tractor units and trailers came jointly from Costain and Taylor Woodrow for use on an extension to the Dubai port, in the initial construction of which Foden had played a key role. They could carry 48 tons of aggregate, having a gross weight of 63 tons and a top speed of 55mph.

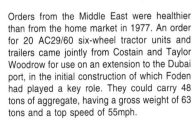

became a fleet failure and the Foden field service personnel who were later allocated to this operation were advised accordingly.

In March 1977, a convoy of five Foden vehicles left Elworth on a long journey to Munich to take part in the Bauma European Transport and Contractors' Plant Exhibition. The vehicles in the Foden convoy included a 36 ton six-wheel end tipper, an MoD 6 x 6 gun tractor and 4 x 4 recovery vehicle, an S.90 rigid eight-wheeler, an FC 35A six-wheel dumper on a low loader and finally an eight-wheeler equipped with a snowplough and gritter body made by Atkinsons of Clitheroe. Hitching a lift on the first part of the journey to London, was Phil Reed of *Motor Transport* who praised the standard of our drivers in a subsequent article.

On the Brenner Pass some 25km. south of Innsbruck the eight-wheeler snowplough was able to demonstrate its efficiency by clearing 4ft-high snowdrifts. All the vehicles completed the journey without further incident and the Foden Stand looked quite impressive.

During the Show orders were received from France, Tunisia, Greece and Turkey, but unfortunately none from Germany where the commercial vehicle market was apparently depressed. On the other hand there were signs that in the UK, commercial vehicle sales were improving and this impression was endorsed by customer comments at the Harrogate Tipper Convention and the principal dealers' shows traditionally held at that time of the year. This increasing confidence in the UK commercial vehicle industry in general, and Fodens' future prospects in particular, was further endorsed at this time by a series of take-over bids from Rolls Royce, which at the same time was attempting to obtain a controlling interest in Gardners.

The subsequent Financial Report for the year ending 2nd April 1977 showed the increasing confidence in Fodens' future to be well founded. Group turnover totalled a massive £47,150,000 with group trading profit £3,139,000 and group profit before tax £1,738,000.

To further endorse Fodens' future prospects it was announced that the Company had outstanding orders for military vehicles with a total value of £10 million and further confirmed requirements for construction vehicles to the total value of £2 million. 23% of the company's total output during the 1976/77 financial year had been exported and a further 13% had been devoted to military contracts. In the Service Department, in order to meet the field service requirements of Fodens' rapidly increasing overseas vehicle fleets, it was decided to increase substantially the pool of field service engineers available on call from our Sandbach service workshops. Personnel selected for this work were experienced mechanics, well able to handle all aspects of Foden vehicle servicing and with a sound knowledge of spares stocking and procurement procedures. The selected personnel were controlled by area service managers, who, in turn were responsible to the Overseas Field Service Manager based at Sandbach.

In a similar manner, the UK Field Service Manager based at Sandbach controlled area service managers located in various parts of the country, usually in close proximity to a Foden Service Depot. To receive and distribute service information with our own and our distributors spares and field service personnel, we held quarterly meetings at Sandbach which were also attended by representatives of the Design Department. In this capacity I had attended Service meetings on a regular basis for many years, so, in effect, I was still playing for the same team, but in a different position.

Part of the famous Fodens band under conductor James Scott at the Jubilee Gala day in June 1977. At that point, the company's prospects looked bright and *Foden News* conveyed this in its pages.

The total number of Foden vehicles in service, both in UK and overseas areas, had increased significantly in the mid-'seventies despite our occasional production problems and the demand for spares and service repairs had increased accordingly. A good deal of time and money had been spent on our Production organisation, but very little on the Service Spares and Repair facilities at Sandbach. In mid 1977 work was started to extend and improve this situation by the addition of new buildings to accommodate an extension to the Repair Shop, a new customer engineering section and additional space for parts storage, packing and despatch. The new buildings were scheduled for completion by February, 1978.

In the last week of June 1977, to mark the Jubilee Year, we held a Sports and Gala Day at the Company sports ground in Sandbach. Over 1,500 people attended the celebration and enjoyed a varied programme of entertainment and competitive events which continued for some four or five hours.

The Sports and Gala Day was so obviously enjoyed by all who attended that it was subsequently decided to make it an annual event. At this point in time, Fodens' immediate prospects appeared to be reassuring and full of future promise as this extract from a

The Fleetmaster, introduced in November 1977, was readily identifiable by its single-piece curved windscreen. It was designed for 32-ton gross operation and had a choice of Cummins or Rolls-Royce engines.

Champion trucks that meet the challenge
The Truckmasters

Fleetmaster
Foden Truckmasters pack a punch with style

Haulmaster
Foden Truckmasters can go the distance comfortably

Super Haulmaster
Foden Truckmasters built to take all the punishment

Foden News publication of the period illustrates:- 'Our future is bright. We have the right vehicles, we have the right people and our difficult periods involving loss-making military contracts, high interest rates and high new model costs are hopefully behind us. We are on the road again and Fodens will still be a name to be proud of in a future of continuing success'. This was strong stuff and somewhat over-emphasised, but there was no doubt that the future for Fodens looked more reassuring at this time. In the Service Department a new parts information system based on microfilm produced from computer output tape had been devised and was due to become operative from December 1st, 1977.

The Haulmaster, intended mainly for the home market, had a two-piece windscreen using flat glass. This example was for William Gaskell, of Upholland, near Wigan.

The information provided from the system included customer details, the original vehicle building instructions, which listed all units incorporated in the vehicle specification, together with the date the vehicle was built and entered service. A secondary data base provided details of the individual parts used in each element of the vehicle specification. Terminals were being installed at all Foden Depots and Distributors' Service Stores and arrangements were made to update this data on a continuous basis.

On 3rd November 1977 at the Europa Hotel in London, a new range of Foden tractor units was introduced to the press and selected customers. Code named 'Fleetmaster' and 'Haulmaster' there were significant variations in the vehicle specifications to suit the particular market for which it was intended.

Vehicles in the Fleetmaster range, easily identified by the curved single piece windscreen, were built primarily from well proven proprietary components so that the production rate could be varied without resultant problems in our own unit manufacturing areas. The Fleetmaster tractor unit, designed for both UK and

The heavy-duty range intended for export markets had now become the Super Haulmaster and, as it happened, a repeat order for 60 was received from Bahattin Goren for work on an irrigation scheme in Iraq on the day the new overall range was announced – two of the six-wheel end tippers are seen before dispatch.

international haulage up to gross vehicle weights of 38 tonnes, was offered with either day or sleeper composite cab, Cummins or Rolls Royce 290 bhp engines, Fuller nine-speed RT 9509A gearboxes and Rockwell hypoid bevel drive rear axles.

The Haulmaster range, identified by the flat two piece windscreen and initially, large diameter single headlights, was intended primarily for the UK market. The specification included an all-steel tilt cab somewhat similar in shape to that of the Fleetmaster tractor, but the specified engine was a Cummins 250 bhp unit with Foden eight-speed gearbox and Foden front and rear axles.

The Super Haulmaster vehicles, built either as rigid six-wheelers or as three-axle tractor units were normally produced in left-hand drive form with Cummins 290bhp engines and S.90 day or sleeper steel cabs, Foden eight-speed gearbox and Foden axles. As a tractor unit with a suitable twin axle articulated trailer the total maximum gross train weight was increased to 63.97 tons. On the same day as the Foden 'Truckmasters' were introduced in London, a further order for 60 Super Haulmasters was received from the Turkish Bahattin Goren organisation in the Middle East which had been awarded an irrigation scheme contract by the government of Iraq.

As part of the contract, the Service Department was required to allocate three experienced personnel to train the customer's maintenance personnel and drivers.

After the customary Scottish Show, at which I noted that Scottish hauliers tended to favour the Haulmaster range, retaining their faith in the Foden transmission, I began a comprehensive visit to the Middle East, together with David Roberts, Overseas Service Manager and Tony Twemlow, my successor as Design Department Manager. I had visited our dealers and customers in Greece, Cyprus

The full extent of the overloading of the front axle of this Super Haulmaster six-wheeler was not immediately obvious, save that it appeared to be riding low, but a change of use to carrying high-density rock with no tailgate on the body had forced the front springs into permanent contact with the frame, the rubber bump stops having disintegrated. Continued operation in such a state could well have resulted in frame failures and similar lack of normal operational standards accounted for reported service problems of kinds not encountered in Britain.

and the Emirates in November and December of 1976 and had identified a number of problems at that time which, although prevalent under overseas conditions, were not noted in the UK.

We now had Super Haulmaster vehicles entering service in the Middle East with specifications more suited to the more demanding operational conditions and with sufficiently high mileage to judge their performance objectively. Our market area had also expanded to include the Kingdom of Saudi Arabia with a completely different working environment from that of the Emirates.

We arrived in Dhahran on the East coast of Saudi Arabia to finalise service and spares agreements with our newly appointed dealers for the Kingdom and then visited the operating sites of our existing customers, Foster Yeoman, Algosaibi Engineering and Fairclough.

Foster Yeoman was the first company to operate the new Super Haulmaster six-wheelers in Saudi Arabia, 21 of these 38 ton six-

Lack of a high level of after-sales service and instruction of operating staff results in rapid deterioration. Here a six-wheel double-drive tractor unit with S.40 cab has come to the end of the road.

wheelers and tippers having been delivered early in 1977 to deliver crushed limestone to various sites on the coast from a quarry located some 10 kilometers inland.

The customer found it more profitable to convert some of the tippers to tractor units for general delivery work and use the remainder in the quarry as dumpers to deliver stone from the quarry face to the crusher. Body tailgates had been removed, a body designed for crushed limestone was now overloaded with high density rock with the payload centre of gravity so far forward that the front springs were in contact with the underside of the frame.

The problems experienced by Algosaibi Engineering with its fleet of twelve tractor units and two dumpers that had been supplied in August 1976 were mainly due to poor driving and inadequate maintenance. Al Medani-Fairclough, our largest operator in South Arabia, with a total of 57 Super Haulmasters benefited from field service engineering based where they operated. Most of the troubles experienced related to very poor road conditions and agreement to grade the roads and add a tarmac surface helped matters considerably. The Fairclough operation was a prime example of the necessary manufacture/customer working relationship to ensure a successful operation under difficult overseas conditions.

Without this high level of after sales service and instruction, heavy commercial vehicles in this working environment, however well built, very soon deteriorate to the condition illustrated here.

Many of the original fleet of eight-wheel dump trucks supplied to Costain for the initial Dubai Harbour contract were still in use, some having covered well over half a million miles. Their dependability had done much to encourage other operators in the area to buy Foden vehicles.

The visit continued with calls to Riyadh and Dubai, the Foden vehicle population in the Emirates having increased during 1977. The Dubai Transport and Balfour Beatty consortium, DUCTO was about to take delivery of 35 more Super Haulmasters.

Among other users, Gulf Rock had been experiencing clutch failures which were accepted as being due to poor driving standards, and an Allison automatic gearbox was being fitted to one vehicle. Similar experience had led Costain Taylor Woodrow to convert two tractor units and two eight-wheel tippers with Allison type 750 gearboxes though its Dubai Harbour extension contract was almost complete.

Costain, the original Foden customer in Dubai, was still operating a high proportion of the original Rolls-Royce-powered eight-wheel dump trucks. A propeller-shaft and centre-bearing modification had been found beneficial but a great deal of the credit for their successful operation was due to the local Costain Transport Director, Jim Reagan, and his Engineering Manager, Allan Cook.

During the five years spent in the Service Department from 1975 to 1980 under the Foden regime, I spent as much time as possible with the field service engineers both at home and overseas. Service reports, however detailed and well presented, are rarely as informative or as satisfying to the customer as a face-to-face discussion on his reported problems and an explanation of the corrective measures to be taken. In addition, it was possible during a comprehensive tour similar to the series of Middle Eastern customer visits recently completed, to form an impression of the future sales prospects in the area.

Two of the special 'Dockspotter' tractors built for South African Railways and sent out in kit form from Sandbach for assembly in the Foden plant in Johannesburg are seen at Capetown harbour.

In the early months of 1978 our future prospects in the Emirates and Saudi Arabia remained promising with a fleet of Haulmaster six-wheel concrete mixers ordered for Unimix of Dubai and encouraging reports of sales prospects from our regional sales manager in Saudi Arabia. The situation elsewhere in the world was patchy. At home, our Scottish dealer, Beaverbank of Edinburgh, secured an order for 33 four-wheel tractor units for Transfleet Truck Rental.

In South Africa, the market was depressed, but the Johannesburg Plant tendered for the manufacture of specialised tractor units for use by South African Railways and secured a contract – they were called 'Dockspotter', being designed for shunting duty in and around the docks.

In Australia and New Zealand, competition from America and

Japanese makers was growing, but a special launch of the Fleetmaster range was arranged with demonstrations by the respective dealers.

However, at the Annual General Meeting in April, Fodens appeared to be competing effectively with their many competitors. With a £47,150,000 group turnover, trading profit totalled £3,828,000, a significant increase on the previous year. The value of Fodens' export business had increased by almost £3 million to a total of £13,155,000 and represented 27% of our total UK production. In addition, vehicles to the value of approximately £3 million had been supplied to the Ministry of Defence.

The only serious negative sign noted in the final quarter of the financial year was a depression in the UK construction industry, a sector which, in previous low points in the road haulage business, had provided Fodens with a considerable measure of support.

Demonstrating that the Army's description 'Medium Mobility' was a considerable understatement, this 6x6 gun tractor, with FH70 field gun on tow, was of the type of which a further 116 were ordered in June 1978.

Fodens' European vehicle sales were again limited; indeed since the early activity in Holland and the later sale of crane carriers and other items of contractors' plant, our activities in Europe, despite the more recent Foden/Faun marketing arrangement, had proved to be less effective than anticipated.

In June, just prior to the opening of the British Army Equipment Exhibition at Aldershot, it was announced that Fodens had secured a further order, valued at £5 million, for 116 Medium Mobility 6 x 6 Gun Tractors and Limbers, bringing the total value of Military vehicle orders received since 1973 to a staggering £23m.

However, in the Service Department at this time, following a flying visit to West Germany, we were modifying the transmission driveline on a fleet of eight-wheel MoD low mobility vehicles at Ashchurch by fitting a centre bearing assembly and two shorter propshafts. It was a sharp reminder that warranty claim costs on extensive fleets are completely proportional, and inevitably costly.

At that time, the importers, led by Volvo, had grown to take about 15% of the total eight- and six-wheel market (2,000 and 3,000 respectively on 1977 UK registrations) but an anticipated increase in registrations would allow Foden to maintain required production levels. The overseas market was also subject to competition but was generating enough business to remain viable.

We were in discussions with Caterpillar on the service and spares implications of fitting their engines in Foden chassis, a measure due to be announced at the forthcoming Commercial Vehicle Show.

The first ever combined Motor and Commercial Vehicle Show was held at the National Exhibition Centre from the 20th to 29th

The Foden stand at the first NEC Motor Show, October 1978, with a Super Haulmaster six-wheeler nearest the camera. This picture was taken before the Show was open to the public, but the combination of the commercial vehicle show with the car show brought immense crowds, few of whom were seriously interested in our products, and the upper floor area had the virtue of allowing us to talk to our friends and potential customers in relative peace.

A new development for the Haulmaster eight-wheeler was the latest fibreglass and aluminium alloy tilt cab which revived the designation S.10, as had been used for the standard Foden cab of the late 1930s and early post-war era.

October 1978. The eventual total attendance exceeded 908,000 and fell just short of a world record. The attendance figures showed a 68% increase above the combined total of the previous separate shows held in 1976 and had Fodens' stand designers not incorporated a substantial upper floor area in their layout, it would have been impossible to carry out our normal business on the stand. A new and purposeful feature on the stand was a display of genuine Foden spare parts, with the emphasis on *genuine*.

The one completely new Foden feature introduced at this time was a completely redesigned, Foden built, composite material cab, designated the S.10. The cab was manufactured entirely at Fodens using a combination of fibreglass and alloy as the basic materials and it was designed to be utilised across the whole range of 4, 6 and eight-wheeler vehicles in day cab and sleeper configuration.

In October 1978 a new Marketing Department was created to incorporate the responsibilities of market research, product planning and publicity. Up to this time product planning at Fodens had been generated primarily by legislative change and customer demand, and in turn, customer demand had often been activated by technical innovation.

One of the fleet of 66 snowplough/gritter vehicles developed jointly with Atkinsons of Clitheroe supplied to the Department of Transport is seen in use in the winter of 1978-9, soon after delivery. There were six- and eight-wheel versions, all with the Rolls-Royce 265 Mark III engine, Foden eight- or nine-speed gearbox and double-drive rear bogie with differential lock. The six-wheelers had the S.85 fibreglass cab as shown here, but the eight-wheelers had the steel S.90 cab, similar to the MoD pattern, these vehicles being derived from the military 'Low Mobility' specification.

In time for the winter of 1978, Fodens handed over a special vehicle type in this latter category to the Chief Mechanical Engineer of the Department of Transport at that time, Mr. John Furness. The vehicle was a special six-wheel snowplough-gritter, one of a range developed jointly by Fodens and Atkinsons of Clitheroe and the Ministry had placed an initial order for 66 units.

In January 1979 there were changes to the top management structure which resulted in Sales, Service, Production, Engineering, Personnel and Marketing all reporting to a single Managing Director. With this company structure change it was obviously easier to settle inter-departmental problems and attain joint objectives. One of the problems we identified in the Service Department at that time was a significant reduction in overseas spares requirements, particularly in the Middle East area. On 13th February, accompanied by Dennis Hockenhull, at that time our overseas field service manager, I set off on another tour of our dealers and customers in this former highly lucrative area. In Dubai, our dealer, GENAVCO, reported a significant reduction in activity in the Trucial States for the very simple reason that all the main construction projects in the area were either completed or nearing completion. In the Dubai rock quarry, the source of all the raw material used in the harbour and dry dock project, and normally the scene of considerable heavy vehicle activity, there was a single six-wheel Foden dumper operating.

The situation with other operators in the Dubai area was not optimistic. Most of our customers in the area had been engaged directly or indirectly in the major construction projects of the harbour and dry dock in Dubai and the new port and industrial complex at Jebal Ali. With the completion of these projects the requirement for heavy road vehicles in the area diminished accordingly and a sizeable proportion of the transport requirements remaining could be handled effectively by the surviving units from the large main contractors' fleets. At the same time, to maintain these vehicles in operational condition there was a continuing demand for Foden spares and it was in this area that we concentrated our efforts with our local dealer and customers.

In Saudi Arabia, the situation was somewhat different, with expanded Sales and Service facilities welcomed by Foden operators. We returned via Cyprus having been informed that some of the four-wheel dump trucks which had become surplus in Dubai had been shipped thence, where their owners had an ongoing contract. However, it transpired that some of them had been damaged in transit.

Apparently the vehicles had been shipped in a shallow draught landing craft and during a rough spell in the Eastern Mediterranean some of the tippers had lost their moorings in the hold and broken free. The list of replacement parts required was extensive and would please both our Spares Department and the dealer, even if bad news for their owners.

From our interviews with major transport operators in the Middle Eastern areas visited, together with our dealers' reports and our own observations, it was clear that, apart from Saudi Arabia, there was little chance of a vehicle sales recovery in the foreseeable future. On the other hand there was still a profitable spares sales market in all the areas visited and in the Service Department we would continue to make the most of these opportunities.

There was no evidence of problems in the home sales market in the spring of 1979, and at the RHA "Tipcon" Exhibition in Harrogate, Fodens again had new automotive engineering features to introduce.

Exhibited on the Foden stand were six S.10 cab eight-wheel Haulmasters, five for individual customers and the sixth, a Foden demonstration vehicle fitted with a newly introduced rubber rear bogie suspension system in place of the standard 'taperlite' rear spring suspension.

The Foden/Rydewell FR20 rubber suspension system was offered as an option on Haulmaster eight-wheelers and used solid beams in place of the normal steel springs but with heavy-duty rubber suspension units at their centres. Rubber-mounted A-frames were used to locate the upper part of the axle casings.

Alfred Hymas Ltd, of Burton Leonard, near Harrogate, was an example of the traditional style of Foden operator, with a fleet of eight-wheelers. In this line-up of Haulmaster models, most of vehicles were fitted with Gardner engines, the most recent examples having the 6LXC type, though a Rolls-Royce engine was fitted to the vehicle third from the right. The rubber suspension bogie was taken up by this and a number of other fleets.

The type of rubber suspension which became standard for the six-wheelers was of Foden design, type FF20, differing from the FR20 in the positioning of the rubber suspension units at the centre of the suspension beams.

The 'site vehicle' was a heavy-duty 24-ton six-wheeler having some of the characteristics of the dump truck but nearer to a road-going vehicle in terms of chassis design. This one was operated by the National Coal Board's Western area, based at Stoke-on-Trent.

The FR 20 type rubber suspension system was a derivative of the Rydewell design featured earlier in this narrative while on field tests with one of our customers in Dubai. It was manufactured under licence by Fodens and incorporated two parallel main beams located at their centres under the chassis by rubber mounting units. The axles were located at each end of the beams by spheralastik bushes in a similar manner to our solid beam suspension on the crane carrier chassis.

The necessary upper links of the suspension system from the frame centre bogie crossmember to each worm gear housing were provided by two rubber mounted 'A' frames.

The Foden/Rydewell rubber suspension system was offered as an option on the eight-wheeler Haulmasters, but on the six-wheel vehicle a Foden rubber suspension system, code-named FF20, was fitted as standard. On this arrangement, the rubber suspension units are mounted in pairs between the main chassis frame and the two suspension beams, which in turn, are attached at each end to the axles. The upper links in the axle suspension system are provided by 'A' frames in a similar manner to the FR20.

The eight-wheeler Haulmaster was now offered with a choice of alternative Rolls Royce 265L or 290L engines, but Alfred Hymas retained his faith in the Gardner, now the 6LXC. Other customers' eight-wheelers on show at Harrogate included Eccles Aizlewood, Heavy Transport, Steetley and Hinckleys.

The Harrogate Show was highly successful, particularly in relation to six and eight-wheeler sales and this event was followed some time later with the SED Contractors' Plant Show at Hatfield where Fodens again had new engineering developments to introduce; on this occasion, the addition of a completely new four-wheeler to the dump truck range, and significant changes to the existing six-wheel dumper specifications.

The 'four-wheeler' specification included a Cummins 280 bhp engine, an Allison fully automatic gearbox and a rubber suspension system on both front and rear axles. The cab had been redesigned to improve insulation from engine heat and noise, and at the same time access for engine servicing had been extended by the fitment of a tilt radiator. High speed tip gear ensured the rapid discharge of the 14 cubic yard capacity body and improved power steering added to manoeuvrability and driver acceptance. The high specification and performance standards achieved by the new dumper design won the *Contract Journal* Silver Award for innovation and good design, and provided an encouraging start to the Show.

The new FC20A four-wheel dump truck introduced in the spring of 1979 had a Cummins 280bhp engine, Allison automatic transmission and rubber suspension for both axles. It had a payload capacity of 20 short tons (40,000 lbs).

The degree to which the manufacture of heavy goods vehicles had become one of international competition was underlined by the other participants in one of a series of comparative trials of tractive units in the 38-ton class organised by *Truck* magazine in conjunction with five European trade journals and conducted in Belgium. As well as the Foden Fleetmaster seen on the right, there were entries from MAN, Ford, Scania and Berliet, lined up in that order in the views above.

The 27 and 35 ton six-wheel dump trucks fitted with Cummins engines and Allison automatic transmissions continued in production with rubber suspension introduced on the rear axle of the FC 27 A and on both front and rear axles of the FC 35 A.

Also continuing in production were the six-wheel 24 ton site vehicle and the FC 17 four-wheel dumper with Cummins 250bhp engine and conventional spring suspension on both front and rear axles. With this range of dump trucks Fodens had a model to suit all of the various contractors' requirements identified at that time and, from the interest evident at the Show, were anticipating a significant number of firm orders.

In May 1979 Fodens entered a Cummins powered Fleetmaster tractor unit in a competitive exercise organised by *Truck* magazine and some five other continental road transport publications to compare the relative performance of various vehicle manufacturers' products operating at 38 tons gross vehicle weight around a specially selected route in Belgium. The Foden Fleetmaster specification included a Cummins E.290 engine, Foden nine-speed gearbox and a dual berth S95 sleeper cab.

Over a period of time, no fewer than 30 European tractor units had been submitted for this specific series of road tests and on this occasion the contestants were Foden, Scania, Berliet, MAN and Ford. In sole charge of the Foden entry was my youngest son, Stuart, at that time a technician in the Experimental Department at Fodens.

The overall performance and fuel economy of the Foden vehicle during the comprehensive Eurotest programme was outstanding, as indicated by the subsequent *Truck* comments:-

'The Euro-Spec. Foden Fleetmaster was in every way an impressive tool, far removed from the traditional Fodens of recent and not-so-recent years. It looked great, went well, and created a powerful impression on the opposition, who had thought that

My son Stuart was in charge of the Foden entry and is seen here, left, with Pat Kennett, founder and editor of *Truck* magazine, repositioning a trailer king pin during the tests.

A display of Foden military vehicles at the Biggin Hill Air Fair in 1979 included a recovery vehicle based on the 6x6 Medium Mobility model with equipment by Eka Recovery Vehicles Ltd, seen here demonstrating a suspended tow, using one of the military eight-wheelers.

the UK independents were not capable of matching Continental standards. The Fleetmaster showed them how wrong they could be.

The Foden Fleetmaster is a potential market winner, fuel economy second only to MAN, an excellent road performance, handling and stability of a very high order. Based on the tests of previous years, we would not have expected a Foden to have done quite so well in this sort of company.'

The test results indicated quite clearly that the Foden product, both in design and performance, was capable of competing, and in many respects beating, the continental opposition and inevitably raised queries in relation to our failure to make any significant impression on the European market.

In addition to the Fleetmaster and Haulmaster development programme, Fodens continued to design and manufacture derivatives of both the 8 x 4 Low Mobility and 6 x 6 Medium Mobility military vehicles for both military and civilian applications, and, at the Biggin Hill Air Fair in mid 1979, examples of each type were on display. The original contract for 1200 Low Mobility eight-wheel vehicles for the Ministry of Defence had now been completed, but alternative applications of the same chassis had been designed and were on display at the Fair.

The Ampliroll hydraulically operated loading device made by Hearncrest Boughton of Amersham had many civilian applications and was a well developed and reliable product. The military applications, particularly the tank loading operation was impressive.

There were also alternative applications on display for the Foden 6 x 6 Medium Mobility vehicle. The superstructure supplied by Eka Recovery Vehicles Ltd., included a 25 tonne main winch, a lifting jib capable of a supported tow up to 8 tonnes and a Fairey 10 tonne front winch. Also on display were examples of the snowplough-gritter on 6 x 4 and 8 x 4 Low Mobility chassis, and for the first time the Cummins engine range was offered as an alternative to Rolls Royce in the military vehicles, a measure intended to widen the potential sales area for this type of vehicle.

In the Service Department our long awaited new Parts Warehouse and computer controlled spares ordering, stocking and despatch systems were almost completed; we had recently held a satisfactory two day service meeting and the works holiday period was due to commence in a week's time. It was Thursday, August 19th, 1979 and all senior executives were called into the Board Room for a special meeting.

The purpose of the meeting was soon revealed. Although the Group turnover for the 1978/79 financial year was very little less than the previous year at £51 million, the small trading profit for the year was not sufficient to cover high interest payments, and a significant Group loss was inevitable.

The main reasons given for the deficit were a reduction in exports to the Middle East, a shortfall in the sales of specialised vehicles in the UK and the high cost of developing and introducing the new Haulmaster and Fleetmaster range with the new S.10 Foden cab. With the new range now in production, it was considered that the future looked far more promising, and, with this reassurance in mind, we moved into the holiday period. In the Service Department, of course, there was no complete shut-down in the holiday periods. The Repair Shop and the Spares Departments had sufficient staff on duty to handle customers' needs, both in the UK and overseas. Also during the holiday period, the opportunity was taken to move the new Parts Warehouse and Control System towards completion.

In order to improve spares availability and spares order processing time all fast moving and standard usage parts had been relocated in a computer controlled store, newly equipped to house 25,000 types of components in varying quantities related to their rate of demand. Computer terminals were located in specific order processing, stock control and despatch areas.

Ordering procedures, stock control and overall spares availability

An unusual form of eight-wheel tractor unit was built in South Africa, with single steering axle but an additional air-suspended axle in front of the double-drive bogie.

were improved to a considerable extent by the new facility, which, in view of the importance and high profitability resulting from spares sales, was long overdue. Unlike vehicle sales which fluctuate in relation to changing legislation, varying operating contracts, modified designs and resultant customer demands, spares sales in the UK for high quality vehicle fleets remain fairly constant.

Overseas, due to operating conditions and lower maintenance standards, there is a certain degree of fluctuation, but overall the demand is predictable, profitable and deserving of a very high priority. Spares shortages lose customers and encourage pirate suppliers. Now we had a modern, efficient spares distribution system well able to compare with the best.

Fodens' overseas sales activities at this time continued to decline in many areas, but in South Africa there were signs of continued activity particularly in the super heavy haulage market.

The four-axle tractor illustrated had a 75,000kg gross load capacity, with Cummins NTA400 engine, Fuller gearbox, single Foden 8-ton front axle and 32-ton four-spring bogie with non-steered air-suspension axle fitted ahead of it. It was one of six for heavy haulage operators in that country. Locally-built cabs were standard on Foden vehicles assembled in South Africa and were well-designed and built.

In October 1979 Fodens participated in a *Motor Transport* sponsored test involving two identical Rolls Royce 290 powered Foden tractor units, one operating at 32 tons GVW with a twin axle trailer, the other at 40 tons GVW with a triple axle trailer.

The object of the exercise was to prove that higher payloads could be carried more economically and with equal safety with little change to the vehicle combination and a considerable benefit in ton miles per gallon. The comparison test, or 'Project Octane' as it was termed by *Motor Transport* provided a good deal of favourable publicity for the two participating Foden tractor units.

The next important event on the calendar was the Scottish Motor Traders Show at the Kelvin Hall, Glasgow in November. The Foden Stand presentation was most impressive with new models and new major features on show, and must have been reassuring to Foden dealers, customers and employees who visited the Exhibition. The new model exhibited was a lightweight six-wheel Haulmaster powered by an equally new Cummins V 504, 207bhp 'Big Cam' engine and fitted with a Fuller R 609 gearbox,

The Scottish Show held at Kelvin Hall, Glasgow, in November 1979 was destined to be the last national exhibition in which Fodens Ltd exhibited, setting a high standard of modern commercial vehicle sales presentation. The new model exhibited was a lightweight six-wheel Haulmaster with the Cummins VT504 'Big Cam' engine, also new and developing 207bhp, Fuller gearbox and S.10 cab. Its low unladen weight of 6100kg allowed a 17.5 ton payload.

Foden F type rubber suspension and S.10 cab. With an allowable payload of 17½ tons and with a two year, 100,000 mile engine warranty, the new model marked Fodens' entry into the lighter, higher volume, sector of the six-wheeler market.

A good deal of publicity was concentrated on the S.10 single bunk sleeper cab which, when fitted to the standard four wheel tractor, would accommodate a 40ft container trailer within the 15 metre legal overall length limit. The Scottish operators demonstrated their faith in Fodens' future during the show period with substantial new vehicle orders, not only for the new vehicle types exhibited, but also for the more traditional eight-wheeler rigid vehicle range.

Back at Sandbach, the outlook was less favourable with continual pressure to increase spares sales, a restriction on non-

Seven Foden NC double-deckers were supplied to six major fleets for evaluation, having entered service in 1976-78, and collectively they had built up over 400,000 miles by the end of 1979. In addition to the original two with Greater Manchester PTE, there were single vehicles with the South Yorkshire, West Midlands and West Yorkshire PTEs, Derby Corporation and Potteries Motor Traction Co Ltd, the last-mentioned acting on behalf of the National Bus Company, of which it was a subsidiary in those days. Northern Counties supplied the bodywork in most cases, though South Yorkshire specified East Lancashire, and all had Gardner 6LXB engines. The West Yorkshire PTE vehicle is seen here.

Although favourable reports on their performance were received, and the Ferodo retarder tried on one of the Greater Manchester buses had been adopted as standard, uncertainties surrounding Foden's future doubtless discouraged the placing of bulk orders. In addition, although the major fleets were still adding large numbers of new buses to their fleets at that time, there was a growing air of caution on the adoption of new bus designs as the national economic situation began to become tighter.

chargeable warranty work and, worst of all, redundancies. Early in January the company half year financial results showed little improvement and the battle for survival continued.

At that stage, there were hopeful signs that one of the six passenger transport operators currently evaluating the Foden NC passenger vehicle would eventually place a substantial order.

In the spring of 1980 Fodens again exhibited at the RHA Harrogate Tipcon show with an impressive range of six and eight-wheel vehicles equipped with all the latest features including rubber suspension, S.10 cabs and a comprehensive choice of Gardner, Cummins and Rolls Royce engines. The Glasgow and Harrogate exhibitions were destined to be the last under Foden management and the 1979 Kelvin Hall Show in particular was a fine example of a modern commercial vehicles sales presentation.

Yet, despite our well equipped modern production plant and a fine competitive range of vehicles, we were finding it increasingly difficult to survive. In the Service Department we were busy with rubber suspension conversions, contract servicing, and a spares sales promotion plan for dealers and customers both home and overseas. We had no way of knowing what the future had in store for the company, but whatever the eventual outcome, there would

Despite the threat to the Company's future, sales in some sectors remained encouraging. Concerns specialising in waste disposal were growing in importance, and Wimpey had set up an organistion specialising in such work, placing a number of 24-ton Gardner-engined refuse collection six-wheelers in service.

be a continuing requirement for spares and service for existing Foden vehicle fleets in the UK and overseas for a considerable time, and to some extent this factor provided a degree of reassurance.

UK vehicle sales appeared to be maintaining a reasonable level at this time with orders from our traditional customers in the bulk haulage, contractors' plant, and refuse collection industries.

Refuse collection was an industry where Fodens' continuous association with operators and equipment suppliers over a considerable period had established a working relationship which almost guaranteed a significant amount of continuous business. In fact, another leading waste disposal company in the London area, A. & J. Bull of Mitcham, had a number of 30 ton eight-wheel refuse container vehicles in progress during the same period as the Wimpey order illustrated.

Despite this continued activity in the UK sales area, which was by no means confined to bulk haulage, contractors' plant and the refuse industry; plus the increased sales of spares and labour in the

Service Department and a significant overall reduction in non-productive personnel in all departments, it was clear that Fodens' financial problems were becoming even more serious month by month and that a complete company failure was almost inevitable. I received confirmation of this critical situation and the inevitable consequences during the evening of Friday, July 11th 1980. Together with two senior Directors, I was attending a retirement presentation evening at Fodens' Recreation Club.

Each retiring employee received an award of his own choice up to an allowable maximum value and I recall that one super fit ex-bandsman had selected a racing bike as his retirement award and consequently received a standing ovation. Such a rejection of decline seemed especially touching in the circumstances.

Later in the evening I learned from my colleagues that Fodens' financial position had become critical and that the company would probably be in the hands of the receivers during the following week. On Monday this information was confirmed and during the week the representatives of the appointed receiver, Cork-Gulley, moved in to supervise the management of the company and, if possible, find a buyer to take over Fodens as a going concern.

Working in Receivership was difficult, particularly in the Service Department where we had problems with questions of spares ownership and warranty continuity, but at least we still had a job and a continuing demand for spares and repairs. The receivers were actively seeking a buyer for the company and from time to time we had visits and inspections of our workshops and stores, together with explanations of our complete service organisation, for various companies which had presumably expressed an interest in taking over all or part of the Foden company. During this period, of course, Fodens continued to build Fleetmaster and Haulmaster vehicles in response to firm orders from our dealers and customers.

One of the companies showing an interest in Fodens was Paccar of Seattle, which built Kenworth and Peterbilt road haulage vehicles in the United States, together with Dart dump trucks, Wagner mining equipment and Braden winch gear.

Several senior personnel from Paccar had visited the factory and appeared to be particularly impressed with the assembly line and store facility, but there was no positive reaction until early October 1980, at which time the receivers finalised the sale of Fodens' assets to the American company and simultaneously made the whole of the workforce redundant, thereby allowing the new owners to offer re-employment to the minimum number required for their primary operational plans.

At the completion of this initial operation the total workforce had been reduced to approximately 350 personnel and only three of the former Foden senior management team had been rehired, the UK Sales Manager, the Production Manager and the Service Manager. The rest of the management team, headed by the Managing Director and including Chief Engineer, Financial Controller, Marketing Manager, Engineering Manager, Data Processing Manager and Materials Manager were all American, all experts at their specific jobs and all, from my own experience, easy to work with.

The company title at this time was changed to the 'Sandbach Engineering Ccompany' and one of our first activities under the new title, and with the new management team, was attendance at the 1980 Commercial Vehicle Show at the NEC. At the time of the Paccar acquisition, stand space and equipment had been booked, show models were in production, and although the new management

Despite the dramatic change of ownership which had occurred earlier that month, the Foden display at the Commercial Motor Show held in October 1980 at the National Exhibition Centre continued as planned. The Show catalogue had already been printed and the Foden entry still bore the name Fodens Ltd that had been current since 1901 rather than the new company title Sandbach Engineering Company, but the marque name Foden was to continue. This exhibit maintained a long-standing tradition in being a Gardner-engined eight-wheeler, though the RG20/30 had the 6LXC engine developing 201 bhp at 1920rpm, almost exactly twice the power output of the 6LW in its pre-war form as had been used to power the first Foden eight-wheeler in 1935. The 1980 Show chassis had Lipe Rollway twin-plate clutch and Fuller RTO 9509B gearbox, a Foden 20-ton bogie with double overhead-worm drive and FF20 rubber suspension, with tapered leaf suspension of the front axles and S.10 cab.

These two scenes at outdoor shows date from almost half a century earlier, a few years before the author joined the firm, conveying earlier ventures at sales presentation and giving an indication of progress over that period. The upper view, evidently at an agricultural show, dates from 1931, judging by the registration numbers, and hence from the days when steam still ruled supreme. Speed Six models were on display but, despite the copious presentation of evidence of customer approval by repeat orders and confident expressions, Ted Johnson and Sydney Smith would not have found it easy to secure orders for steam wagons at that period. The vehicle nearest the camera, GO 4514, was No. 63 of Murrell's Wharf, of Blackfriars Bridge Wharf, London. In the middle was one for Shipstones Ltd, of Nottingham, a loyal Foden customer well into the diesel era, while the vehicle farthest from the camera, LG 7005, was probably a demonstrator.

This scene in Scotland dates from 1934, judging by the Roxburgh registration number, KS 6223, of the R-type 6-ton model at the left of the picture. Steam has gone, and diesel reigns supreme – even the 2-ton model in the centre is a diesel – the same chassis design in petrol form is illustrated on page 35. The 10-ton model on the right would doubtless have been a six-wheeler, among Foden's first in diesel form. Stand staff seem conspicuous by their absence, but note the prominence given to the 'By Appointment' royal coat of arms. The neighbouring stand, selling Austin vans, was occupied by David Carlow & Sons Ltd, of Glasgow.

The end of the road. Among several farewell events was a lunch given by senior officials of the Freight Transport Association, on whose technical committee I had served for some years, and here I am with Roger Bird, Terry Goldrick and Ron Plant on that occasion in November 1982.

were of the opinion that dealer shows were of more long term value than National Exhibitions, it was decided to go ahead with the existing plans on this specific occasion. The principal exhibits were the 6 and eight-wheeler Haulmasters.

Considering the situation at the time, the 1980 Show was remarkably successful and the new company was off to an impressive start. This satisfactory trend continued and by the commencement of the new year, 1981, a further 150 workers had been taken on to bring the total workforce up to around 500.

I continued to work for Sandbach Engineering Company as Service Manager through to July 1982 when, shortly after My 62nd Birthday, I decided to retire and spend more time with our family which had now grown to include seven grandchildren, a total which was destined to increase to eight in due course.

There were other, rather more formal reactions to my decision to retire from Fodens, which were recorded at the time. I had served on the technical committee of the Freight Transport Association for a number of years, and the senior officials gave me a farewell lunch soon after my retirement, as a token of appreciation.

There was a final departmental farewell party at the Recreation Club which I thoroughly enjoyed and that was the final event in the 45 years which constituted 'My Time at Fodens'.

INDEX